Berlin Divided City, 1945–1989

Culture and Society in Germany
General Editors: Eva Kolinsky and David Horrocks

Volume 1: *Turkish Culture and German Society Today*
Edited by David Horrocks and Eva Kolinsky

Volume 2: *Sinti and Roma: Gypsies in German-Speaking Society and Literature*
Edited by Susan Tebbutt

Volume 3: *Voices in Times of Change: The Role of Writers, Opposition Movements and the Churches in the Transformation of East Germany*
Edited by David Rock

Volume 4: *Coming Home to Germany?: The Integration of Ethnic Germans from Central and Eastern Europe in the Federal Republic*
Edited by David Rock and Stefan Wolff

Volume 5: *The Culture of German Environmentalism: Anxieties, Visions, Realities*
Edited by Axel Goodbody

Volume 6: *Berlin Divided City, 1945–1989*
Edited by Philip Broadbent and Sabine Hake

BERLIN DIVIDED CITY, 1945–1989

Edited by
Philip Broadbent and Sabine Hake

Berghahn Books
New York • Oxford

First published in 2010 by
Berghahn Books
www.BerghahnBooks.com

©2010, 2012 Philip Broadbent and Sabine Hake
First paperback edition published in 2012

All rights reserved.
No part of this publication may be reproduced in any form or by any means without the written permission of Berghahn Books.

Library of Congress Cataloging-in-Publication Data
Berlin divided city, 1945–1989 / edited by Philip Broadbent and Sabine Hake.
   p. cm. – (Culture and society in Germany v. 6)
   Includes bibliographical references and index.
   ISBN 978-1-84545-755-6 (hbk.) – ISBN 978-0-85745-802-5 (pbk.)
   1. Berlin (Germany)–History–1945–1990–Congresses. 2. Berlin (Germany)–Social conditions–20th century–Congresses. I. Broadbent, Philip, 1972– II. Hake, Sabine, 1956– III. University of Texas at Austin. IV. Title.
   DD881.G486 2008
   943'.155087–dc22
                                                                        2010023806

British Library Cataloguing in Publication Data
A catalogue record for this book is available from the British Library.

Printed in the United States on acid-free paper

ISBN 978-0-85745-802-5 (paperback)   ISBN 978-0-85745-818-6 (ebook)

Contents

List of Illustrations — vii

Acknowledgments — ix

Introduction *Philip Broadbent and Sabine Hake* — 1

PART ONE Cold War Beginnings

1. Life Among the Ruins: Sex, Space, and Subculture in Zero Hour Berlin *Jennifer V. Evans* — 11

2. The Propagandistic Role of Modern Art in Postwar Berlin *Maike Steinkamp* — 23

3. Back to the Future: New Music's Revival and Redefinition in Occupied Berlin *Elizabeth Janik* — 34

4. The Nylon Curtain: Architectural Unification in Divided Berlin *Greg Castillo* — 46

5. Mediascape and Soundscape: Two Landscapes of Modernity in Cold War Berlin *Heiner Stahl* — 56

PART TWO East Berlin, the Socialist Capital

6. Painting the Berlin Wall in Leipzig: The Politics of Art in 1960s East Germany *April A. Eisman* — 69

7. "You Have to Draw a Line Somewhere": Tropes of Division in DEFA Films from the Early 1960s *Mariana Ivanova* — 78

8. Constructing a Socialist Landmark: The Berlin Television Tower *Heather Gumbert* — 89

9. Transparency in Divided Berlin: The Palace of the Republic *Deborah Ascher Barnstone* — 100

PART THREE West Berlin, Showcase of the West

10 The Woman Between: Hildegard Knef's Movies in
    Cold War Berlin *Ulrich Bach* 115

11 Benno Ohnesorg, Rudi Dutschke, and the Student Movement
    in West Berlin: Critical Reflections after Forty Years
    David E. Barclay 125

12 Berlin and Post-Meinhof Feminism: Yvonne Rainer's *Journeys
    from Berlin/1971* *Claudia Mesch* 135

13 Daniel Libeskind's Jewish Museum in Berlin as a
    Cold War Project *Paul B. Jaskot* 145

14 Beyond the Berlin Myth: The Local, the Global and
    the IBA 87 *Emily Pugh* 156

PART FOUR Berlin After Unification: Looking Back and Beyond

15 Stereographic City: Berlin Photography in the *Wende* Era
    Miriam Paeslack 171

16 Divided City, Divided Heaven? Berlin Border Crossings in
    Post-*Wende* Fiction *Lyn Marven* 184

17 Interview with Barbara Hoidn *Philip Broadbent and
    Sabine Hake* 194

Notes on Contributors 204

Index 209

Illustrations

Figure 1.1 During a February 1945 bombing raid in a Berlin air raid shelter. Courtesy of Bildarchiv Preussischer Kulturbesitz/ Arthur Grimm.   14

Figure 2.1 Friedrich Seidenstücker: Documentary photograph of the exhibition *La sculpture française de Rodin à nos jours*, Zeughaus, Berlin, spring 1947, © bpk/ Friedrich Seidenstücker.   25

Figure 2.2 Exhibition on Soviet Painting at the Soviet Union House of Culture, Summer 1949. Courtesy of German Historical Museum Berlin.   26

Figure 2.3 Catalogue of *Künstler schaffen für den Frieden* (1951). Photograph by the author.   30

Figure 4.1 Stalinallee in East Berlin during the late 1950s. Courtesy of Rheinisches Bildarchiv.   48

Figure 4.2 Hansaviertel in West Berlin during the late 1950s. Courtesy of Landesarchiv Berlin.   49

Figure 6.1 Klaus Weber, *The Morning of 13 August (Der Morgen des 13. August)*, oil on canvas, 1962. Courtesy of Museum der bildenden Künste Leipzig and Klaus Weber.   70

Figure 6.2 Collective work of the laymen's circle of Altscherbitz, *Socialism Wins*, tapestry, 1961. Current location unknown. Reproduction from *Bildende Kunst* (Dec. 1961): 833.   72

Figure 6.3 Jochen Nusser, entry for the *13 August 1961* painting competition, 1966. Courtesy of Sächsisches Staatsarchiv, Staatsarchiv Leipzig, SED-BL Leipzig.   75

Figure 7.1 Film still, *And Your Love, Too*. Courtesy of Deutsche Kinemathek, Filmmuseum Berlin.   84

Figure 7.2 Film still, *Divided Heaven*. Courtesy of Deutsche Kinemathek, Filmmuseum Berlin.   87

Figure 8.1 Looking south from the 123-meter-tall Interhotel "Stadt Berlin" on the construction sites around the not-yet-completed television tower. 5 March 1969. Bundesarchiv, Bild 183-H0605-0020-001, Photographer: Eva Brüggmann. 97

Figure 9.1 Sketch of the Palast der Republik as a suspended structure. Courtesy of The Getty Foundation. 101

Figure 9.2 Palast der Republik seen from the Karl-Marx-Platz with the Fernsehturm in the background. Courtesy of Bundesbildstelle. 102

Figure 10.1 Hildegard Knef in front of the Brandenburg Gate. Courtesy of The Granger Collection. 117

Figure 12.1 Film Still, Yvonne Rainer, *Journeys from Berlin/1971* (1979). Courtesy of Yvonne Rainer. 140

Figure 13.1 Daniel Libeskind, The Jewish Museum within the Berlin Municipal Museum, Competition Entry, ground floor plan (1989). Courtesy of Studio Daniel Libeskind. 151

Figure 13.2 View along the Lindenstrasse, showing from left to right: Kreis, Schad and Schad, Wohnpark am Berlin Museum (1986), Gerlach, Kollegienhaus (1735), and Libeskind, Jewish Museum (1989). Photograph by the author. 153

Figure 14.1 View of squat in Kreuzberg in 1980. Photo by Jochen Moll. Courtesy of Bildarchiv Preussischer Kulturbesitz. 159

Figure 14.2 O. M. Ungers, apartment complex on Lützowplatz (1979–1981). Photo by author. 162

Figure 15.1 Helga Paris, *Berliner Kneipen*. Courtesy of Helga Paris, Fotografien. 175

Figure 15.2 Michael Schmidt, *Wall*. Courtesy of Studio Michael Schmidt. 176

Figure 15.3 Wiebke Loeper, *Lad*. Courtesy of Studio Wiebke Loeper. 179

Figure 15.4 Wiebke Loeper, *Lad*. Courtesy of Studio Wiebke Loeper. 180

Figure 15.5 Elisabeth Neudörfl, *Der Stadt*. Courtesy of Studio Elisabeth Neudörfl. 181

Acknowledgments

This volume is the product of the Second German Studies Workshop on "Berlin Divided City, 1945–1989," which took place at the University of Texas at Austin. With the exception of the contributions by Ulrich Bach, Heiner Stahl, and Elizabeth Janik, all essays included here were initially presented as talks at the workshop. Both the workshop and the present volume would not have happened without the support of numerous individuals and institutions. The biannual German Studies Workshop was made possible through the generous support of the Texas Chair of German Literature and Culture Endowment. We are grateful to the chair of the Department of German Studies, John Hoberman, for supporting the event, and to the staff for help with organizational matters. Bradley Boovey did an excellent translation of the interview with Barbara Hoidn. Marion Berghahn's commitment to publishing in German studies remains awe inspiring, and we are honored to be part of her catalogue. We are particularly grateful to the second anonymous reviewer for suggesting a different chapter lineup. Ann Przyzycki saw the project through with great efficiency, and Kristine Hunt improved the manuscript considerably through her meticulous copy editing. Thanks to all the contributors for making their research available for the volume and for being so patient, responsive, and collegial during the editing and reviewing process. And for keeping them amused throughout, the editors would like to thank two four-legged creatures, Daisy and Bones.

Introduction

Philip Broadbent and Sabine Hake

Potsdamer Platz in 1962: a vast urban wasteland, divided by metal fences and antitank barricades soon to be replaced by the more impenetrable steel and concrete of the Berlin Wall. In the brief moment captured by this snapshot, we can still detect a dialogic relationship between looking and being looked at, a relationship that would soon become more one-sided, with the point of view increasingly associated with that of the West. The spatial configuration captured by the photographer at once reflects and rehearses some of the scenarios of confrontation and rhetorics of difference that defined the Berlin Wall era from 1961 to 1989. In the spatial articulation of what since has become almost a critical cliché, urban space in Berlin appears at once burdened by its own history of destruction and empowered by the political meaning of construction and reconstruction. Both sides of the fence remain haunted by the devastations of war, with the emptiness of the site a painful reminder of what once was Europe's busiest intersection. Yet both sides also boldly assert the competing political and urban visions emerging from the cataclysm of the Third Reich. In the foreground, we see an advertising board depicting Potsdamer Platz in 1932, evoked here as the symbol of a democratic Germany—and a dream of classical urbanity that, more than thirty years later, would again animate plans for urban renewal. In the background, we can identify the unadorned facade of the Nationalrat on Wilhelmstrasse (then: Otto-Grotewohl-Strasse), maintaining the illusion of democratic process through a building that once belonged to Goebbels's Propaganda Ministry. And in the central picture plane, we can observe some of the modes of engagement that defined the East-West relationships during the Cold War, beginning with the forms of looking, watching, and framing the Other that provided ample opportunity for projections as well as strategies of imitation and demarcation.

The legacies of the Weimar Republic and the Third Reich, the clash between tradition and modernity, the interplay of representation and perception, the dynamics of remembering and forgetting, and the construction of sameness and difference: these constitute the main discursive elements and strategies in the making of Cold War Berlin. Images such as the one on the cover have contributed to the perception, formed since German unification in 1989, of Berlin as a haunted place divided by walls, defined by voids, and predestined for palimpsestic and allegorical readings (Huyssen 2003). Yet as this anthology shows, Cold War Berlin is also a place where the future is being planned, built, imagined, and defended; it is a space of artistic experiments and competing ideologies, of political struggles and social upheavals. In short, it is a profoundly modern and self-consciously modernist site. Departing from the centrality of culture in the ideological divisions of the Cold War, the sixteen essays assembled here examine the heightened role of art, architecture, music, literature, photography, and film in East and West Berlin between the end of World War II in 1945 and the fall of the Berlin Wall in 1989. Yet the contributions by art historians, architectural historians, film scholars, literary scholars, musicologists, and historians not only produce a cultural history of Cold War Berlin based on the similarities that, despite the antagonistic rhetoric, continued to inform aesthetic sensibilities, artistic experiments, and urban practices. By reconstructing the specifically urban landscape of Cold War politics and its East-West rivalries, this volume also asserts, through interdisciplinary readings of city images, narratives, practices, and ideologies, the central role of Berlin within postwar discourses of urbanism, modernism, and postmodernism. Last but not least, through its interdisciplinary perspective, comparative method, and mixture of historical case studies and close textual analyses, the volume hopes to open up new perspectives on mass culture, urban space, and the politics of the aesthetic in the postunification period as well.

Berlin Divided City, 1945–1989 builds on the rich body of scholarship on Berlin's layered and contested topography and the overdetermined role of urban literature, film, art, and architecture produced during the last two decades. The fall of the Berlin Wall in 1989 brought renewed attention to the Cold War as a period of international tensions, replete with espionage stories, military confrontations, and difficult negotiations concerning the most mundane problems before 1949 and after 1961 (Elkins 1988; Taylor 1989; Wyden 1989). The primacy of the political in many popular histories of the Berlin Wall has since given way to more complicated narratives that emphasize the centrality of both elite and popular culture in representing the differences between East and West Berlin and in facilitating the many movements and encounters across borders (Braun and Treichler 2006). Just as the early years after 1945 allowed some scholars to revisit the geographical and ideological terrain on which intellectual and commercial life would assume new functions

(Schivelbusch 1981; Steege 2007), the institutionalization of the division after 1961 prompted others to trace its long-term effects on civil society and family life (Davey 1998; Borneman 1998). The proliferation of studies on postunification Berlin (Costabile-Heming, Foell, and Halverson 2004; Gerstenberger 2008) have brought growing awareness of the city's role in organizing public and private memory and providing a space for the staging of contemporary subjectivity and cultural heritage (Verheyen 2008; Williams 2008). Following Brian Ladd's seminal study, *The Ghosts of Berlin: Confronting German History in the Urban Landscape* (1998), architecture has assumed the function of a master discourse allowing scholars both to read urban topographies as special manifestations of German history and identity and to probe the politics of urban space through alternately archeological, allegorical, and critical materialist readings (Till 2005; Jordan 2006).

Berlin Divided City, 1945–1989 shares a number of key assumptions with these studies: a belief in interdisciplinary approaches and comparative readings; an emphasis on the continuities of urban culture beyond historical ruptures and spatial divides; an awareness of the centrality of Berlin's divided history in postunification approaches to urban life and city marketing; and an interest in the ongoing revisions and representations of the city's troubled past in contemporary practices and texts. At the same time, several of the contributors to this volume introduce questions and perspectives often neglected in the preoccupation with national history, memory, and trauma. Three points deserve to be emphasized. First, the culture of Cold War Berlin cannot be understood without adequate recognition of the centrality of modernism, in its high art and vernacular forms, to the rebuilding of the urban infrastructure after the war and the staging of the ideological divisions between the capitalist West and the socialist East. Second, the importance of culture in articulating this ideological confrontation cannot be appreciated in all its complexities without taking into account the overlapping binaries of East and West, German and European, and European and American that placed Berlin at the geographical/geopolitical center of the Cold War and that produced the city's competing but also corresponding political imaginaries. Third, the politicization of high art, mass culture, and counterculture cannot be assessed properly without recognition of the formative power of the aesthetic, especially in the ensemble of art forms and mass media, to transform the urban environment and influence the perception and experience of the divided former capital.

Reflecting the volume's interdisciplinary nature, its four parts are organized in a chronological manner that at once documents the politicization of art, music, architecture, film, and popular culture from 1945 to

1989 and identifies moments of resistance and difference; throughout, the similarities between artistic media and cultural practices on both sides of the ideological divide are highlighted. In recognition of the legacies of World War II that continued to haunt Berlin after the foundation of the two German states, the first part on Cold War beginnings opens with historical snapshots of everyday life among the rubble and early initiatives to restart cultural life. Abandoned bunkers, desolate parklands, and bombed-out buildings set the stage for Jennifer Evans's discussion of the sex trade (gay and straight) of the immediate postwar years; policing this highly contested urban space, she argues, was considered central to social and political normalization. The next three contributions focus on the pivotal role of modernism both in articulating the ideological divisions of the Cold War and in (re)establishing artistic continuities and international connections. Maike Steinkamp examines the propagandistic uses of modern art in a series of art exhibitions organized by French, British, American, and Soviet cultural centers in the late 1940s and discusses the instrumentalization of abstract expressionism and socialist realism in the larger confrontation between capitalism and communism. Mapping a similar trajectory in her account of the postwar appropriation of the Weimar-era tradition of New Music as an alternative to Nazi cultural legacies, Elizabeth Janik diagnoses the growing divide between an Eastern emphasis on amateur musicians and state patronage and a Western insistence on the formal rigors and apolitical nature of New Music, a process that she compares to a musical Iron Curtain. Moving on to postwar architecture, Greg Castillo evokes the image of a nylon curtain to explain the complicated dynamics that made East Berlin's Stalinallee and West Berlin's Hansaviertel not only competing designs in the 1950s debate over the ideology of modernism but also equal parts in a hidden dialogue throughout the 1960s on modern architecture and city planning that involved German architects Hermann Henselmann and Egon Eiermann as well as international stars Le Corbusier and Oscar Niemeyer. A similar dialogue can be found after 1962 in the intense competition over the airwaves. As Heiner Stahl shows in his study on youth programming on East and West Berlin radio stations (SFB, RIAS, Berliner Rundfunk), "the soundscapes of pop" projected the ethos of Western consumerism and individual resistance deep into East Berlin.

The second part brings together case studies on the overdetermined function of film, art, and architecture in organizing cultural life in East Berlin after the building of the Berlin Wall on 13 August 1961. The first two contributions deal with the representation of the Berlin Wall in East German art and film. April Eisman reconstructs the reception history of Klaus Weber's socialist realist painting, *Am Morgen des 13. August* (On the Morning of 13 August), from its initial acceptance by the SED to its exclusion from the 1962 Fifth German Art Exhibition in Dresden within the larger context of cultural policies and aesthetic debates. Mariana Ivanova looks at several DEFA films, Kurt Maetzig's *Septemberliebe* (September Love, 1961), Frank Vogel's *Und deine Liebe auch* (And Your Love Too, 1962), and Konrad Wolf's *Der geteilte Himmel* (The Divided Heaven, 1964), that insist on the wall's presumably unifying effect on GDR society through their documentary aesthetics and reconfiguration of public and private life. Moving to the late 1960s, Heather Gumbert documents the discussions surrounding the construction of the famous East German television tower (1965–69) and shows its overdetermined function as a symbol of the official project of building socialism, the GDR's expanding broadcasting infrastructure, and the modernization of the historical center in the East. Continuing this exploration of urban architecture as a privileged place for official images of nation and state, Deborah Ascher Barnstone analyzes the Palace of the Republic (1973–76), designed by Heinz Graffunder, within the history of an ideology of transparency that extends from the glass architecture of the expressionists to the Bundeshaus in Bonn and the 1961–1964 renovation of the Reichstag in West Berlin.

Developments in West Berlin after 1961 are the focus of the volume's third part. The postwar career of Hildegard Knef, the actress and singer most closely associated with West Berlin, allows Ulrich Bach to trace the relationship between cinema, urbanism, and femininity from the DEFA film *Die Mörder sind unter uns* (The Murderers Are Among Us, 1945) to several British Cold War spy thrillers and her last appearance in *Jeder stirbt für sich allein* (Everyone Dies Alone, 1976). David Barclay affirms the significance of the Cold War for the student movement and its impact on cultural life in West Berlin between 1966 and 1972, but also points to other Berlin-related developments such as the 1972 signing of the Four Power Agreement in assessing "1968" and its resonances in the present. Adding an international perspective, Claudia Mesch's close reading of Yvonne Rainer's *Journeys from Berlin/1971* (1979) uncovers the function of West Berlin in highly formalized reflections on feminism and terrorism and the politics of identification organized around the controversial figure of Ulrike Meinhof. Paul Jaskot challenges prevailing accounts of Daniel Libeskind's Jewish Museum as one of the founding sites of the city's postunification identity by drawing attention to both its Cold War origins as an integral part of the 1987 Internationale Bauausstellung (IBA) and its initial conception as an extension of the Berlin Museum. Introducing decidedly local concerns, Emily Pugh further complicates the standard account of IBA's international ambitions by reading its exhibition projects primarily as a response to the squatter movement in Kreuzberg.

The volume's fourth part concentrates on the resonances of the pre-1989 period in postunification artistic practices. Miriam Paeslack uses the metaphor of the stereoscope to consider the formal and thematic affinities between the photographic representation of East and West Berlin neighborhoods from the 1970s to the 1990s. Against the familiar distinction between social documentary photography in the East and subjective photography in the West, Paeslack insists on the strong sense of political disillusionment and growing attachment to notions of place, of the city as *Heimat,* shared by East Berliners Helga Paris and Wiebke Loeper and West Berliners Michael Schmidt and Elisabeth Neudörfl. Looking at the representation of Berlin border crossings in post-1989 fiction, Lyn Marven similarly rewrites the history of the city's division through the unified topographies and imaginary journeys depicted in Irina Liebmann's *In Berlin* (1994), Monika Maron's *Geburtsort Berlin* (Place of Birth Berlin, 2003), and Emine Sevgi Özdamar's *Seltsame Sterne* (Strange Stars Stare Toward Earth, 2003) and *Mein Berlin* (My Berlin, 2001)—all examples of the inherent ambiguity of retrospective views that reinscribe the future of reunification into the city's divided past. Last but not least, the concluding interview with Barbara Hoidn, Head of the Architecture Workshop of the Senate Building Director of Berlin during the early 1990s, sheds light on the dismantling of the spatial order imposed by the Cold War and its absorption into a very different unified cityscape, a cityscape that, as this anthology sets out to show, can only be understood through a historical reconstruction of the culture of the divided city.

Notes

Borneman, John. 1992. *Belonging in the Two Berlins: Kin, State, Nation.* Cambridge: Cambridge University Press.

Braun, Jutta and Hans J. Treichler, eds. 2006. *Sportstadt Berlin: Prestigekämpfe und Systemwettstreit.* Berlin: Ch. Links.

Costabile-Heming, Carol Anne Kristie A. Foell, and Rachel J. Halverson, eds. 2004. *Berlin: The Symphony Continues Orchestrating Architectural. Social, and Artistic Change in Germany's New Capital Berlin.* Berlin and New York: Walter de Gruyter.

Davey, Thomas. 1987. *A Generation Divided: German Children and the Berlin Wall.* Durham, NC: Duke University Press.

Elkins, Thomas Henry. 1988. *Berlin: The Spatial Structure of a Divided City.* London: Routledge.

Gerstenberger, Katharina. 2008. *Writing the New Berlin: The German Capital in Post-Wall Literature.* Rochester, NY: Camden House.

Huyssen, Andreas. 2003. *Present Pasts: Urban Palimpsests and the Politics of Meaning.* Stanford, CA: Stanford University Press.

Jordan, Jennifer A. 2006. *Structures of Memory: Understanding Urban Change in Berlin and Beyond.* Stanford, CA: Stanford University Press.

Ladd, Brian. 1998. *The Ghosts of Berlin: Confronting German History in the Urban Landscape*. Chicago: University of Chicago Press.
Schivelbusch, Wolfgang. 1998. *In a Cold Crater: Cultural and Intellectual Life in Berlin, 1945–1948*. Trans. Kelly Berry. Berkeley: University of California Press.
Steege, Paul. 2007. *Black Market, Cold War: Everyday Life in Berlin, 1946–1949*. Cambridge: Cambridge University Press.
Taylor, Frederick. 1989. *The Berlin Wall: A World Divided, 1961–1989*. New York: Simon & Schuster.
Till, Karen E. 2005. *The New Berlin: Memory, Politics, Place*. Minneapolis: University of Minnesota Press.
Verheyen, Dirk. 2008. *United City, Divided Memories? Cold War Legacies in Contemporary Berlin*. Lanham, MD: Lexington Books.
Williams, John Alexander, ed. 2008. *Berlin since the Wall's End: Shaping Society and Memory in the Germany Metropolis since 1989*. Newcastle, UK: Cambridge Scholar's Publishing.
Wyden, Peter. 1989. *Wall: The Inside Story of Divided Berlin*. New York: Simon & Schuster.

PART ONE

Cold War Beginnings

CHAPTER 1

Life Among the Ruins
Sex, Space, and Subculture in Zero Hour Berlin

Jennifer V. Evans

Upon returning to his apartment in the once-tony district of Charlottenburg, British observer Lieutenant Colonel W. Byford-Jones described what he had witnessed in a recent tour of the city center:

> I saw the Kurfurstendamm, a miserable colourless heap of ruins . . . the Dom . . . its broken ribs spiking the sky . . . the Tiergarten, littered with wreckage, its elms and firs blasted and shattered, its gardens churned up, its pool grey and smeared with oil. . . . My room, from which I could look out north, east and west over the grey ruins of the city and watch, among them, the troglodytes creeping over piles of rubble or burrowing their way into cellars, was on the Kurfurstendamm, Berlin's Piccadilly. . . . From beneath it, rising on the heat of the day to my bedroom, came a hideous smell of dampness, of charred remains, of thousands of putrefying bodies (Byford-Jones 1947: 19).

With little doubt, area bombing, street fighting, mass rape, and occupation put a violent end to Berlin's metropolitan trappings. In the central districts, those most heavily affected by the two-year bombing campaign, very little remained of Berlin's former glory. Over 350 air attacks dropped more than 45,000 tons of explosives on the waiting city. With over 28 square kilometers of its prewar surface area destroyed generating anywhere between 55 and 100 cubic meters of rubble—one sixth of all the rubble in Germany proper (Fichtner 1977: 5)—Berlin was a debris field, "the greatest pile of rubble" the world had ever seen (Howley 1950: 8). Nightly bombing completely transformed the physical geography of the city, leveling buildings, leaving behind mounds of rebar, concrete, and sand. The hustle and bustle of Potsdamer Platz, once the symbol of the city's modernity with its automobiles and six-sided traffic light, had been completely devastated, creating a preindustrial steppe inside the city limits that would remain undeveloped until unification (Roth 2003). The Tiergarten's ponds, lined with sunbathers in seasonable summers, were choked with oil (Byford-Jones 1947: 19); craters and cesspools existed where parkland and canals once beckoned flaneurs in search of urban escape. Of the city's inhabitable space, a full one-third of all prewar apartment houses lay in tatters with even more tenements damaged beyond repair (Bohleber 1990: 15; Rürup 2005: 59–60).

Berlin had survived the last days, but its infrastructure, its housing, and its spirit were broken. What remained was a shattered cityscape, pockmarked with bullet holes, charred and rotting. To many, like journalist Curt Riess, it was "a dying city" (1952: 72), a veritable necropolis that historians Monica Black and Brian Ladd have described as inhabited by phantoms of the fallen and the felled (Black 2010; Ladd 1998). As Berliners crawled out from their hiding places, emerged from their cellar communities, or returned from the front or exile, they encountered the physical ravages of war everywhere they turned (Mierendorf in Martin and Schoppmann 1996: 139). Seizing on the corrupting influence of the destroyed landscape, police, and city planners, architects, and welfare workers worked quickly to develop strategies to deal with what they saw as "the criminality of the ruins" (von Hentig 1947: 338). The urgency was great as critics feared Germany was not simply a "rubble heap in a material sense but had reached an exceptional low point in a moral sense as well" (Weingartner 1951).

Drawing on strands of research in historical geography, this essay examines the overlapping place of Berlin's rubblescape as a highly gendered and sexualized contact zone (Bell and Valentine 1995; Hubbard 1998, 2000; Mort and Nead 2000). Relished by teen gangs, frequented by rent boys, and sought out by prostitutes, Berlin's ruined bunkers and bomb cellars served as emblems of the chaos and lawlessness of defeat. But they also played host to the reflowering of Berlin in terms of irregular sexualities and transgressive identities. In analyzing the shifting meaning of Berlin's subterranean world, first as a hybrid military and civilian space designed to engender support for the war, then as a site of chaos and disorder, and finally as part of an underground economy of cruising and the sex trade, I will show how the quest to control these sites resulted in multiple struggles and contradictions, shedding light on the role of danger and desire in the process of rebuilding.

Trumpeted as a symbol of the capital's resistance to its enemies, the 1940–1942 bunker-building campaign had been designed on Hitler's order to create between seven hundred and one thousand large- and small-scale concrete facilities with sleeping arrangements for over 160,000

Berliners (Arnold et al. 2003: 13). In addition to the over forty large vertical bunkers commissioned in 1942, plans were made to integrate civilians into existing flak towers, build bunkers adjacent to major transit arteries and train stations, and reinforce neighborhood shelters in both the city center and the outlying districts. Rarely was the building of bunkers framed in terms of the state's moral obligation to protect its civilian population in times of attack. Instead, the bunker building program formed part of a preservationist agenda to rationalize the war effort on the home front. Even in the case of increasing vulnerability, the Nazis construed what was essentially a defensive endeavor as a safeguard for future success and a sign of the regime's power, organizational acumen, and strength.

The network of dedicated bunkers and shelters were engineered to deliver a sense of refuge from the hail of bombs just as they served to further align essential social services to the Nazi cause. Monitored by undercover Wehrmacht officers working in tandem with the Propaganda Ministry and staffed by party members and Hitler Youth volunteers, the bunkers extended the reach of the state into the nightly rhythms of Berliners at a time when they were most vulnerable. Indeed, many Berliners preferred to leave the confines of their makeshift apartment cellars for the city bunkers. Hildegard Knef, then just a teenager alternating between her grandfather's cottage in Zossen and her mother's apartment in Schöneberg, recalled an obvious preference for the safety of the large flak tower at the Zoologischer Garten station over the "wobbly cellar in Nr. 6." Then just another face in the anxious crowd she made her way to the bunker, pass in hand, and waited for the Hitler Youth detachment to open up the doors (Knef 1971: 34).

As the population of entire city blocks huddled around makeshift stoves and lanterns, they forged subterranean communities, each with their own "quirks and regulations" and rituals of belonging. These coordinated steps, reenacted nightly, communicated a sense of common experience, local identity, and dwelling in these extraordinary times (Seamon 1979). Although the atmosphere in some bunkers could be plagued by nervousness and anxiety, some Berliners recalled with fondness the times spent in the company of select neighbors. Manfred Woge remembered how children seized the opportunity to form playgroups with neighborhood buddies while others forged lasting friendships with the lady across the way (Arnold et al. 2003: 86). They even provided a context for women to imagine their future fate, as people in the final days of the war discussed the propaganda that circulated in escalating tones about the "Mongol" hunger for retribution.

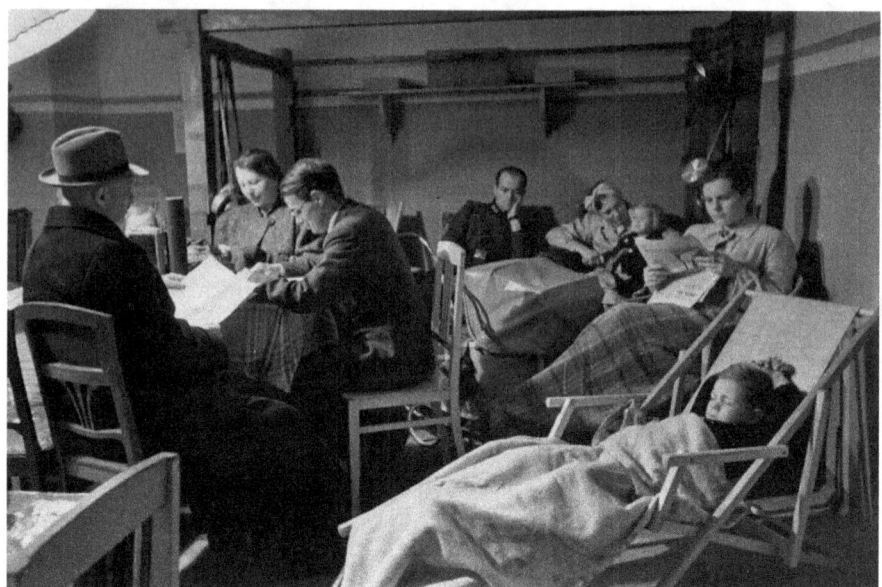

Figure 1.1 During a February 1945 bombing raid in a Berlin air raid shelter. Courtesy of Bildarchiv Preussicher Kulturbesitz/Arthur Grimm.

Soldiers, police, and Hitler Youth led Berliners in orderly fashion to their respective underground cabins. Shelter wardens, usually elderly men or women in uniform, ensured people followed the house rules, including keeping silent and refraining from smoking while spray-painted signs (along with the occasional elbow, groan, or nudge) helped reinforce order and precision. In the larger facilities, select rooms were reserved for the infirm while some were outfitted with electric lighting so people might read or sew (von Kardorff 1962: 95). The goal was to replicate life above ground as accurately as possible. The Charité Hospital had a particularly well-apportioned bunker complete with operating facilities and aftercare chambers, and the national welfare service or NSV maintained a birthing unit in the neighboring Chausseestrasse while many of the larger compounds, like the bunker at the Gesundbrunnen train station, boasted midwifery services. Infants born behind concrete walls received certificates of live birth indicating their first breath was taken "under the protection of the tower in Humboldthain," as one woman recalled, "in a difficult but grand time" (Arnold et al. 2003: 87).

Indeed, for Berlin youths like Knef, the bunkers could be sites of excitement and adventure, especially when looking back through the lens of memory and recollection. Some Berliners even felt smug in the comfort of their concrete dwelling, like the well-heeled guests in the Hotel

Adlon who could savor their cognac under the protection of its famed three-meter-thick concrete wall. Despite the extravagance of the rich, most Berliners languished in what turned out to be less than stellar accommodations, their bedding sullied with flies and bedbugs, rooms overcrowded, short on oxygen and air flow, and infected with hysteria in the final months of the war of Berlin's pending defeat (McGee 2002: 158). By the spring of 1945, most of the watch staff and Wehrmacht had been rerouted to the defense of the city only to be replaced by ill-prepared *Volksturm* who manned the flak gunnery, leaving the task of organizing nightly entry to the ad hoc efforts of the civilians (Foedrowitz 1998: 106). The loss of regular housing meant more people competed for long-term shelter in the already overcrowded facilities, and authorities lost all ability to stifle the swell of gossip that had overwhelmed efforts to clamp down on public opinion (Schäfer 1985: 311).

Designed as an emblem of Nazi war preparedness through the regulation of space and emotion, by the end of the war the bunker evolved into a caricature of itself as these same spaces heralded the absolute collapse of state authority. These "catacombs of fear," designed to embody the principles and ideals of the *Männerstaat* (masculinist state) were transformed into feminized spaces, inhabited nightly by a hodgepodge of women, the elderly, the underage, and the discarded—those men and boys whom the anonymous diarist of *A Woman in Berlin* suggests were "unwanted at the front, rejected by the *Volkssturm*." The bombast of Nazi Germany—"ruled by men, glorifying the strong man—(was) beginning to crumble, and with it the myth of the 'Man'" itself (Anonymous 2005: 9–10, 43). Perhaps the bitterest irony of all was the fact that these protective havens turned into the deadliest of sanctuaries given the concentration of people seeking shelter, not to mention the incendiary effect of a *Volltreffer* (direct hit) and the ubiquitous calls of "Frau komm" ("woman come") once the Russians arrived.

As "bedrooms, living rooms, and reception rooms for the first to enter Berlin," the shelters became host to private degradations carried out in plain sight. In the extreme, the wave of rapes that gripped the city transformed the spatial meaning of the bunker from one of protection and community to one of danger and depravity (Menzel 1946: 177). The violence of bodily assault underscored not just the feminization of the space through defeat but also a particular vision of femininity. Some desperate women tried to exert control over their environment by selecting which of their fellow bunker dwellers might placate Russian desires (Schrade 1977). Others attempted to transcend their own sexuality, donning men's pants and waistcoats and cutting their daughters' faces while darkening their own with coal. While the raping was often indiscriminate, some accounts suggest the Russians gravitated toward a particular vision of womanhood in choosing, for example, the robust over the skeletal (Ryan 1966: 337). While the very old, the very young, and even the infirm did not always escape unharmed, the bespectacled and mannish lesbian in the shelter managed to avoid their attention, as did some pregnant women. Recasting the space according to a culturally bound sense of sexual preference, the Russians were, in her words, "horribly normal" (Anonymous 2005: 77).

How do Berlin's cellars, bunkers, and ruins become transformed from places of sexual violence to sites of sexual subversion? Turning to a discussion of the ways in which police and social services regulated sexual delinquency, I will demonstrate how a particular segment of Berlin's population, street youth, used the opportunities provided by the broken physical landscape to harness the spaces opened up by defeat to suit their own purposes.

While city architects designed plans for Berlin's future, MPs, criminal police, railroad police, and public health and welfare workers combed through the rubble day and night to provide a sense of order and rule of law. The bombed-out bunker was no longer simply a symbol of Nazi war bluster; it was now a tangible sign of the perceived immorality of victor's justice and the depths to which Germany had sunk in defeat. In the weeks after capitulation, it began to take on new meaning as well, as a site of communal identity for the legions of children and youths left orphaned, homeless, or in the care of psychically damaged parents. More than a physical shelter for Berlin's large number of street youth, the bunkers provided emotional relief from the quotidian challenges of life after Hitler with black marketeers, rent boys, and fallen women camping out together in subterranean cliques and gangs.

Just as the rapes solidified in public consciousness the danger and immorality of these underground spaces as sites of racial mixing and bodily assault, the bunkers posed unique challenges to German sensibilities. When in November 1946 Officer Behr of the women's police detachment was called to investigate the clique that had barricaded itself in an abandoned bunker near the Schlesische station, what she found there flew in the face of German mores on a number of fronts. Six youths, two girls and four boys, ranging in age from eleven to fifteen, had been living in the bunker for the better part of a year (Raid Report, C Rep 303/9 Polizeipräsident in Berlin, Nr. 259. Landesarchiv Berlin, 1947). The youths did not posses proper identification. Without any form of ID, they sidestepped Allied de-Nazification strategies and shirked enrollment in school, two important sites of ideological reorientation for the Americans and Soviets respectively (Blessing 2006). More tangibly, they would be unable to take part in the rebuilding of Berlin through the clearing of rubble or industrial employment. In living beyond the boundaries of the family or the state, these youths created their own nascent community, stealing to survive, prostituting themselves if necessary, and confirming in the minds of police and welfare authorities that the ruins had become a "hotbed of asocial elements." (Raid Report, C Rep 303/9 Polizeipräsident in Berlin, 1945–48, Nr. 259, 1948).

Living in underground clusters of ten to fifteen, street youth created a world unto their own with their own distinctive hierarchies, ranks, and rules. Although forged out of necessity, when parents could no longer provide for their children, these cliques provided some of their members with a sense of adventure and romanticism, if tempered by the recent experience of war. As one chain-smoking, teenaged "gangster's moll" remarked to a journalist in the underground hideaway she shared with other street youth, "you know, we haven't forgotten what the Russians did when they came in" (Riess 1952: 110). Ever mindful of the space's dark history, one boy reminded the journalist, "For Christ's sake, where do you think you are? This is Berlin." What may have seemed like a carefree existence without parental control was not far from Rossellini's depressing images of abandoned children in *Germania Anno Zero;* for the legions of youths, many of whom were former members of the *Volkssturm* and League of German Girls and raised "in a world of slogans, of resounding phrases, of wild curses and promises," this hunger "for life, for love, even for vice" came at a cost, with prostitution and stealing the only ways to earn a semblance of a living (Riess 1952: 111).

While public streets, bars, and clubs gained the scrutiny of MPs and health authorities on the look out for girls "on the make," the rubble provided shelter for another underground activity—the male sex trade. In this regard, the city's semidestroyed train stations were a natural draw for Berlin's bombed-out youth. Bustling with life at a time when entire city blocks remained idle and deserted, train stations served as important nodes of activity. An engineering marvel given the Mark Brandenburg's sandy plane, the turn-of-the-century construction of these stations formed part of the modernization project to aid with the flow of human traffic, streamlining how people moved from domestic to commercial space. In addition to lending shape to traffic and travel, these stations were urban stages not unlike the street or boulevard, where the flow of people forced the creation of a new language to better organize, standardize, and regulate which actions, styles of clothing, postures, gaits, or facial expressions would be countenanced as suitable to that particular space (Benjamin 1999 and 2006). While transit police and vice cops might try to dictate the pace of circulation and proper behavior, these spaces did not always lend themselves to control and management (de Certeau in Edensor 2005: 82). The sheer number of the dislocated compounded the problem and in a sense democratized deviance as even wait staff at train station restaurants could not help but notice the throngs of soiled youths loitering around the waiting rooms, accosting would-be passengers with knowing glances and sideways looks, and heading out among the rubble in search of a private site of exchange (e.g., case against Klaus S. in C Rep 341 Stadtbezirksgericht Mitte, Nr. 5635 Landesarchiv Berlin, 1949).

Beat cops were well versed in how to spot male prostitutes (Evans 2003; Pretzel 2002). They also had access to Nazi-era investigation files and a photo album of rent boys. Despite this arsenal of knowledge, they struggled to contain the problem due to the fluidity of the internal boundary, the general level of debasement in German society, and differing notions of deviant masculinity. Without a clearly coded gender map, they turned their attention to the spaces of contact: the ruins themselves. Focusing on suspects in station waiting rooms, watching how they (using their terminology) gadded about (*sich umhertrieben*), with whom they shared glances, if they winked and motioned hither, police tagged their perpetrators-in-the-making and surreptitiously followed them as they ambled out on to the street. When beat cops followed Enrico P. and Gunter M. to a bunker ruin along the Reichstagsufer, it did not matter that they had yet to have sex. Boldly Enrico declared at the scene that he "leaned toward homosexuality" and the boy had been observed leaving the station with another man earlier in the night (Operation Report, 1948. C Rep 303/9 Polizeipräsident in Berlin, 1945–48, Landesarchiv Berlin).

Although the police tried hard to find physical evidence of transgression to substantiate charges, sometimes even collaborating with colleagues from the other sectors, this was not a prerequisite for questioning or even arrest. Where it mattered most was the sentencing. While men and boys served time and paid heavy fines for sex in the rubble, sometimes judges evoked the shadowy character of the ruins themselves as spaces that at least fell outside of the public eye, as in the 1950 case against Gerhard P. (B Rep 069 Jugendstrafanstalt Plötzensee, Landesarchiv Berlin, 1950). Obtaining evidence of sex acts in the rubble proved invariably difficult, at least for the off-duty *Volkpolizist* Werner W., whose case before the central Berlin district court was dismissed for lack of evidence since the holes in the ceiling of the ruin he had sought out allowed rain to collect precisely where the act had taken place, preventing the forensic chemist from collecting incriminating semen samples (C Rep 341 Stadtbezirksgericht Mitte, Nr. 4433, case 98 Ds 34/50, June 23, 1950). Given the haphazard application of the law against homosexuality, it is not difficult to understand why rent boys and their johns believed to find at least shelter if not protection in the cavernous insides of the city's bombed-out bunkers and ruins.

If forced into a detention facility to await further investigation by child protective services (since youths under the age of twenty-one were considered minors), in the Eastern sector boys could be sent to the Dircksenstrasse police station's youth wing at Alexanderplatz, itself a ruin, chronically overcrowded, and outfitted with beds and bedding from a neighboring bunker. In the West, they were often channeled into a detention facility that had been built in the Fichtebunker in Kreuzberg, a former gas tank measuring twenty-six meters in diameter and twelve meters in height. Constructed as part of the Nazi program to create three giant bunkers to house up to six thousand people, its basement had been converted during the war so police could house inmates without fear that they might flee. "Liberated" by the Soviets on 27 April 1945, its official postwar function was to provide temporary shelter to displaced persons. But it also jailed delinquents like "Freddy," whose case was documented in *Der Telegraf* in 1948. "Seventeen years old, small, undernourished, mentally slow—a mixture of feeble-mindedness and smarts"—Freddy had spent time in the Fichtebunker youth jail for avoiding work, burglary, and "stealing anything that wasn't nailed down." When he began "socializing with known homosexuals," he acquired money to buy cigarettes and chocolate. "The best thing for him," the reporter suggested, "would be a stint in the countryside" where, ostensibly, he would learn the error of his ways while regaining his physical and mental strength (*Der Telegraf* 17 January 1948).

While the Fichtebunker or the Dircksenstrasse facilities might provide temporary holding for what *Der Tagesspiegel* called the "Besprisornies of Berlin" (a term that emerged out of the Russian Revolution for the street children of Moscow and Petrograd), as Freddy's example shows, many youth advocates believed long-term rehabilitation was best achieved outside the city's corrupting spaces in one of the neighboring youth remand homes and institutional facilities—like Struveshof in Brandenburg—resurrected in 1946 as a means to neutralize youth itinerancy by enforcing the values of hard work and healthy living (*Der Tagesspiegel* 7 August 1947 and Evans forthcoming). Despite attempts by the divided city administration to reclaim the ruins, positioning them to serve productive purposes as prisons and detention centers, they could not yet fully rehabilitate those who occupied them. In a sense, only a limited order could be imposed on these physical spaces through social welfare, policing, and the law. The desires of the ruins could not be redeemed within the ruins themselves. Only hard labor in an industrial or agricultural setting outside the city offered true reformation and a connection to healthful and productive manhood.

In other words, although Berlin's underground was built as a testimony to a "rationalizing" state, the physical transformation of the bombing campaigns and the experience of occupation transformed these same sites into spaces of irrationality and confusion. In the events leading up to capitulation, the Nazi state lost its ability to rationalize the space, to organize it, the behaviors it inspired, and the memories it engendered. In the immediate postwar period, attempts to regulate the comings and goings in the ruins likewise proved challenging, as Berlin youth chose their subcultural identification over official attempts at buttressing the family and channeling ideological renewal. In thinking about the place of gender in these spaces of conflict and desire, we also see evidence of a shift in orientation. While the underground "caves," as the *Woman of Berlin* calls them, were feminized hosts of male violence, they remained highly charged places of sexual exchange albeit of a different kind. In the postwar orbit, these spaces continued to play host to shifting notions of femininity (in this case effeminacy) and masculine desire, and an evolving homosexual subculture.

Inextricably linked to the recent terror of war's end, the ruins of Berlin were host to predation, crisis, death, and decay. As spaces of disorder, however, they emerged as much more than a passive backdrop to postwar rebuilding. Certainly, they represented the breakdown of traditional authority (Fisher 2005). But they also helped shape the dynamics of a wide range of human sexualities, reflecting a host of concerns about the way in which sex, gender, and immorality was represented, perceived, and remembered at war's end. In some instances, those memories gained expression through official channels, in diaries and memorial projects. In others instances, the ruins foregrounded experiences that remained truly subterranean, buried in archived police ledgers and dusty court dockets. This onion-skin effect shows quite clearly that geographer Doreen Massey's claims for contemporary Berlin also hold true for the immediate postwar period: that the city's story is a product of "intersections of multiple narratives" (1999: 22). Hidden in plain sight; fragmented; decaying; pointing to a lost, invisible world; yet heralding something still to be articulated, Berlin's ruins were, in the words of Lieutenant Byford-Jones, much more than a "fossilized region where life no longer existed." In the face of death and decay, Berlin's "troglodytes" (as Byford-Jones calls them) used these spaces to map out their desires, connecting the ruins' shadows with those of the prewar city. In other words, the city's ruins were not only spaces of violence and death; they were also sites of subversion, nonconformity, and visibility for a host of sexual subcultures, proving that the rupture of war's end was also accompanied by continuities as well. Byford-Jones conceded as much when after scrutinizing the city below, he turned from his apartment window and "went down amid its ruins" since "there was much to learn from its secrets" (1947: 19).

Works Cited

Andreas-Friedrich, Ruth. 2005. *Battleground Berlin: Diaries, 1938–49.* New York: Holt.
Anonymous. 2005. *A Woman in Berlin: Eight Weeks in a Conquered City: A Diary.* New York: Picador.
Arnold, Dietmar, and Reiner Janick, Ingmar Arnold, Gudrun Neumann, and Klaus Topel. 2003. *Sirenen und gepackte Koffer: Bunkeralltag in Berlin.* Berlin: Ch. Links.
Bell, David, and Gill Valentine, eds. 1995. *Mapping Desire: Geographies of Sexualities.* London: Routledge.
Benjamin, Walter. 1999. *The Arcades Project.* Cambridge, MA: Bellknap Press.
———. 2006. *A Berlin Childhood Around 1900.* Cambridge, MA: Bellknap Press.
Black, Monica. 2010. *Death in Berlin from Weimar to Divided Germany.* Cambridge, MA: Cambridge University Press.
Blessing, Benita. 2006. *The Antifascist Classroom: Denazification in Soviet-occupied Germany, 1945–49.* New York: Palgrave.
Bohleber, Wolfgang. 1990. *Mit Marshallplan und Bundeshilfe: Wohnungsbaupolitik in Berlin 1945–1963.* Berlin: Duncker und Humblot.
Byford-Jones, Wilfred. 1947. *Berlin Twilight.* London: Hutchinson.
Edensor, Tim. 2005. *Industrial Ruins: Space, Aesthetics and Materiality.* New York: Berg Press.
Evans, Jennifer V. 2003. "*Bahnhof Boys:* Policing Male Prostitution in Post-Nazi Berlin." *Journal of the History of Sexuality* 12, no. 4 (October): 605–36.
———. "Repressive Rehabilitation: Crime, Morality and Delinquency in Berlin-Brandenburg, 1945–1958. In *Crime and Criminal Justice in Modern Germany,* ed. Richard Wetzell. New York: Berghahn, forthcoming.
Fichtner, Volkmar. 1977. *Die anthropogen bedingte Umwandlung des Reliefs durch Trümmeraufschüttungen in Berlin (West) seit 1945* Band 21. Berlin: Selbstverlag des geographischen Instituts der Freien Universität Berlin.
Howley, Frank. 1950. *Berlin Command.* New York: Putnam.
Fisher, Jaimey. 2005. "On the Ruins of Masculinity: The Figure of the Child in Italian Neorealism and the German Rubble-Film." In *Radical Fantasy: Italian Neorealism's Afterlife in Global Cinema,* ed. Laura E. Ruberto, Tomas Taraborrelli, and Kristi M. Wilson, 25–54. Detroit: Wayne State University Press.
Foedrowitz, Michael. 1998. *The Flak Towers in Berlin, Hamburg, and Vienna, 1940–1950.* Trans. Don Cox. Atglen, PA: Schiffer.
Hubbard, Phil. 1998. "Sexuality, Immorality and the City: Red-Light Districts and the Marginalization of Female Street Prostitutes." *Gender, Place and Culture* 5, no. 1 (September): 55–72.
———. 2000. "Desire/Disgust: Mapping the Moral Contours of Heterosexuality." *Progress in Human Geography* 24, no. 2: 191–217.
Kardoff, Ursula. 1962. *Berlin Aufzeichnungen aus den Jahren 1942 bis 1945.* Munich: Biederstein.
Knef, Hildegard. 1971. *The Gift Horse.* New York: McGraw-Hill.
Knopp, Lawrence. 1995. "Sexuality and Urban Space: A Framework for Analysis." In *Mapping Desire: Geographies of Sexualities,* ed. David Bell and Gill Valentine, 149–164. New York and London: Routledge.
Ladd, Brian. 1998. *The Ghosts of Berlin: Confronting German History in the Urban Landscape.* Chicago: University of Chicago Press.
Martin, Angela, and Claudia Schoppmann. 1996. *"Ich fürchte die Menschen mehr als die Bomben" Aus den Tagebüchern von drei Berliner Frauen 1938–1946.* Berlin: Metropol.

Massey, Doreen. 1999. "Imagining Globalisation: Power Geometries of Time–Space." In *Global Futures: Migration, Environment and Globalization*, ed. Avtar Brah, Mary J. Hickman and Mairtin Mac an Ghaill, 27–44. New York: Macmillan.
McGee, Mark. 2002. *Berlin: A Visual and Historical Documentation from 1925 to the Present.* Woodstock, NY: Overlook Press.
Menzel, Mathias. 1946. *Die Stadt ohne Tod.* Berlin: Carl Habel Verlagsbuchhandlung.
Mort, Frank, and Lynda Nead. 2000. "Sexual Geographies." *New Formations* 37: 5–129.
Pretzel, Andreas. 2002. *NS-Opfer unter Vorbehalt: Homosexuelle Männer in Berlin nach 1945.* Berlin: LIT.
Riess, Curt. 1952. *The Berlin Story.* New York: The Dial Press.
Roth, Nadine L. 2003. "Metamorphoses: Urban Space and Modern Identity, 1870–1933." PhD dissertation, University of Toronto.
Rürup, Reinhard. 2005. *Berlin 1945: A Documentation.* Berlin: Willmuth Arenhövel.
Ryan, Cornelius. 1966. *Der letzte Kampf.* Munich: Droemer/Knaur.
Schäfer, Hans Dieter. 1985. *Berlin im Zweiten Weltkrieg: der Untergang der Reichshauptstadt in Augenzeugenberichten.* Munich: Piper.
Schrade, Willi. 1977. LAB Rep. 240 Kleinschriftgut Zeitgeschichtliche Sammlung. Erlebnisberichte aus der Berliner Bevölkerung über die Zeit des Zweiten Weltkrieges und danach. Acc. 2651, Nr. 419.
Seamon, David. 1979. *The Geography of the Lifeworld.* London: Croom Helm.
Statistisches Landesamt Berlin. 1951. *Berlin in Zahlen.*
Von Hentig, Hans. 1947. "Kriminalität des Zusammenbruchs." *Schweizer Zeitschrift für Strafrecht* LXII.
Weingartner, Egon. 1951. "Die Notzucht. Eine kriminologische Untersuchung unter besonderer Berucksichtigung des Erscheinungsbildes der Notzuchtskriminalität in der heutigen Nachkriegszeit." PhD dissertation, University of Freiburg.

CHAPTER 2

The Propagandistic Role of Modern Art in Postwar Berlin

Maike Steinkamp

Immediately following the liberation of Berlin by Soviet troops on 2 May 1945 and the surrender of the Nazi regime on 8 May, Berlin's cultural life resumed. In this development of cultural renewal, a special role was attributed to modern art and particularly artists whom the National Socialists had defamed as "degenerate." Lauded in press reports and numerous exhibitions, these artists would become active players in the cultural reconstruction of the city and the country. Modern art in postwar Berlin can be understood as a political act, a statement—a break from the National Socialist regime and its cultural politics. With the beginning of the Cold War, the promotion of modern art reached a new dimension. It was no longer solely concerned with demonstrating liberty and the variety of artistic work after twelve years of Nazi dictatorship, but with aiding the formation of new cultural identities, which, in East and West Germany, had different meanings. Art exhibitions in particular served as substantial mediating institutions and events. In the following discussion, I would like to show to what extent modern art was elevated by these propagandistic means and how this contributed to the simultaneous formation of a new cultural and political self-image in the socialist East and democratic West. Varying political and cultural agendas of the occupying powers, changing political circumstances, and the central role played by modern art throughout this process were especially evident in Berlin's four occupation sectors.

Berlin's culture scene was, however, greatly determined by Soviet cultural officers at least during the first months following German capitulation. Their ambitions were characterized by openness, pragmatism, and a close cooperation with the German communist intelligentsia. By the time the Western Allies arrived in July and August 1945, the Soviet Military Administration (SMAD), in cooperation with the "Ulbricht Group," presented the situation as a fait accompli (Ribbe 2002). Municipal authorities, political parties, and trade unions had been set up, newspapers licensed, and libraries and museums created and again made accessible to the public (Reichhardt 1987: 87ff). Moreover, as Heiner Stahl argues in his contribution to this volume, broadcasting had been initiated, cinemas supplied with films, and the Kulturbund zur demokratischen Erneuerung Deutschlands (Cultural League for the Advancement of the Democratic Renewal of Germany) created. Berlin soon had considerably more possibilities for political and artistic articulation than any other area within occupied Germany (Reiche 1989: 43; Schulmeister 1977). Upon their arrival in the city, the Western Allies initially accepted those structures that had been created by the SMAD, though very quickly divergent developments were already appearing within Berlin's four sectors. With regard to cultural and educational policy, the Allies were pursuing different goals. Each of them, however, attached substantial meaning to the "reeducation" of the German people (Schivelbusch 1995: 52ff; Hinz 2000). Especially the French and Soviet occupying powers attributed a major role to fine arts in this process.[1] Alongside establishing contacts and cooperating with local individuals engaged in the cultural scene, the cultural centers of the respective occupying forces also took on an important role. The Amerika Haus (US Information Center) opened as early as February 1946, followed by the opening of the Haus der Kultur der Sowjetunion (Soviet Union House of Culture) one year later. In April 1948 and 1950, respectively, the British Information Center and the Maison de France took up their work. Through these centers, public lectures, exhibitions, and theater performances, the cultural achievements of the respective states were presented to the citizens of Berlin (Genton 2000: 37ff).

Even before the completion of the Maison de France, the French had already caused a sensation with their ambitious program of events—events that did not simply make international (French) modern art again accessible to the citizens of Berlin but also affirmed the French as the preeminent cultural force among the other occupying powers (Schieder 2005: 44). Paintings of French postimpressionists such as Paul Gauguin and Paul Cézanne, cubists such as Georges Braque and Pablo Picasso, as well as sculptures by Auguste Rodin, Constantin Brancusi, and Ossip Zadkine were highlighted in three large exhibitions of modern French art presented between 1946 and 1947.

This large number of French art exhibitions was quite characteristic. Only the Soviets between 1947 and 1949 offered comparable presenta-

Figure 2.1 Friedrich Seidenstücker: Documentary photograph of the exhibition *La sculpture française de Rodin à nos jours,* Zeughaus, Berlin, spring 1947, © bpk/Friedrich Seidenstücker.

tions of Soviet artworks at the Soviet Union House of Culture. Neither the Americans nor the British showed larger exhibitions of their country's modern artworks in the initial postwar period.[2] Instead, the United States started a cultural exchange program in October 1946. This program sought to exchange highlights from German and American art, literature, theater, and music in order to contribute to the internationalization of German culture (Ruby 1999: 52ff). Aside from presentations initiated by the occupying powers, local authorities in all sectors and the city's arts council attempted to exhibit the work of artists who had been vilified by the Nazis as well as young artists promoting what was to become the new artistic perspective.[3] New private galleries and the Kulturbund, founded in July 1945, contributed immensely to Berlin's cultural renewal (Heider 1993: 55ff; Schulmeister 1977). The Kulturbund in particular praised the pre-1933 artistic movements and presented this cultural heritage in form of exhibitions and lectures. The large number of exhibitions in these years demonstrated the will to renounce the National Socialist art doctrine. Especially Karl Hofer and Max Pechstein—like many artists residents of Berlin—gained great popularity and performed a role-model function not only as painters but also as teachers

Figure 2.2 Exhibition on Soviet Painting at the Soviet Union House of Culture, Summer 1949. Courtesy of German Historical Museum Berlin.

of the next generation.[4] The catalogue published for the 1946 Pechstein exhibition at the Admiralspalast on Friedrichstrasse stated:

> Pechstein is back. Homeless and pursued just a short time ago, he is working tirelessly again in our Berlin. He now spreads out before us what remained from the massive destruction of the war. Unfaltering and unaffected by Hitler art, Pechstein has forged his own way.... The work of forty years of a leading master reflects the most recent artistic developments and documents our path into the future. Pechstein belongs to us once again. (Jannasch 1946: 4, 7)

This feeling that the artist was an integral part of Berlin again not only involved Pechstein, but many other artists. Modern art from the beginning of the twentieth century stood for liberal, democratic values and was seen as an expression of the actual political orientation in all four sectors of Berlin and Germany. By returning to what had previously been dismissed as so-called degenerate art, they removed any lingering vestiges of Hitler's influence on art. By this time, the first signs of a new cultural and political course could already be seen in the Soviet sector.

Glimpses of the emerging cultural and political direction became clearer between 1947-48 as tensions arose among the victorious Allies. The withdrawal of Soviet representatives from the Allied Control Council on 16 June 1948 sealed the end of the Four Power administration in Berlin and advanced the division of the city and its administrative structures. The Berlin Blockade, lasting from June 1948 to May 1949, led to the foundation of two separate German states and marked the peak of the crisis (Weber 2003: 133; Ribbe 2002: 63ff). It is beyond question that this political discord became noticeable in the cultural area as well. While the politicians in the western sectors, and later in West Germany, sought a close connection with modern Western art and its alleged aesthetic autonomy, the SMAD and the SED in the Soviet sector, and later in the GDR, explicitly promoted a *wirklichkeitsnahe* and *volksverbundene* art, a realistic art connected to the people as defined by the doctrine of socialist realism in the Soviet Union. One result of this was that the Kulturbund was banned in the western sectors on 1 November 1947.[5] While the Kulturbund now operated exclusively in the eastern parts of Berlin, new cultural organizations and structures developed in the western districts (Schivelbusch 1995: 161). Mechanisms were set up on both sides independently of one another. In the Soviet sector, the structures relied heavily on the SED's exclusive claim to leadership (Köhler 1994: 253). The SMAD was said, as quoted in the West Berlin daily *Tagesspiegel* in January 1948, to have "opened" the population of Berlin, thereby increasing the people's access to their "intellectual world":

> If it were for the sheer quantity of exhibitions and expenditure of rhetoric and leaflets, the winner of the Allies competition for the sympathies and cultural awareness of the Berlin people would have to be the Soviet occupying powers. Because in the Soviet House of Culture, a place where propagandistic goals are actively pursued, exhibitions and lectures follow each other in quick succession (Schimming 1948).

The cultural events organized by the Soviets were indeed considerable. Although the American Joint Chiefs of Staff Directive 1779 of 11 July 1947 placed a higher value on cultural affairs within Germany's politics, it did not primarily address the visual arts (Davies 2006: 18). Even private initiatives, as the exhibition *Abstract Painting from America,* organized by Hilla Rebay from the holdings of the Museum of Non-Objective Painting (Guggenheim) in New York, which toured the western zones between 1948 and 1951, were not shown in Berlin. The French interrupted their exhibition activities during the Berlin Blockade (Zauner 2000: 91). With the exhibit *French Painting and Sculpture: 1938–1949,* which opened in the summer of 1950, France repeated the success of its earlier exhibitions of 1946–47, though by this time, they had lost their cultural preeminence to the Americans. Even if the Americans already dominated popular culture, they obtained an even more influential position in the visual arts with the escalation of the East-West conflict. It was in autumn of 1951 that they showed the exhibition *American Painting: Past and Present* in the course of the Berlin festival, presenting American paintings from the eighteenth century to the present day. A small historical section introduced artists such as John Singleton Copley and Gilbert Stuart to the German public. But it was mainly art from the twentieth century that was on view. The exhibition showed the magic realists Edward Hopper, Charles Sheeler, and Ben Shahn, whose works conveyed, as Will Grohmann wrote in his review in September 1951, a candid view of reality and did not develop a "false romanticism" as did their German counterparts of the New Objectivity (1951: 7). However, it was overall the abstract tendencies represented by Robert Motherwell, Georgia O'Keeffe, Jackson Pollock, Mark Rothko, and Mark Tobey that dominated the show.

Those responsible for selecting pieces for the exhibition had paid close attention to the guiding principle of the day, that only artists and works that the Soviets could not use for propagandistic means should be considered. Burton Cummings from the US State Department wrote in July 1951: "In discussing the contents of the show, he [Sergeant B. Child, US State Department] told me that for political reasons it would be a mistake to exhibit paintings whose subject matter could be used against us by the Russian propaganda machine. He felt that the only kind of individual artist who could possibly make any trouble would be one who was a reputed Pinko. He did not give any examples" (1951, in Ruby 1999: 296).

Fear that the Soviet propaganda machine could use the exhibition against the United States was not the only principle guiding the selection of works. In fact, the exhibition served American purposes precisely because the works presented were intended to attract audiences from both East and West Berlin.[6] Until the construction of the Berlin Wall in 1961, Berliners could visit art exhibitions and cultural events in all sectors of the city. But cultural officers on either side, as early as the Berlin Blockade, had been paying close attention to individual artists, noting which part of the city they came from, where they were teaching, and where they were showing their work. Artists who taught at an art academy in the eastern part of the city also had to take up residency there.

Conversely alleged socialist leanings or participation in exhibitions or programs in the Soviet sector could be used as reason for excluding people from employment at art academies in West Berlin (Fischer-Defoy 1989: 146).[7] Considering the fluctuations among the teaching staff during this period, it becomes abundantly clear just how many artists and other members of the cultural scene either wanted or were required to switch sides because they could not realize their political and artistic ideals (i.e., in the West) or because they found themselves confronted with increasingly restrictive cultural policies (i.e., in the East) compromising their artistic freedom.

In general, cultural functionaries of the SMAD and SED increased their influence on the direction of art production in the Soviet sector. In the course of the infamous Formalism Debate of 1948–49 and 1951–52, they demanded a clean break from what was seen as the "methods of formalism" and the "reactionary tendencies" of the past, including nearly all art from the first third of the twentieth century. An article in the *Tägliche Rundschau* in December 1950 described this as a break from the "integral component of cosmopolitan ideology, the official dominant ideology in American circles" (Alex 1950: 4). According to this article, abstract formalist tendencies were raising form as an end in itself and thus destroyed any historical or national content, as they were not incorporating the life of the people and the interest in peace and democracy in their works of art. But exactly what was expected of art production in the Soviet sector? It was expected that realistic art address the concerns of the day. The political recourse of this art expressed itself in a number of state-initiated art projects. One example was the so-called *Wandbildaktion* (mural event) of Horst Strempel at Friedrichstrasse station. His mural painting *Trümmer weg! Baut auf!* (Clear the Rubble! Rebuild!), finished in 1948, meant to represent the reconstruction of the city after the end of World War II showing the achievements of the SED regime. Only two years later his painting was no longer considered suitable, neither in form nor in expression, to symbolize the building of the new socialist state. The mural became a victim of the antiformalism campaign and was removed in February 1951.

Politically motivated exhibitions also increased. Two exemplary shows where the exhibitions *Mensch und Arbeit* (People and Work) in May/June 1949 and *Künstler schaffen für den Frieden* (Artists for Peace) in December 1951.[8]

Carefully selecting the themes, artistic media, and manner of presentation, the organizers exerted great influence over the way the artworks were received. For example, artists had to represent the emerging socialist society, focusing on themes such as work and the so-called progres-

Figure 2.3 Catalogue of *Künstler schaffen für den Frieden* (1951). Photograph by the author.

sive human condition. By now a majority of the artists had distanced themselves from formalist tendencies, which had been denounced as outdated. Artists who would not fulfill these requirements were no longer considered for inclusion in exhibitions. Indirectly, this official approach also implied a repudiation of artistic developments in the western sectors.

In the West, abstract expressionism was praised as the guarantor of artistic freedom since it seemed entirely removed from politics. Expressionist artists from the prewar period and painters such as Heinz Trökes, Mac Zimmermann, Alexander Camaro, or Hans Uhlmann achieved considerable success in numerous exhibitions. While the ideals of artistic freedom were praised and their values explicitly stated in exhibition catalogues, artists following a realistic style were nevertheless rarely included in exhibitions. The allegiance to freedom was not to be demonstrated through realist artworks. This became obvious at the first show presented by the West German Art Federation in Berlin 1951, an exhibition dominated by the abstract expressionist paintings of Max Ackermann, Willi Baumeister, and Ernst Wilhelm Nay. "Justly Chosen for Freedom's Noble Fight" (Redslob 1951), the exhibition catalogue stated, these artists were celebrated as representatives of the new political order and the will of artistic expression. In the exhibition catalogue, Jakob Kaiser, minister for All-German Affairs, declared: "This exhibition as a whole is an image, a mirror of the visual arts of our day: free from the bondage of dictators old and new, free from all those influences and aims foreign to art, and solely subject to our own responsibility, with mutual respect and mutual toleration of everything different" (Kaiser 1951).

Berlin had not simply become a "stage for the Cold War" with the establishment of the two German states in 1949. The different interests of occupying powers had already become apparent when Berlin was liberated in May 1945. In staging the political divide, the visual arts, and culture more generally, took on an important role. The large number and great variety of exhibitions in both East and West Berlin attests to this strategic role. A new cultural landscape, appropriate to the new political circumstances, was created with the help of art and its institutions. As shown, the Allied occupying powers contributed considerably to the formation of the art historical canon by supporting German projects as well as by promoting their own art. On either side, both in the West and East of Berlin and in Germany, modern art was used simultaneously to stabilize the political situation and to aid the formation of national identity. This phenomenon was particularly apparent in Berlin where two political systems, two *Weltanschauungen* (world views), and two diametrically opposed concepts of art confronted each other face to face.

Notes

1. As Trommler notes, the Americans attributed only a minor role to culture in reaching German intellectuals. They mainly focused on disseminating a positive image of the United States (Trommler 2001: 571). For the cultural politics of the British, see Davies 2006.

2. Only the addendum to the US Allies Charter in February 1949 listed art exhibitions and museum shows as suitable areas for reeducation in Germany.
3. As early as the summer of 1945, the Kammer der Kunstschaffenden (Chamber of Artists) showed the First Exhibition of the Chamber of Artists in the badly damaged Royal Palace. One year later, in May 1946, the First German Art Exhibition opened in the former Armory on Unter den Linden. Between 1945 and 1948 the Department of Fine Arts at the magistrate in Berlin organized numerous modern art exhibitions; see the documentation by Vierneisel 1989. District departments of culture, as for example the department in Steglitz, also organized several exhibitions and other cultural events.
4. The popularity of Max Pechstein is apparent in the large number of articles dealing with Pechstein exhibitions and his position at the Academy of Fine Arts in the western sector. See the press clippings on Pechstein at the Zentralarchiv, Staatliche Museen zu Berlin, Stiftung Preußischer Kulturbesitz.
5. The catalyst for the ban was a scandal at the Erste Schriftstellerkongress (First Congress of Authors) on 8 October 1947. The American writer Melvin J. Lasky criticized censorship in the Soviet Union, whereupon he was verbally attacked by a member of the Soviet delegation. On the same day, public notices of the ban of the Kulturbund circulated in the western sectors of Berlin. Beginning on 1 November 1947, the Americans prohibited any activity of the Kulturbund in their sector. This prohibition was expanded to the British sector on 11 November 1947; the French soon followed suit.
6. It was the explicit wish of HICOG that the catalogue of the exhibition could also be purchased with Ostmark by visitors from the eastern sector. See the comment on the exhibition American Painting Past and Present, Hauptamt Kunst II/2, Bericht über die Ausstellung "amerikanische Malerei," gez. GL, 6. Februar 1952 (Landesarchiv Berlin, B Rep. 014, Nr. 1614)
7. See for example the dismissal of Heinrich Ehmsen from the Academy of Fine Arts in the western sector of Berlin. The cause of his dismissal was, among other things, his signature under the welcoming address of the German "intellectuals" to the World Peace Congress in Paris. Karl Hofer had also signed it. Hofer had also accepted "Pajoks," food packages, from the Soviets, for which he was criticized in the press (Fischer-Defoy 1989: 146).
8. Other exhibitions dealing explicitly with the building of socialism were *150 Jahre soziale Strömungen in der bildenden Kunst* (150 Years of Social Tendencies in the Fine Arts), *Der schaffende Mensch* (Productive Man), and *Künstler sehen die Großstadt* (Artists See the City), all three in 1947; *Die Arbeit in der Kunst* (Work in Art) in 1948; and *Soziale Kunst: Mexikanische Revolutionsgrafik* (Social Art: Mexican Graphic Arts of the Revolution) and *Berlin lebt–Berlin ruft* (Berlin Lives–Berlin Calls) in 1949 (Vierneisel 1989).

Works Cited

Alex, S. 1950. "Verfall der bildenden Kunst im Westen." *Tägliche Rundschau* 20, 20 December: 4.
Davies, Veronica. 2006. "German Initiatives and British Interventions 1945–51." In *Kunstgeschichte nach 1945: Kontinuität und Neubeginn in Deutschland*, ed. Nikola Doll et al., 13–20. Cologne: Böhlau.
Feist, Günter. 1989. "Das Wandbild im Bahnhof Friedrichstrasse. Eine Horst Strempel Dokumentation 1945–1955." In *Zone 5. Kunst in der Viersektorenstadt 1945–1951*, ed. Eckehard Gillen and Diether Schmidt, 92–137. Berlin: Dirk Nishen.
Fischer-Defoy, Christine. 1989. "Die Neugründung der HfBK Berlin im Ost-West Konflikt 1945–51." In *Zone 5. Kunst in der Viersektorenstadt 1945–1951*, ed. Eckhard Gillen and Diether Schmidt, 138–50. Berlin.
Französische Malerei und Plastik 1938–1948. 1950. Berlin: n. p.
Genton, Bernard. 2000. "Berlin als Theater der Nationen." In *Die vier Besatzungsmächte und die Kultur in Berlin 1945–1949*, ed. Hans-Martin Hinz, 29–40. Leipzig: Leipziger Universitäts-Verlag.

Grohmann, Will. 1951. "Die Neue Kunst in der Neuen Welt. Amerikanische Malerei im Schöneberger Rathaus." In *Die Neue Zeitung* 219, 20 September: 7.
Heider, Magdalena. 1993. *Politik–Kultur–Kulturbund: Zur Gründungs- und Frühgeschichte des Kulturbundes zur demokratischen Erneuerung Deutschlands 1945–1954 in der SBZ/DDR*. Cologne: Wissenschaft und Politik.
Hinz, Hans-Martin. 2000. *Die vier Besatzungsmächte und die Kultur in Berlin 1945–1949*. Leipzig: Universitäts-Verlag.
Jannasch, Adolf. 1946. *Pechstein-Ausstellung*. Berlin: n. p.
Kaiser, Jacob. 1951. "Preface." In *Deutscher Künstlerbund 1950. Erste Ausstellung 1. August–1. Oktober 1951*. Berlin: n. p.
Köhler, Roland. 1994. "Die Behandlung Berlins als kulturelles Zentrum durch die sowjetische Besatzungsmacht." In *Kulturpolitik im besetzten Deutschland 1945–1949*, ed. Gabriele Clemens, 237–54. Stuttgart: Steiner.
Redslob, Edwin. 1951. "Idee und Geschichte des Deutschen Künstlerbundes." In *Erste Ausstellung 1. August–1. Oktober 1951*. Berlin: n. p.
Reiche, Jürgen. 1989. "Berlin. Zukunft nach dem Ende." In *So viel Anfang war nie: Deutsche Städte 1945–1949*, ed. Hermann Glaser, 36–49. Berlin: Siedler.
Reichhardt, Hans J. 1987. "... raus aus den Trümmern." *Vom Beginn des Wiederaufbaus in Berlin*. Berlin: Transit.
Ribbe, Wolfgang. 2002. *Berlin 1945–2000: Grundzüge der Stadtgeschichte*. Berlin: BWV Berliner Wissenschaftsverlag.
Ruby, Sigrid. 1999. *"Have We An American Art?" Präsentation und Rezeption amerikanischer Malerei in Westdeutschland und Westeuropa der Nachkriegszeit*. Weimar: Verlag und Datenbank für Geisteswissenschaften.
Schieder, Martin. 2005. *Im Blick des Anderen: Die Deutsch-Französischen Kunstbeziehungen 1945–1959*. Berlin: Akademie.
Schimming, Wolfgang. 1948. "Vorbilder zum Guten." *Tagesspiegel*, 21 January.
Schivelbusch, Wolfgang. 1995. *Vor dem Vorhang: Das geistige Berlin 1945–1948*. Munich: Fischer.
Schulmeister, Karl-Heinz. 1977. *Auf dem Weg zu einer neuen Kultur: Der Kulturbund in den Jahren 1945–1949*. Berlin: Dietz.
Trommler, Frank. 2001. "Neuer Start und alte Vorurteile. Die Kulturbeziehungen im Zeichen des Kalten Krieges 1945–1968." In *Die USA und Deutschland im Zeitalter des Kalten Krieges 1945–1990: Ein Handbuch*, ed. Detlef Junker, 2: 567–91. Stuttgart: Deutsche Verlags Anstalt.
Vierneisel, Beatrice. 1989. "Berliner Ausstellungschronologie 1945–1951." In *Zone 5: Kunst in der Viersektorenstadt 1945–1951*, ed. Eckehard Gillen and Diether Schmidt, 235–71. Berlin: Dirk Nishen.
Weber, Hermann. 2003. *Geschichte der DDR*. Erftstadt: AREA.
Zauner, Stefan. 2000. "Die französische Kulturmission in Berlin." In *Die vier Besatzungsmächte und die Kultur in Berlin 1945–1949*, ed. Hans-Martin Hinz, 87–101. Leipzig: Universitäts-Verlag.

CHAPTER 3

Back to the Future
New Music's Revival and Redefinition in Occupied Berlin

Elizabeth Janik

This essay will explore the reconstruction and eventual East-West division of Berlin's musical community after 1945, using as its leading example the reception of New Music in the city's American- and Soviet-occupied sectors. Berlin's postwar cultural authorities strove to promote music that would represent and support a new Germany. To define the post-Nazi musical future, they turned backward in time, encouraging musical expressions that had been a hallmark of the interwar era, in Germany and abroad.

The term "New Music" (*Neue Musik*) entered into widespread use in the German musical press of the 1920s (Stephan 1969; Thrun 1995; Ballstaedt 2003). Perhaps most prominently, New Music described the harmonic and formal experiments associated with modernist composers like Arnold Schoenberg and Igor Stravinsky. The German section of the International Society for New Music (IGNM), one of the first and most active national affiliates, was founded in Berlin in 1922. The society's annual festivals sought to promote international understanding through the performance of new musical works. Equally important, the IGNM provided a friendly platform for the performance of avant-garde chamber works that were unlikely to find favor among wider concert audiences.

Other New Music initiatives in Weimar Berlin questioned the very basis of traditional concert performance. These included Paul Hindemith's work with the youth music movement and other forms of *Gebrauchsmusik* (music for use), Bertolt Brecht's and his collaborators' politically oriented

Lehrstücke (learning plays), as well as Hanns Eisler's overtly socialist *Kampfmusik* (literally, battle music) and ties to the workers' music movement. As diverse and sometimes incompatible as these musical expressions were, all found a voice in Berlin institutions associated with New Music, including the IGNM, a radical artists' society called the November Group, the music journal *Melos,* and the festival New Music 1930.

In the aftermath of World War I, New Music became a rallying cry for young progressives who sought to challenge the musical norms and traditions of an older generation. For cultural conservatives, it was a symbol of aesthetic and moral degeneracy. The best-known artists associated with the New Music movement, including Schoenberg, Hindemith, Brecht, and Eisler, were compelled to emigrate soon after the National Socialists' rise to power. Yet less-prominent New Music enthusiasts (with acceptable racial and political credentials) remained active in Berlin's musical life before and after 1933. Despite the rhetoric of Nazi ideologues, Hitler's regime never pursued consistent policies to stamp out twelve-tone, jazz, and other "cultural bolshevist" music. While open advocacy of such idioms was intolerable, supposedly taboo harmonies and rhythms continued to sound throughout the Third Reich, as long as they were linked with musicians acceptable to the regime, and were placed in an appropriate German nationalist context instead of that of the Weimar-era New Music (Levi 1994: 82–123; Kater 1997: 177–188; Potter 1998: 16–25).

After 1945, then, a core of now middle-aged New Music enthusiasts in Berlin was poised to take up the cause with renewed vigor. Because New Music had never gained a wide following among German audiences, it could be touted as an antidote to Nazi cultural policy, in the city's eastern and western sectors alike. Berliners who demonstrated their longtime support for the musical avant-garde typically enhanced their status as political resisters before Allied de-Nazification tribunals. Soviet and American officers, meanwhile, used New Music as a means of demonstrating their cultural sophistication and goodwill. Only after Cold War tensions had divided the city politically did separate conceptions of the German musical future take root in eastern and western Berlin, each buttressed by a differing interpretation of the Weimar musical heritage.

As the headquarters of Germany's postwar military government and home to the country's most prestigious institutions of the arts, Berlin was pivotal to the Allied occupiers' mission of cultural and political reform. All four Allied authorities maintained propaganda or information control divisions that were responsible for registering artists, approving concerts and theatrical productions, and determining best how to de-Nazify the local arts community. Allied military officials also provided Berliners with positive cultural examples from their own national traditions, particularly works that had been discouraged or banned by Nazi authorities. New Music fit this bill nicely, although in practice it presented the two postwar superpowers with some unusual challenges.

The Soviets arrived in Berlin first, assuming sole administrative responsibility for the city in May and June 1945. The Soviet Military Administration in Germany (SMAD) was a chaotic entity, plagued by internal rivalries, unclear lines of authority, and makeshift decision making. The Soviet occupiers were an unpredictable and often fearsome variable in the lives of Berliners, yet they cultivated an altogether different image when it came to matters of arts and culture. Sergei Tjulpanov, Alexander Dymshits, Sergei Barsky, and other officers in SMAD's Administration for Propaganda and Censorship quickly earned the respect of local artists and intellectuals. They spoke fluent German and were well versed in the European cultural canon; they elevated art and music to a matter of high priority within the Soviet administration (Schivelbusch 1995: 58–60; Hartmann and Eggeling 1998: 147–152, 165–174). In the first postwar weeks, Soviet authorities oversaw a comprehensive reactivation of the city's elite musical institutions. The Berlin Philharmonic Orchestra recommenced its regular performances on 26 May 1945; the city's two major opera houses reopened their doors soon thereafter.

Musical performances in Soviet-occupied Berlin typically featured both Russian and German classics (Tchaikovsky, Beethoven, and Mozart prevailed), with German works easily outnumbering Russian ones. Contemporary music was more problematic. With the exception of a handful of works by Shostakovich and Prokofiev, almost no twentieth-century Russian or Soviet music was performed in Berlin in 1945–46.[1] There were good reasons for this hesitation: recent party crackdowns on "formalism" in the Soviet arts community had discredited much of the country's latest creative output.

The interwar New Music movement had not been limited to Weimar Germany; Russian cities such as Moscow and Leningrad had cultivated vibrant New Music scenes that united the ideals of radical aesthetic and social change. Changes set into motion by Stalin's rise to power replaced the musical eclecticism of the 1920s with more rigid state control. A Union of Soviet Composers replaced all rival music organizations, promoting socialist realism as the standard to which all musicians ought aspire. Socialist realism merged reverence for the classic-romantic heritage with new genres like the mass song, resulting an inspirational musical idiom that was intended to reflect the progressive development of Soviet society.

After 1945, similarities between Stalin's and Hitler's cultural policies were readily apparent to Berliners and their Western occupiers. Both regimes had generously funded the arts but clamped down on artistic freedom, emphasizing instead the artist's obligation to society, although Nazi cultural authorities had been less doctrinaire in their attempts to engineer new musical standards. Thus Soviet officials in Berlin were in the awkward position of representing a regime that was in many ways more culturally repressive than that of the National Socialists. In the first postwar year, they glossed over this dilemma as much as possible. Instead, they supported the local arts community magnanimously, emphasizing their similarities, rather than their differences, with German high cultural tradition.

The American Office of the Military Government for Germany (OMGUS) operated according to more clearly defined objectives and lines of authority than the Soviet military authorities on the opposite side of the city. Overall the American occupation regime was much more benign than that of the Soviets, but the occupiers' roles reversed with respect to their monitoring of the local arts community. The Americans' initial priority was to close down cultural activities, not to restart them. Local artists were required to register with OMGUS's Information Control Division (ICD), and all music and theater groups had to obtain a license demonstrating their de-Nazification before recommencing performances.[2]

Few American compositions of any era were heard on Berlin stages in the first postwar year; a stand-out exception was the Berlin Philharmonic Orchestra's presentation of William Grant Still's *Afro-American Symphony* in September 1945. Berliners apparently considered the piece more a novelty than a serious contribution to the symphonic repertoire; it was not performed again throughout the duration of the Allied occupation. And herein the lay the American cultural officers' dilemma. John Bitter, Benno Frank, and others were sent to "reorient" the German people and introduce them to the achievements of American culture, yet the world of classical music had been dominated by Europeans—and particularly Germans—for well over a century. If the officers had not themselves received their musical training in Germany, their mentors most likely had. They rarely questioned accepted standards of European high culture. The propagation of jazz and other American popular music in occupied Germany occurred primarily through channels intended for the American troops. For German audiences, ICD officers promoted jazz most readily when integrated within "legitimate" orchestral pieces like the *Afro-American Symphony* or Gershwin's *Rhapsody in Blue*.[3]

The Americans had good reason to encourage the performance of these and other contemporary works. Until the early twentieth century, relatively few American composers had enjoyed international recognition. American conservatories, opera houses, and professional symphony orchestras were younger than their European counterparts, and they received little if any public subsidy. The interwar New Music movement leveled the international playing field by challenging the existing musical establishment. New Music provided American composers with the tools to develop a distinctive musical idiom, just as the Europeans were reinventing theirs. Thus ICD officers promoted New Music not only to counteract the Nazis' suppression of musical modernism, but also because they believed that the latest generation of American composers compared most flatteringly to their European colleagues. These officers sought to demonstrate that American music by modernist composers like Aaron Copland, Roy Harris, Samuel Barber, and Walter Piston was sophisticated enough to be performed by the elite ensembles under their supervision. Their efforts began to bear fruit in the second postwar year.

Berlin's unusual status as a musical Mecca and the headquarters of Germany's military occupation compelled American and Soviet authorities alike to modify their cultural-political agendas by 1946–47. Americans consented to more lenient de-Nazification standards than they had initially intended, while the Soviets tolerated modernist sounds in Berlin that would have been unacceptable in their home country. In competition with each other and seeking the loyalties of their German charges, the Allies encouraged Berlin to become a lively—and heavily subsidized—center of New Music activity.

Before and after 1945, Berlin's elite ensembles tended a repertoire that was overwhelmingly dominated by German masters from the eighteenth and nineteenth centuries. Yet New Music, loosely defined as the work of composers who came of age in the 1920s and later, as well as that of older experimenters like Schoenberg and Stravinsky, made an impressive comeback on the city's stages in 1946–47. The term *New Music* did not necessarily refer to the most recent musical works. "Much of the music from yesterday—yes, even from the day before yesterday—is still new, because it was denied to us for the past twelve years," explained one critic. "In this respect our concert programs are gradually beginning to regain color." (Kroll 1946: 3) Stravinsky and Hindemith were the most frequently performed New Music composers, followed by Britten, Prokofiev, and Shostakovich. Intriguingly, little difference existed between the kinds of contemporary music performed by the city's eastern and western ensembles in 1946–47. The American music officer John Bitter conducted Shostakovich with eastern and western sector symphony orchestras, and the Soviet-administered German State Opera premiered the first American opera in postwar Berlin.

Berlin's leading music critics of the immediate postwar era, including Erwin Kroll, Kurt Westphal, Hans Heinz Stuckenschmidt, and Herbert Graf, had established their journalistic careers as New Music enthusiasts twenty years previous. The young rebels of Weimar Berlin became the experts and elder statesmen of the postwar musical community. Yet their promotion of New Music was more cautious than it had been a generation earlier. They wrote informative, evenhanded accounts about neoclassicism and primitivism, chamber music and mechanical music, atonality, pantonality, and even the return to traditional tonality. Few aligned themselves with any one musical cause, and they paid careful tribute to the musical accomplishments of the four Allied powers. After the failed National Socialist cultural experiment, modesty was the order of the day.

Such reserve notwithstanding, many of these critics held strong convictions about New Music's nature and purpose. The composer and author Paul Höffer explained that

> the fundamental achievements of this music include: Incorporating twelve-tone chromaticism without the dominance of the leading tone, liberating rhythm and meter from centuries of confining symmetry, abandoning the supremacy of regular periodic structure, and regenerating all small and large forms. These elements are, so to speak, the hammer, pliers, and nails given to us by new music from the very beginning. The use and full exploitation of this material is our task, and the task of the coming generation (Höffer 1947a: 4).

From this perspective, the essence of New Music was absolute: it lay in the (re)discovery of new sounds, rhythms, and forms, not in the exploration of music's representational or social capacities. Conspicuously absent in the musical press of 1946–47 was discussion of workers' music, the youth music movement, and the other kinds of "music for use" that had occupied New Music enthusiasts in the 1920s.

The reluctance to reexplore these musical paths was not altogether surprising. The leftist workers' and youth music movements of the Weimar era had thrived with only minor modifications under the auspices of National Socialist organizations like the Hitler Youth and Strength Through Joy (Kraft durch Freude, or KdF). In the first postwar months, therefore, most critics took pains to reassert music's essentially apolitical nature. According to one author, the popular KdF concerts had been one of the "greatest aberrations" of the Nazi era. "Music was presented to the masses in forms that did not correspond to them. Just because the KdF brought them into contact with the heights of musical achievement, this did not promote actual understanding" (Herzfeld 1946: 183–84). If the Third Reich had been an aberration in German musical development, then government intervention and the exploitation of music as a means of social and political activism were among the era's primary failings.

Berlin's earliest New Music initiatives promoted a cultural ideal that was self-consciously nonpolitical despite the fact that most found their homes in the American occupation sector. Zehlendorf district authorities sponsored contemporary chamber concerts at the Haus am Waldsee, as well as an International Music Institute that sought to reacquaint German music students with modernist techniques. Stuckenschmidt led a Studio for New Music at the American-sector radio station RIAS. In 1947, he and his colleague Josef Rufer received American licensing to publish their own music journal, *Stimmen*, which aggressively promoted the cause of New Music.

There was, however, an important exception to the American sector's New Music monopoly—a well-attended series of contemporary chamber concerts sponsored by the Kulturbund zur demokratischen Erneuerung Deutschlands (Cultural League for the Democratic Renewal of Germany). Inspired by the antifascist cultural leagues of the 1930s, the Kulturbund had been established by local cultural leaders and returning émigrés from the Soviet Union in June 1945. Unlike art organizations that were licensed by Berlin's Western occupiers, the Soviet-sponsored Kulturbund emphasized that art could and should play a political role in Germany's democratic renewal (Pike 1992: 80–88; Heider 1993; Schivelbusch 1995: 117–128).

In 1946 the Kulturbund's central administration established advisory committees of leading Berlin artists in fields such as music, theater, literature, and the visual arts. The Kommission Musik, under the leadership of Heinz Tiessen, was practically a "Who's Who" of the local New Music community. The committee soon organized a series of contemporary music evenings, which were held at the Kulturbund's Club der Kulturschaffenden in the Soviet sector. The concerts showcased a cross-section of New Music composers, including Bartók, Britten, Copland, Eisler, Hindemith, Milhaud, Prokofiev, Schoenberg, Stravinsky, and Webern, as well as the works of Kommission members Tiessen, Höffer, and Max Butting. More contemporary American chamber music was performed at the Club der Kulturschaffenden than at the American-sector Haus am Waldsee in 1946–47.[4]

So what did the contemporary music evenings have to do with Germany's democratic renewal? "Very much," answered Höffer: "Narrow-mindedness, inflexibility, and the inability to adopt an unprejudiced outlook are the worst enemies of democracy; they are equally bitter enemies of new music" (1947b: 3). The Kulturbund's leadership was less certain. Its general secretary praised the high artistic standards of the committees, but he expressed concern over their lack of engagement in cultural-political issues; their intended role as advisors to local Kulturbund groups had been largely forgotten.[5] The first signs of political strain were evident in New Music's postwar revival.

The Allied Four-Power Administration of Berlin broke down irreparably in the spring of 1948. The municipal government splintered into eastern and western halves by the year's end, and the local musical community gradually followed suit. In this polarizing political environment, New Music lost its appeal as an all-purpose antidote against fascism and a "bridge between nations." (Kroll 1946: 6) Western proponents of New Music disowned the term's pre-1933 social (and particularly socialist) content, refashioning it as a bulwark against politically manipulated art. Eastern authorities disassociated themselves from the phrase altogether, adopting instead the parole of "realism" as their road map for the musical future.

This transition did not occur all at once. Although the Soviet Central Committee had recently resumed its crusade against formalism in the arts and culture, SMAD officers made few serious efforts to discipline wayward artists in occupied Berlin. Barsky and Dymshits promoted discussions of socialist realism in the eastern-sector press, but they appear to have censored no performances on musical grounds alone (Barskij 1948: 3; Dymschits 1948: 4; Hartmann and Eggeling 1998: 157–162). The German State Opera staged local premieres of operas by Hindemith and Gottfried von Einem, while the Soviet-administered Berlin Radio Symphony Orchestra performed "absolute" works by Shostakovich and Khachaturian that had fallen out of favor in the USSR. The murkiness of the formalism concept notwithstanding, these and other pieces should have set off bells of warning for even the laxest of cultural watchdogs. The greater caesura in eastern-sector concert programs occurred after the first generation of Soviet cultural officers were sent home, and German SED administrators took the lead in monitoring local performances. The city's first great public controversy over musical formalism, concerning Bertolt Brecht's and Paul Dessau's opera *Das Verhör des Lukullus* (The Trial of Lucullus), took place under the instigation of SED authorities in 1951.

The parting of ways of Berlin's musical elites was reflected through the changing face of the Kulturbund, which the Western Allies banned from their occupation sectors at the end of 1947. The organization's contemporary music evenings continued unabated, but the concerts were increasingly overshadowed by very different musical initiatives. In October 1948, the Kulturbund and the FDGB cosponsored a conference entitled "The Two-Year Plan and Producers of Culture." Delegates discussed the sponsorship of factories by musical conservatories, the establishment of touring orchestras to perform at local workplaces, as well as the formation of working-class choirs. Founding members of the Kommission Musik began to distance themselves from the organization, and new members stepped in to take their places. Ernst Hermann Meyer and Nathan Notowicz had been committed socialists since the 1920s; they had only recently returned to Germany after years in exile. Max Butting and Karl Laux, on the other hand, had enjoyed relatively successful careers in Nazi Germany. In 1948–49, this unlikely quartet found common ground in the Kulturbund. All four were suspicious of American popular culture, and they eschewed the esoterism of the international avant-garde in favor of a more practically oriented "music for use." They believed that state intervention was necessary to protect the unity and integrity of German musical tradition in the postwar era. In short, all four men were budding members of a new eastern German cultural elite: Butting was the head of the composers' section in the FDGB; Laux a music critic at the east-sector newspaper *Tägliche Rundschau;* Meyer a professor of music sociology at Humboldt University; and Notowicz soon to be appointed to the faculty of the new (East Berlin) conservatory. All were residents of eastern Berlin; all except Butting were members of the SED. The Kulturbund's contemporary chamber evenings grew fewer and farther between; the twenty-second and final concert was held in June 1949.[6]

The Kommission Musik was defunct by the end of 1949, but several of its members had already shifted the focus of their musical initiatives elsewhere, to the refounded German chapter of the International Society for New Music (IGNM). Ironically reestablishment of the IGNM in Germany had been one of the Kommission Musik's earliest goals. As late as September 1947, Höffer, Butting, and Tiessen were engaged in negotiations to reestablish the German chapter *within* the Kulturbund's institutional framework. When the chapter was formally established in the summer of 1948, however, it was as a "nonpolitical organization" in the American sector. The chapter's founders were all residents of West Berlin or West Germany. Tiessen announced the reestablishment of the IGNM as fulfilling one of the Kommission Musik's earliest goals, but it was a hollow victory for the Kulturbund.[7] The IGNM's chamber music series, which commenced in December 1948, drew audiences as well as performers away from the Kommission Musik's eastern-sector concerts. The Haus am Waldsee was home not only to the IGNM concerts, but also to the Kulturbund's western rival, the Liga für geistige Freiheit

(League for Intellectual Freedom). New Music in Berlin had begun to demonstrate a distinctly anticommunist slant.

In the summer of 1948, Stuckenschmidt and Rufer devoted nearly an entire issue of *Stimmen* to rebut the Soviet Central Committee's resolutions against formalism. Stuckenschmidt asserted that the resolutions

> correspond factually, down to the details of their formulation, with the artistic maxims of the National Socialists from whose spiritual terror we have been free only three years. "Decay," "alienation from the people" (*Volksfremdheit*), "subjectivism," and "atonal dissonance" were reasons why the performance of works by Paul Hindemith and Alban Berg were forbidden, and why a war of annihilation was declared against all who interceded for them. And this campaign was conducted in the name of the people (*Volk*) as well, in the name of the millions of workers who found the *l'art pour l'art* games of a handful of intellectual snobs to be incomprehensible (Stuckenschmidt 1948: 211).

These were fighting words; association with Nazi cultural policy was the ultimate condemnation in Berlin's postwar musical community. A few months later, Stuckenschmidt embarked upon a two-month, coast-to-coast tour of the United States through an OMGUS cultural exchange program. His upbeat observations on American musical life appeared regularly in the western newspaper *Die Neue Zeitung* throughout the spring of 1949.[8]

Earlier that year, the composer Hanns Eisler returned to Berlin on the invitation of SED officials. Eisler had been a powerful presence in Weimar Berlin's New Music community. He had studied twelve-tone composition under Arnold Schoenberg, collaborated with workers' choirs and agitprop troops, and even befriended Stuckenschmidt. Resident in Southern California since 1942, Eisler returned to Europe six years later after an unfriendly encounter before the House Committee on Un-American Activities in its investigation of communist subversion in Hollywood. Unsurprisingly, Eisler's thoughts on music—and the United States—deviated sharply from Stuckenschmidt's. In an address to Humboldt University students, Eisler took direct aim at the latest activities of Berlin's New Music leadership. He argued that socially responsible composers could not content themselves with producing "sophisticated chamber music" for a small circle of musical experts. Rather creative artists had to strive to dissolve the "old opposition between entertainment and art, *Bildung* and amusement" by turning their attentions to the working class, "the most progressive stratum of the people (*Volk*)" (Eisler 1949: 205–6). Soon thereafter, Eisler received a National Prize for composing the German Democratic Republic's national hymn. His name all but disappeared from American and West German musical life for years to come.

In 1949, Hanns Eisler seemed well on his way to becoming the honored elder statesman of the GDR musical community. His subsequent relationship with SED authorities, however, was far from smooth. Party officials deemed much of his work too complex or pessimistic for public performance. The 1953 controversy surrounding his unfinished opera, *Johann Faustus*, marked the height of the Soviet-style campaign against formalism in the young GDR. Like his colleague and fellow reemigrant from the United States Paul Dessau, Eisler's nuanced thoughts on music clashed with the black and white spirit of the early Cold War era.

The interwar New Music movement had sought to revolutionize musical practice through a variety of innovations—some purely aesthetic, others involving social and political change. In the polarizing atmosphere of early Cold War Berlin, all middle ground fell away between these divergent paths of musical progress. Eastern party officials underscored the role of musical amateurs and the necessity of state patronage and intervention. Western critics promoted a modernist musical ideal that was intellectually challenging (perhaps even unpleasant to the untrained ear) and free from political interference. Both sides viewed the musical practice of the other Berlin as an illegitimate perversion of German tradition. A musical Iron Curtain separated the two Berlins until at least the late 1960s, when a growing core of musicians from both city halves began to revisit neglected Weimar-era legacies and embrace musical influences from the United States, the other Germany, and elsewhere around the world.

Notes

1. This and subsequent references to Berlin's musical repertoire are drawn from Janik 2005: 305–21.
2. National Archives (NA) 260/390/46/17/4/248, "Reorientation Activities of ODIC in Germany: Theater and Music," 15 April 1947. See also Monod 2005.
3. NA 84/350/56/35/5/1, Memo to the Berlin Kommandatura, 3 August 1945. See also Poiger 2000: 38–43.
4. Concert programs are available at the Haus am Waldsee and the Bundesarchiv-Stiftung Archiv der Parteien und Massenorganisationen der DDR (BA-SAPMO), DY 27/215. See also Köster 2002: 123–34.
5. BA-SAPMO, DY 27/122, Protokoll der Sitzung der Kommissionsvorsitzenden, 28 February 1947.
6. BA-SAPMO, DY 27/433, Protokoll der Sitzung der Kommission Musik, 16 November 1948; and Stiftung Archiv der Akademie der Künste (SAAdK), Ernst Hermann Meyer-Archiv, 196, "Aufgaben der Musik im Zwei-Jahr-Plan." See also Notowicz 1949; and Thacker 2007: 105–18.
7. SAAdK, Heinz Tiessen-Archiv, Butting to Tiessen, 11 Sept. 1947; NA 260/390/48/10/4–7/97, Petition of "Internationale Gesellschaft für Neue Musik e.V.," 21 May 1948; and BA-SAPMO, DY 27/433, Protokoll der Sitzung der Kommission Musik, 3 September 1948.

8. NA 260/390/46/16/6-7/214, "GERMAN CONSULTANTS CA BRANCH," and 260/390/42/16/5-6/70, Van Delden to Director, ECRD, 5 October 1949. See also Stuckenschmidt 1979: 192-209; and Beal 2006: 41-44.

Works Cited

Ballstaedt, Andreas. 2003. *Wege zur Neuen Musik: Über einige Grundlagen der Musikgeschichtsschreibung des 20. Jahrhunderts*. Mainz: Schott.

Barskij, Sergej. 1948. "Für eine volksverbundene Kunst." *Tägliche Rundschau*, 13 February: 3.

Beal, Amy C. 2006. *New Music, New Allies: American Experimental Music in West Germany from the Zero Hour to Reunification*. Berkeley: University of California Press.

Dymschits, Alexander. 1948. "Warum wir gegen Dekadenz sind." *Tägliche Rundschau*, 21 March: 4.

Eisler, Hanns. 1949. "Hörer und Komponist." *Aufbau* (3): 200-208.

Hartmann, Anne, and Wolfram Eggeling. 1998. *Sowjetische Präsenz im kulturellen Leben der SBZ und frühen DDR 1945-1953*. Berlin: Akademie.

Heider, Magdalena. 1993. *Politik-Kultur-Kulturbund: Zur Gründungs- und Frühgeschichte des Kulturbundes zur demokratischen Erneuerung Deutschlands 1945-1954 in der SBZ/DDR*. Cologne: Wissenschaft und Politik.

Herzfeld, Friedrich. 1946. "Deutsches Musikleben auf Neuen Bahnen." *Aufbau* (2): 177-87.

Höffer, Paul. 1947a. "Die neuen Grenzen: Zur Situation der neuen deutschen Musik und den Berliner Musiktagen." *Berliner Musik Bericht* (May): 3-4.

———. 1947b. "Neue Musik und demokratische Erneuerung." *Die Aussprache* (May): 3-4.

Janik, Elizabeth. 2005. *Recomposing German Music: Politics and Musical Tradition in Cold War Berlin*. Leiden: Brill.

Kater, Michael H. 1997. *The Twisted Muse: Musicians and Their Music in the Third Reich*. New York: Oxford.

Köster, Maren. 2002. *MusikZeitGeschehen: Zu den Musikverhältnissen in der SBZ/DDR 1945 bis 1952*. Saarbrücken: Pfau.

Kroll, Erwin. 1946. "'Kleine Ewigkeit' in der Musikgeschichte: Konzerte mit neuer Musik." *Der Tagesspiegel*, 9 February: 3.

———. 1946. "Musik—Brücke zwischen den Nationen." *Der Tagesspiegel*, 2 October: 6.

Levi, Erik. 1994. *Music in the Third Reich*. New York: St. Martin's.

Monod, David. 2005. *Settling Scores: German Music, Denazification, and the Americans, 1945-1953*. Chapel Hill: University of North Carolina Press.

Notowicz, Nathan. 1949. "Kommission Musik." *Der Zweijahrplan und die Kulturschaffenden*. Berlin: Kulturbund.

Pike, David. 1992. *The Politics of Culture in Soviet-Occupied Germany 1945-1949*. Stanford, CA: Stanford University Press.

Poiger, Uta G. 2000. *Jazz, Rock, and Rebels: Cold War Politics and American Culture in a Divided Germany*. Berkeley: University of California Press.

Potter, Pamela M. 1998. *Most German of the Arts: Musicology and Society from the Weimar Republic to the end of Hitler's Reich*. New Haven, CT: Yale University Press.

Schivelbusch, Wolfgang. 1995. *Vor dem Vorhang: Das geistige Berlin 1945-1948*. Munich: Carl Hanser.

Stephan, Rudolf. 1969. "Das Neue der Neuen Musik." In *Das musikalisch Neue und die Neue Musik,* ed. Hans-Peter Reinecke, 47-64. Mainz: Schott.

Stuckenschmidt, Hans Heinz. 1948. "Was ist bürgerliche Musik?" *Stimmen* (7): 209-13.

———. 1979. *Zum Hören geboren: Ein Leben mit der Musik unserer Zeit*. Munich: Piper.

Thacker, Toby. 2007. *Music after Hitler, 1945-1955*. Aldershot, UK: Ashgate.

Thrun, Martin. 1995. *Neue Musik im deutschen Musikleben bis 1933*. Bonn: Orpheus.

CHAPTER 4

The Nylon Curtain
Architectural Unification in Divided Berlin

Greg Castillo

Architectural historians have long privileged binary opposition as the trope through which to chronicle divided Berlin's building culture. East Berlin's Stalinallee and West Berlin's Hansaviertel districts are the most cited case studies in this adversarial tale of two cities, a pairing that persuasively argues for an Iron Curtain dividing postwar German design practices. However, cultural cross-fertilization was another fundamental characteristic of the relationship between the two Berlins (Ladd 2005). Until the notorious Berlin Wall went up in 1961, Berliners crossed a permeable border to construct daily lives that transgressed the Cold War's geopolitical realms.

Inspired by the ways consumers exploited the porous boundary for their own ends, propagandists devised new strategies to reach target audiences on both sides of the urban and ideological divide. As this essay documents, East German reconstruction specialists followed suit. On day trips to West Berlin, they evaluated the capitalist world's innovations in architecture and building technology: a research method rich in socialist precedent. Soviet reverse engineering—called the "Western option" by technology historian Raymond Stokes (1997: 227)—was the USSR's tried-and-true method of achieving industrial parity at a fraction of the cost of original research and development. Soviet attempts to ship samples of American building materials to Moscow for inspection began as early as 1935, architectural historian Richard Anderson (unpublished manuscript) has discovered. Nowhere was the Western option easier to put into practice than in the postwar world's only adjacent socialist capital and capitalist metropolis. East Berlin's transition from the neoclassical architecture of the Stalin era to what Susan Reid calls "Khrushchev

Modern" (2006) owed much to the open city border of the 1950s, raising questions about cultural histories based on Cold War discourses of ideological quarantine. Before it was an Iron Curtain, the barrier separating the two Berlin's was, as György Péteri puts it, the "Nylon Curtain": a membrane that separated yet enticed; a barrier intended to divide, but which promoted a scopic regime of cross-cultural voyeurism. Historian John Connelly has noted that "the precise function of the open border is one of the most pressing questions in the historical sociology of the GDR" (2004: 332), an assertion reinforced by the city's use as an architectural entrepôt.

As East Germany's flagship reconstruction project, the Stalinallee proclaimed the nation's adoption of Soviet socialist realism, a creative method "socialist in content and national in form." Begun in 1951, the new Soviet-style boulevard served as East Berlin's triumphal approach from the land route to Moscow. Its kilometer-long run of neoclassical facades, ennobled by travertine sheathing and Doric columns, consciously recalled the architecture of imperial Prussia. Lustrous ceramic tiles made by the Meissen porcelain works sheathed the upper stories of the boulevard's apartment blocks. Residences were serviced by ground-floor shops displaying luxury products from across the Eastern Bloc: Bulgarian cigarettes and feta cheese, Romanian Riesling and Hungarian Bikaver wines, Polish eggs, and canned pineapple from China (Böhm-Klein 1966). From a perch on a pedestal at the edge of the boulevard, Stalin's statue presided over the cultural and economic intersections of a socialist hemisphere. East German newspapers compiled plans, panoramic views, photojournalism, and poems to convey the new townscape in its ideological totality. "Stalinallee," by Kuba, the nom de plume of Kurt Barthel, was one of many state-sponsored works of art created to celebrate the boulevard and unpack its symbolic content:

> On this street, peace came to the city. / The city was dust, / we were dust and shards, / and dead tired. / But tell me, how should one die? / Stalin himself took us by the hand / and bid us. / Hold our head high— / and as we cleared rubble and made plans, / Planted the greensward, built the housing blocks, / there we were victors, / and the city began to live. / Straight to Stalin led the path, along which the friends came. / Never will these windows, / these new glinting panes, / shimmer with flame! / Tell me, how should one thank Stalin? / We gave this street his name. (Barthel 1953)

Walking the broad sidewalks, gazing into well-stocked storefronts, residents of both Berlins would undergo a conversion experience—or so it was hoped. The Stalinallee was East Germany's ultimate marketing tool: a model of the socialist future built at one-to-one scale.

Critics in West Berlin remained unimpressed. According to an anonymous editorial in the West Berlin daily *Der Tag*, the rows of columns grac-

Figure 4.1 Stalinallee in East Berlin during the late 1950s. Courtesy of Rheinisches Bildarchiv.

ing Stalinallee apartment facades were endemic to dictatorial regimes, revealing "the characteristic of this 'German' style: soullessness!" (Anon. 1953). The project's model residents also attracted editorial criticism. They included "party functionaries . . . ministry employees, worker-activists, award-winning inventors," and other assorted elites. Despite their status, these ideal socialist citizens would be living in a less-than-ideal setting, *Der Tag* claimed. Deficits cited in the model apartments thrown open to visitors ranged from illogical room layout to sloppy construction. The West German newspaper declared the Stalinallee indeed great, in the sense that its housing represented "the world's greatest rental barracks! [*Mietskaserne*]." *Der Tag*, it should be pointed out, was by no means an impartial observer of the East Berlin's socialist realist import efforts, having championed an American exhibition of modernist home furnishings a year earlier. In fact, just weeks before the journal's reporter crossed the city's internal border to examine the future of socialist housing, West Berlin's Senate had announced a grand modernist reconstruction project in the form of an International Building Exhibition (Internationale Bauausstellung), soon known as Interbau. According to Karl Mahler, the city senator in charge of residential construction, it would constitute "a lucid declaration of the architecture of the Western world. It should demonstrate what we understand to be modern urbanism and proper housing, in contrast to the false ostentation of the Stalinallee" (1956: 683). The site chosen for the exhibition was the Hansaviertel, at the west end of the

Tiergarten park. Although the formerly elegant residential district had been devastated by bombs, the Cold War made it immensely attractive, ideologically speaking. As Mahler explained, "Due to its immediate proximity to the sector border, the exhibition will provide for those in the east a powerful testament of the West Berlin's will to rebuild" (1956: 683).

Figure 4.2 Hansaviertel in West Berlin during the late 1950s. Courtesy of Landesarchive Berlin.

A design collaborative headed by Willi Kreuer and Gerhard Jobst—the latter, a former officer in Albert Speer's Third Reich staff of reconstruction planners—took first prize in the Hansaviertel planning competition. They proposed that its housing blocks be scattered "in open nature ... and, through this unforced arrangement, should prove an obvious antipode to buildings designed for dictatorial needs" (Howell-Ardila 1998: 72). The East German press pounced upon their redevelopment proposal as incontrovertible proof of socialist realism's superiority. "A glance at the design," announced *Neues Deutschland*, "reveals a complete muddle, without point or objective, as if a child had played with building blocks and left them scattered" (Stern 1954). "Comparing the Stalinallee ensemble with the site plan and views of the premiated design [for the Hansaviertel], no one of sound mind would find beauty in this fantasy from a decaying world," announced Kurt Liebknecht, the president of East Germany's state-managed architectural institute, the Deutsche Bauakademie. "I am convinced that our workers would reject such buildings" (1954: 74). Interbau's housing commissions called upon architectural talents from Austria, Brazil, Denmark, England, Finland, France, Israel, Italy, Sweden, Switzerland, the United States, and West Germany to demonstrate "the free world's technology and creative strength in its wide variety of forms" (Lampugniani 1987: 96). Residential interiors invoked the new lifestyle of West Germany's economic miracle, exhibiting "an ingenuity to which the East had no counterpart" (1992: 235) as the architectural historian Anders Åman has observed. Apartments ranged from efficiency flats and two-story maisonettes to garden townhouses. Model kitchens were stocked with electric appliances. Interiors flaunted the chic modernist appointments condemned by East German SED party leader Walter Ulbricht as "formalist," and the modular cabinetry he derided as "crate-like furniture" of "primitive design" (1952). East German agitators crossed the border to infiltrate Interbau, launching disparaging comments at opportune moments. Excoriating the design of a chair, one of them announced: "This thing is an example of the cultural decay of the West. No human being could possibly sit in this; it's an abstract design out of a modern painting at best" (Wandersleb 1958: 110). Echoing an accusation made of the Stalinallee by the editors of *Der Tag*, an editorial in the East's *Berliner Zeitung* proclaimed Interbau "Berlin's biggest rental barracks" (Anon. 1957). East and West seemed to have achieved a perfect state of symbiosis, in which artifacts expressing the core values of one provided a perfect propaganda foil for the other.

Among Interbau's exemplars of free world housing, the contribution by the French architect Le Corbusier provoked controversy the moment plans were unveiled. Too big to fit on the Hansaviertel site, his building was constructed in Charlottenburg, miles away from the main exhibition. Ceiling heights in the French architect's *machine à habiter,* critics complained, were too low to work in Berlin, where men and women were on average ten centimeters taller than in southern France. Le Corbusier dismissed all objections with a breezy affirmation of his universal modernist solutions. "My buildings are good for Zulus and Eskimos," he insisted. "They are neither dependent on the height of people nor on century-old cultural structures" (Siedler 1987: 22). But were they, along with the rest of Interbau's model housing, compatible with the new people and cultural structures of socialism?

West Berlin's *Tagesspiegel* reported the arrival of a fresh collection of undercover East German housing officials at Interbau daily. Their "object of special interest" (Anon. 1956) was reported to be a specific apartment block: "Object 1," a concrete monolith designed by Gerhard Siegmann and Klaus Müller-Rehm and built using high-speed construction innovations. Its predominantly one-bedroom apartments were compact, averaging thirty-two square meters, but included a telephone, garbage chute, and central heating—standard amenities today, but notable features for 1950s Berlin. The mystery of why members of the East German Bauakademie would congregate around a building so lavishly condemned by their government and professional leaders deepened when considered in tandem with the behavior of another visitor to West Berlin, the Brazilian architect Oscar Niemeyer. In addition to three weeks spent at the Interbau site overseeing the construction of his sculpturally daring housing slab, Niemeyer made time for trips to East Berlin, where he toured the Stalinallee, and to Prague, where he opened an exhibition of his work. The East Bloc debut was unusual for a designer—even with communist party affiliations—whose creative output was a case study of the "formalism and kitsch," as defined by party cultural authorities, which served "only the misanthropic interests of imperialism and its politics of warmongering" (Deutsche Bauakademie 1953). "The many messages of the last month appear to mean, in fact, that Soviet architecture is set to make a 180 degree turn from 'socialist realism' to functionalism" (1982: 101), architect Hans Schoszberger surmised in the West German professional journal *Bauwelt.* Seen in this light, there could be little doubt that Bauakademie agents were evaluating Interbau exhibition displays for their potential application in socialist housing and reconstruction practices.

East German housing officials evaluated Interbau building by building, scrutinizing layout and function. They found galley kitchens too small and located "with astonishing carelessness" far from windows, thus requiring artificial light and mechanical ventilation. They pronounced Interbau floor plans unacceptable for providing little space for domestic tasks like baking and child care. Such shortcomings revealed the true nature of Interbau's "indistinctly defined 'modern lifestyle'": "Principally, the question that must be asked is: for which portion of the population are these designs intended? They are not based upon the lifestyle of the majority population, but rather the needs and living patterns of the propertied class and the 'well-situated' petty bourgeois. This especially expresses itself in the notion of design based on leisure use." In short, East German state representatives found Interbau modernism incompatible with socialism. "One cannot start from the principle that the home serves only consumption—either individual or collective; of a material or an ideal sort—instead, the home is linked to productive tasks" (Sekretariat des Beirates für Bauwesens 1958). A socialist definition of functional design focused on the home as a workplace, not a space devoted to leisure pursuits or modern consumer practices.

On 3 August 1961, Walter Ulbricht flew to Moscow for a secret meeting in the Kremlin. Khrushchev reluctantly approved a plan that would resolve East Germany's border problem, but which would also confirm the SED's loss of popular support. At midnight on 13 August 1961, military commanders in East Berlin received instructions to rouse their troops and secure the border. Three days later, masons began building a concrete divider. An official guide to East German architecture described the wall as a noteworthy piece of national infrastructure: "The protective measures establish reliable conditions for the quick and successful economic, political, and cultural development of the GDR and its capital city. It opens a new chapter in German history" (Palutzki 2000: 193).

Two months after the wall turned East Germany into a sealed socialist ecosystem, a Bauakademie design collective set out to revolutionize the nation's mass housing. Charged with designing a cost effective solution to the housing crisis, the collective proposed a new residential prototype, the P2, that reduced the standard two-and-one half room, four-person dwelling to fifty-five square meters (592 square feet). This was accomplished by merging living and dining into a single open area, and moving an adjacent galley kitchen far from exterior walls and windows: the formula advanced at Interbau four years earlier, and roundly dismissed by Bauakademie critics. By 1962, East German architects would manage to shave another 10 percent from the floor plan. Apologists were forced to retract the propaganda of a previous decade, the new line being: "A widely shared but mistaken idea is that, with the expanding construction of socialism, apartment size must also grow" (Gruner et al. 1996: 92). The East German homemaking magazine *Kultur im Heim* informed readers that in Sweden, where the smallest apartments were about the same size as P2 units, "mass housing is built no larger than ours" (Gruner et al. 1996: 92). The party, taste professionals, and the East German media agreed: learning to think small was a big part of the future for the socialist home.

The Bauakademie unveiled its first P2 prototype at the *neues leben-neues wohnen* (new life-new dwelling) exhibition. Fifteen model units emphasized "openness and lightness," furnishings conforming to "the international standard," and wall-mounted modular storage providing storage space for new emblems of proletarian prosperity: "technical devices and hardware, such as the radio, phonograph, audio tape system, television, and film and slide projectors" (Könitzer and Jordan 1962: 532). "Considered all in all," furniture designer Horst Michel effused, "the new living-new dwelling exhibition demonstrates the progress, the great turning point that has come to pass in the German Democratic Republic's style of living" (1962: 598). The public seemed to agree. More than thirty-two thousand, including a handful from West Berlin, toured the model units. One in a hundred visitors recorded their impressions in the show's guest book. Most found the "apartments of the future" enchanting: "The exhibit shows how space can be put to better use than in the other [housing] types built in Berlin. I'd move into one of these beautiful apartments immediately." The compact kitchen garnered several critical responses: "One can easily prepare a salad or mixed drinks in the little kitchen, but I think that a home-cooked dinner would leave it a mess." But the most common complaints stemmed from unrequited desire, plain and simple. "When will such furnishings finally appear on the market? When will officials in industry and retailing take into account the wishes and tastes of their customers?" And: "Once and for all, we want to put an end to being satiated only by exhibitions. We want the modern, rational way of life that is rightfully ours." Considering the similarity of P2 dream home interiors to those showcased at Interbau, the visitor who wrote, "Why not this ten years ago?" in the new living-new dwelling guest book hit the mark in more ways than she or he realized (Anon. 1962). The East German project to inculcate socialist modernism had come to seemed more like a finishing school for proletarian disenfranchisement.

In the early 1960s, housing projects assembled from precast concrete panels literally and figuratively "finished off" the last stretch of the Stalinallee. With the Stalin-era vision of a socialist realist utopia abandoned, entire residential districts went up quickly and at great savings. New apartments offered residents new identities as socialist consumers, opportunities to become the "active engineers" of domestic modernization, and reason to compare their experiences with perceptions of "world class" living outside the Soviet Bloc (Harris 2003: 265). But rather than producing enfranchised socialist citizens committed to living out that role in the public realm, the norms and forms of domestic modernity produced the insular outposts of a "niche society"—in German, *Nischengesellschaft*. Wrapped in a cocoon of privacy, provisioned by a shadow economy made necessary by the inefficiencies of its centrally planned counterpart, East Germans withdrew in mass from the public sphere, disrupting the teleological Marxist narrative of progress. In György Péteri's memorable formulation (2008: 937), "the rebellious project of socialism not only failed to be 'antimodern' (which it never wished to be), but it also failed to provide a workable way toward an *alternative* modernity. It lost the race for modernity as it failed to assert its systemic exceptionalism by way of offering viable alternatives for everyday life."

Works Cited

Åman, Anders. 1992. *Architecture and Ideology in Eastern Europe during the Stalin Era: An Aspect of Cold War History*. Cambridge, MA: MIT University Press.
Anderson, Richard. Unpublished Manuscript. "1939 and the Soviet House of Tomorrow."
Anon. 1953. "Stalinallee—die größte Mietskaserne." *Der Tag*, 6 March.
Anon. 1956. "Ost Architekten im Hansaviertel." *Tagespiegel*, 2 September.
Anon. 1957. "Berlin's größte Mietskaserne auf der Interbau." *Berliner Zeitung*, 22 September.
Anon. 1962. "Meinungen, Kritik und Hinweise zum Versuchsbau P2." *Deutsche Architektur* 11, no. 9: 543–46.
Böhm-Klein, Johanna. 1996. "Wohnen, Geschäftsleben und Infrastruktur der Stalinallee." In *Karl-Marx-Allee: Magistrale in Berlin*, ed. Helmut Engel and Wolfgang Ribbe, 141–52. Berlin: Akademie.
Connelly, John. 1997."Ulbricht and the Intellectuals." *Contemporary European History* 6, no. 3: 329–59.
Deutsche Bauakademie. 1953. "Thema: Innenarchitektur im Wohnungsbau." DH2 VI/61/8, SAPMO, Bundesarchiv Berlin-Lichterfelde.
Gruner, Petra et al. 1996. "P2 macht das Rennen." In *Alltagskultur der DDR: Begleitbuch zur Ausstellung Tempolinsen und P2*, ed. Stadt Eisenhüttenstadt Dokumentationszentrum, 87–102. Berlin: Be-Bra.
Harris, Steven. 2003. "Moving to the Separate Apartment: Building, Distributing, Furnishing, and Living in Urban Housing in Soviet Russia, 1950s–1960s." PhD dissertation, University of Chicago.
Howell-Ardila, Deborah. 1998. "Berlin's Search for a 'Democratic' Architecture." *German Politics and Society* 16, no. 3: 87–102.
Könitzer, Ernst und Jordan, Jacob. 1962. "Die Ausstellung 'neues wohnen-neues leben' im Muster- und Experimentalbau P2 in Berlin." *Deutsche Architektur* 11, no. 9: 523–32.
Kuba [Kurt Barthels] 1953. "Stalinallee." *Neues Deutschland*, 29 November.
Ladd, Brian. 2005. "Double Restoration: Rebuilding Berlin After 1945." In *The Resilient City: How Modern Cities Recover from Disaster*, ed. Laurence J. Vale and Thomas J. Campanella, 117–57. Oxford: Oxford University Press.
Lampugnani, Vittorio Magnano. 1987. "The 'Zero Hour': Reconstruction's Goals and Premises." *Domus* 685: 25–31.
Liebknecht, Kurt. 1954. *Die nationalen Aufgaben der deutschen Architektur*. Berlin: Deutsche Bauakademie.
Mahler, Karl. 1956. "Internationale Bauausstellung 1956: Wiederaufbau eines inneren Stadtviertels." *Bauwelt* 44, no. 35: 681–83.
Michel, Horst. 1962. "Moderne Wohngestaltung." *Bildende Kunst* 7, no. 11: 593–99.
Palutzki, Joachim. 2000. *Architektur in der DDR*. Berlin: Reimer.

Péteri, György. 2004. "Nylon Curtain—Transnational and Transsystemic Tendencies in the Cultural Life of State-Socialist Russia and East-Central Europe." *Slavonia* 10: 113–17.

Péteri, György. 2008. "The Occident Within—or the Drive for Exceptionalism and Modernity." *Kritika* 4: 929–37.

Reid, Susan E. 2006. "Khrushchev Modern: Agency and Modernization in the Soviet Home." *Cahiers du Monde Russe* 47, no. 1–2: 227–68.

Schoszberger, Hans. 1982. "Oskar Niemeyer von außen und innen." In *Oscar Niemeyer: Selbstdarstellung, Kritiken, Oeuvre,* ed. Alexander Fils, 100–102. Berlin: Fröhlich + Kaufmann.

Sekretariat des Beirates für Bauwesen. 1958. "Analyse der Interbau." Bundesarchiv SAPMO, DH2 DBA/4/48.

Siedler, Wolf Jobst. 1987. "Città e Utopia." *Domus* 685: 17–24.

Stern, Katja. 1954. "Ganz Berlin soll schön werden." *Neues Deutschland,* 25 November.

Stokes, Raymond. 1997. "In Search of the Socialist Artefact: Technology and Ideology in East Germany, 1945–1962." *German History* 15, no. 2: 221–39.

Ulbricht, Walter. 1952. "Die grossen Ausgaben der Innenarchitektur beim Kampf um eine neue deutsche Kultur." Bundesarchiv SAPMO, DH2 DBA A 141.

Wandersleb, Hermann. 1958. *Neuer Wohnbau,* volume 2. Ravensburg: Otto Maier.

Chapter 5

Mediascape and Soundscape
Two Landscapes of Modernity in Cold War Berlin

Heiner Stahl

The various zones of contact, conflict, and tension between publishing houses, television, and broadcasting stations in East and West Berlin determined Cold War Berlin's mediascape in the 1950s and 1960s. Arjun Appadurai uses the term *mediascape* to describe the production of media content, symbols, and narratives in a competitive setting of distribution channels, such as broadcasting stations (2000: 27–47, 33). The producer of content is keen on securing the transmission of an intended meaning to viewers and listeners without being distorted through acts of consumption or by adding additional meaning.

This essay examines these zones by discussing the organizational structure of radio broadcasting in Berlin in the 1950s and 1960s and by further focusing on the strategies of West and East Berlin broadcasting stations adapting to new kinds of programs, and realigning and modernizing specific areas of broadcasting, especially youth and music programs. The very sound of the music broadcast by radio stations provides a field in which they can claim a distinct identity, and in which the political purpose of a radio station must negotiate with its fundamental need to attract the majority of a target audience. This essay argues that the commercially competitive agenda of the media market is a crucial force that drives broadcasting institutions to redefine themselves in a constantly shifting environment of listening behavior. The consumption of music via small devices that are capable of receiving and replaying music is a prominent feature of popular culture. For the purpose of this argument Raymond Murray Schafer's term *soundscape* (1973) is defined as a space in which melodies, tunes, and riffs are received and interpreted by audiences, and in which the location of the listener shapes the interpretation of these sounds. The listener imbues the soundscape with individual meaning and relevance.

This understanding of the contest of meanings that takes place in a given soundscape can be illustrated by the historical account of radio broadcasting in Cold War Berlin. Radio stations in both West Berlin and East Berlin provided the soundtrack for everyday life, but neither faction could control the ways in which listeners appropriated the sounds of the broadcasts. West Berlin's Sender Freies Berlin (Radio Free Berlin, SFB), Radio in the American Sector (RIAS), and Berliner Rundfunk (Berlin Radio) in East Berlin aimed to defend their own territory against "competitors" based in the same geographical area, while simultaneously trying to attract listeners from the other side of the Iron Curtain. I do not intend to neglect the political dimensions of radio broadcasting in Cold War Berlin but will focus primarily on applying the concepts of mediascape and soundscape to the radio broadcasting milieu of the city at that time, which was a market characterized by the relations of competition between broadcasting stations that were offering competing acoustic and visual texts to their audience.

Taking a step back at this point to consider the wider mediascape of Cold War Berlin, it is possible to view this mediascape as a product of Allied decisions in the sectors of publishing, newspapers, and broadcasting—certainly for the first three years of occupation before 1948. During the decade leading up to World War II, the German mediascape had changed insofar as the medium of wireless transmission had become an increasingly significant means of disseminating information and promoting the *Volksgemeinschaft* (racial community) (Dussel 2002). Broadcasting was centralized in 1932 by the von Papen cabinet, which was to benefit the Nazi propaganda machine in later years, and Nazi rule was to develop the German mediascape significantly.

Berliner Rundfunk first began broadcasting at the end of May 1945, following the Soviet army's occupation of the premises of the Reichsrundfunk in Charlottenburg. Competition was to emerge in the form of RIAS in November 1946, which, within one year, would commandeer the strongest frequencies in the former capital for evening programming (Dussel 2004). Although the Nordwestdeutscher Rundfunk (NWDR), or Northwest German Radio, was based in Cologne and Hamburg in the British zone of occupation, it also ran its own studio in Berlin. Its organizational structure was modeled on that of the BBC, and British journalists working for the British Military Administration in Germany were tasked with reeducating German professionals to promote the ethic of commitment to an independent public sphere on which their own training had been based.

There was no federal body to regulate the broadcast landscape of West Berlin, and local politicians pushed to establish a radio station under the supervision of the Senate of West Berlin toward the end of the 1940s (Schaaf 1971). Before June 1954, when SFB went on the air, the Allied Control Authority in Berlin denied several attempts by the Berlin Christian Democratic Party and Social Democratic Party to allocate a medium wave frequency, and to pass legislative proposals for public broadcasting. The opportunity to challenge political opponents, and dominate the agenda-setting process, proved to be excellent "selling points" through which broadcasting institutions negotiated with the agencies of the military administration that governed the media. After 1949, the Senate of West Berlin, various political parties in Berlin, and anticommunist humanitarian organizations in West Berlin (Heitzer 2008) used their on-air presence on RIAS to broadcast their messages to the Soviet sector. The stations offered slots of airtime for the specific purpose of disseminating political messages, which was referred to as either "information" or "propaganda" (Riller 2004; Galle 2003).

During the 1950s, the US State Department considerably reduced its financial support for RIAS (Riller 2004), but the Senate of West Berlin was prepared to keep the station running by any means possible. The reassuring existence of RIAS meant that the US Information Agency remained interested in Berlin's affairs, despite ongoing negotiations between the Soviet Union and the United States to close down RIAS as a symbolic action of détente in the run-up to the Geneva summit of 1958. The cabinet of the Federal Republic of Germany, particularly the Ministry for All-German *Affairs,* intervened by providing the funding for RIAS. Finally, in 1971, RIAS became a federal public broadcasting station that was partly funded by West German radio and television license fees.

Despite having been centralized under the administration of the State Committee for Broadcasting (SRK) in 1952, East Germany's broadcasting stations underwent several major changes during the 1950s. The main focus was to diversify the range of programs targeted at East Germans as well as West German listeners. At this time, the party administration of the Central Committee (ZK) branch of Agitation/Propaganda was regularly negotiating strategies and schemes for future developments with the executive management of the stations.[1] The integration of television services into the GDR media landscape was defined as a crucial task, as shown by Heather Gumbert's essay in this volume. The East German broadcasting media aimed at generating a mass audience in favor of socialist communication and education policies. Within the competitive media market of Cold War Berlin, however, the party functionaries at the level of the Central Committee of the SED and the managing directors of the radio stations negotiated a compromise on what an entertainment and light music program had to include. Although the hierarchies in the centralized socialist state and in the East German State Committee of Broadcasting were asymmetric, they nonetheless demanded rather flexible reactions to set the pace in specific fields of broadcasting, or to keep pace with opponents' efforts in providing uncontroversial entertainment. It was the same basic need to compete for an audience that put all the major players and producers in East and West Germany under significant pressure.

The centralized broadcasting corporation of the GDR recognized the importance of successfully claiming a share of this mediascape, and was willing to demonstrate high levels of flexibility in giving this aim priority, alongside the goal of pushing a specific political agenda. This is especially evident in the entertainment programming, which boasted a significant amount of popular music; and there was no gap in the professionalism of the production to distance socialist "light programs" from those products recorded at West Berlin stations. The department of music at a broadcasting station generally had control over what kind of music was being aired. In his major thesis on the politics of music in postwar Germany, Toby Thacker has examined the cultural economy of attracting stars and reestablishing operas, theaters, and concert venues. Following Thacker's descriptions, I argue that of the sound of Cold War Berlin was shaped and largely dominated by high culture, characterized by classical music concerts in traditional venues such as the Komische Oper in East Berlin and the Städtische Oper, later known as the Deutsche Oper, in West Berlin, a point also made by Elizabeth Janik in her contribution in this volume. The contemporary soundscape of radio broadcasting in the city was dominated by popular dance tunes recorded by large orchestras, and radio stations in West and East Berlin did not differ at all in this respect. The banning of certain types of music from being aired was not exclusive to the centralized socialist broadcasting media in the GDR. The role model of public broadcasting, the British Broadcasting Corporation, also appears to have functioned rather convincingly in this aspect (Stanley 2008).

Light programs were aimed at imagined prototypes of typical male and female listeners and accordingly offered music genres that were deemed appropriate. The refusal to play rock 'n' roll music or specific free jazz styles was a core aspect of this consensus. Nevertheless, some prerecorded DJ sets played on the American Forces Network (AFN) provided a distinctly alternative sound to the mainstream of Germany broadcasts. Especially to young listeners, the AFN was an important distributor of contemporary sounds. Stakeholders in West German public broadcasting were successful in rebranding jazz as cool and rational, as well as an appropriate soundtrack for the young, academically inclined citizens of West Germany (Poiger 2000; Müller, Ortmann, and Schmidt 2004; Schwab 2005; Scharlau and Witting-Nöthen 2006). The seven-inch singles available in jukeboxes in corner cafés or youth clubs dominated the soundscape in which teenagers lived (Maase 1992; Rauhut 1993; Siegfried 2006; Fenemore 2007).

A division between classical and light music in the broadcasting soundscape existed previously and proved to be formative for broadcasting music in general. The emergence and distribution of American and British pop music challenged this arrangement in the late 1950s and continued throughout the subsequent decade of surf beat and rock music. The producers of radio programs in West or East Germany expressed a deeply rooted disgust toward sounds and tunes that they perceived as foreign and non-German. But rock 'n' roll, free jazz, and beat, besides the media hype around juvenile delinquency, had already spread and were very much present on the streets of Frankfurt, Hamburg, Munich, Leipzig, and Berlin (Poiger 2000).

When SFB finally launched *s-f-beat* in March 1967, its first daily program targeting young audiences, the show included explicit references to its socialist competitor, Berliner Rundfunk in East Berlin.[2] Its intention was to challenge an ideological opponent with programming deliberately targeted at the youth segment. Contributing to the so-called communist threat in the war on the airwaves, this line of argument was pushed by the general director of the station and the director of programming of SFB and successfully adopted by members of the program control commission. But it also facilitated the acceptance of new kinds of music, modes of presentation, and political reporting about the student movement or the vibrant alternative scene in West Berlin. Meanwhile in East Berlin, pop music from France, Italy, Britain, and the United States, including their East German cover versions, played a prominent role in such "attractive" programs as *Jugendstudio DT 64*, introduced nearly three years earlier in June 1964.

Although public broadcasting in West Germany had neglected the new aesthetic streams of pop culture during much of the 1960s (Gushurst 2000; Kursawe 2004), SFB and RIAS proved to be the forerunners in remedying the situation. For RIAS, the sound of the postwar decade was based on US swing band tunes, 1920s Tin Pan Alley productions, and new adaptations by domestic dance orchestras. Not forgetting, of course, the poignant sound of the Freedom Bell in the tower of the Schöneberg Town Hall that was rung daily to announce the station's mission. There were the notorious hit song broadcasts, such as *Schlager der Woche,* scheduled as part of RIAS's Monday evening programming, which avoided playing rock 'n' roll and Twist hits like Little Richard's "Good Golly Miss Molly." RIAS promoted predominantly white, male artists and supported those composers and authors who had contributed to the rebuilding of the West German music business.[3] Noisy beat and rock music, American black urban soul released by Stax or Motown, and the international pop music of the decade reached the musical playlist at RIAS as early as 1968, when DJ "Lord Knud" began hosting the weekly pop music broadcast.[4] Before becoming a radio presenter, Knud Kuntze had played bass guitar in the West Berlin beat band The Lords. When it switched from the summer to the winter schedule in 1968, RIAS relaunched its weekly youth program, *RIAS-Treffpunkt,* and consolidated its message by broadcasting in an education-oriented time slot every weekday afternoon.[5]

The Berliner Rundfunk was as reluctant to play pop music as its West Berlin competitors. The process of negotiating what socialist music, and especially light music, should be within the framework of the party's cultural policy[6] triggered various internal disputes among the heads of the music departments of the GDR's broadcasting stations; the managing directors of the Association of Musicians and Composers; the state-owned record label VEB Deutsche Schallplatten; the branches of Culture, Youth, and Propaganda of the Central Committee; and the Politburo as the most important political decision-making body in the GDR.

During preparations for the 1964 Youth Gathering or *Deutschlandtreffen,* the State Committee of Broadcasting launched a broadcasting station called DT 64, the predecessor of *Jugendstudio DT 64* at Berliner Rundfunk; its purpose was to broadcast live reports and news from various festival sites throughout the East German capital. The State Committee of Broadcasting had no intention of continuing this service with regular broadcasts after the event. The Politburo, however, was extremely surprised that this presentation of key issues in domestic policies proved so appealing to audiences, including the catchphrases about liberalization and modernization. Thus the Politburo agreed that the Department of Communication at the Central Committee of the Party (ZK-Abteilung Agitation/Propaganda) should encourage the State Committee of Broadcasting to cooperate with functionaries at the Central Committee's Department of Youth and of the Free German Youth who were in favor of establishing such a program or maintaining the station on a permanent basis.[7]

Jugendstudio DT 64 first aired on 29 June 1964 as an extended version of an afternoon program that had already been running for several years and offered one way of coming to terms with pop music in the GDR. Its programming was modeled on the SED's youth policy of 21 September 1963 that supported all reasonable approaches to playing British (Mr. Acker Bilk), French (Gilbert Bécaud or Jacques Brel), and Italian pop music—and even West German pop music and Afro-American jazz. RIAS examined its rival's program for two weeks in November 1965 and drew the conclusion that only a third of the music played on *Jugendstudio DT 64* was actually produced in the GDR or the Eastern Bloc. It was found that original songs from Western pop stars made up 29.1 percent of the show's content, while cover versions of Western tracks had a 38.2 percent share of airtime. This demonstrates the flexibility of the *Jugendstudio DT 64* music program, although it remained within the legal regulations that stipulated that 60 percent of the music on any program must originate from socialist countries.[8]

The production of light music in the GDR was a relatively slow process, and was hampered by numerous obstacles. A major issue was the fact that acoustic trends came and went faster than GDR composers or arrangers could write suitable pieces. Musicians were required to submit sheet music to the music departments of the broadcasting stations, which would then be evaluated by commissions formed by staff from these departments. Only a number of pieces were approved for recording in East German broadcasting studios and, even then, the facilities had to be prebooked and the dance orchestras or professional musicians working for the stations needed to be available for these recording sessions. The massive administrative costs of producing music in the GDR's broadcasting stations further hindered the development of the industry. At least the existence of this procedure assured some kind of opportunity for the music departments of the radio stations to react to current trends. The East German recording label, VEB Deutsche Schallplatten, which was the main producer and distributor of music for the domestic GDR market, was largely inefficient, but when trying to justify its lack of productivity to high-level party functionaries was quick to allocate blame to the State Committee of Broadcasting.

A report from the Ministry of Culture in 1965 stated that the West German music industry was releasing nearly four thousand titles a year, in comparison with one thousand produced in the GDR—a significant difference indeed.[9] The figure for the GDR was reduced to five hundred songs annually in a second report, which reflected the changes that the Eleventh Plenary of the Central Committee in December had initiated in 1965.[10] Broadcasters in the GDR were successful in mustering support for its initiatives to create a popular music profile. The branch of Agitation and Propaganda of the Central Commune supported them in opposition to the branch of Culture of the Central Commune in order to block their initiatives and to gain more influence over what should be broadcast.

With respect to the production of media texts in the GDR, I have tried to outline that broadcasting stations pursued a pragmatic approach to inserting music in favor of attracting regular listeners and selling political programs. In 1965, the spin of political communication turned again and this approach was then considered counterproductive to the party's core message on the value of a socialist lifestyle. In support of this argument, I refer to a document published by the RIAS Department of Youth Program in November 1965, in response to a rival program broadcast from East Germany. This RIAS document implies that the sound of *Jugendstudio DT 64* was unique in comparison with other areas of socialist broadcasting, and I would argue that, while exposing the sound profile of the competitor, the program directors of RIAS should have been more aware of significant changes in the socialist mediascape. This could have negatively affected the relevance of RIAS, which defined itself as the most important station in Berlin's Cold War mediascape. This document outlines instances in which socialist broadcasting applied and incorporated trends into its youth programming that were characteristic of private and commercial radio with the aim of accommodating the tastes and expectations of young listeners. The advertising of consumer goods was, however, substituted by subliminal political advertising in the socialist broadcasts.

SFB launched a weekly program based on pop music and youth-related information in October 1965. This only lasted until 6 March 1967 when it was replaced by a program called *s-f-beat*, promoting Anglo-American pop music, country, and soul, alongside news of the Berlin student movement and tidbits of travel advice for hitchhikers in West Berlin. Shortly before the regular broadcast started, members of the board of SFB were informed by its head of Radio and Television Programming, Eberhard Schütz, that the new youth program was necessary to reduce the impact of East Berlin's successful station.[11] The members of the board could only accept the changes in programming that the managing director of SFB had approved and initiated. The need to oppose a communist propaganda program that could be successful among working-class youths proved to be the best justification to bring about such a program, even if the autocratic way in which *s-f-beat* was initiated in 1967 was to be cause of some dispute in subsequent years (Stahl 2007).

The producers of media in Berlin were reluctant to adopt pop music as a battleground in the Cold War. Finally, by the late 1960s, they selectively began to use the sound of pop music to challenge each other. Through these tactics, an acoustic setting that had been exclusively linked to urban subcultures at the beginning of the decade moved forward to claim relevance in mainstream broadcasting. From this perspective, the media in Berlin was not divided, but bound together by difference, the pursuit of distinction, and the struggle to adopt new styles of music and new ways of presenting broadcasts.

Notes

1. BArch B, DR 6/463 unpag., [Büro des Komitees] Beschlussprotokoll der Komiteesitzung am 21.4.1959, 1–23, here 7.
2. DRA, P. -Bblg., Schriftgut Hörfunk, Bestand Sender Freies Berlin, Nr. 2016, Protokoll der Sitzung des Programmausschusses des Sender Freies Berlin, Berlin 27.2.1967, 1–4, here 2.
3. DRA, P.-Bblg, Schriftgut Hörfunk, RIAS, A504–02–03, Light Music Program.
4. DRA, P.-Bblg, Schriftgut Hörfunk, RIAS, A504–02–03/0010, Schlager der Woche, Fahrpläne der Musiksendung: "Schlager der Woche mit Lord Knud" 1.11.1968–31.07.1971.
5. DRA, P. -Bblg., Schriftgut Hörfunk, Bestand RIAS, F 404–00–00/0023, Programmdirektion Kulturelles Wort, Herbert Kundler, [an Programmdirektion Bayerischer Rundfunk, Bogner], Jugendprogramm im RIAS, Berlin 19.5.1969, 1–2.
6. SAPMO-BArch, DY 30 IV 2/9.06/285, Sekretär des Verbandes Deutscher Komponisten und Musikwissenschaftler, Gerhard Bab, an Abteilung Kultur des ZK der SED, Peter Czerny, Betr.: Information in Zusammenhang mit den Problemen, die in der Zusammenarbeit des Koordinierungsausschußes für Tanzmusik durch das unverständliche Verhalten des Rundfunks entstanden sind, Berlin 8.6.1960, Bl. 75–76, Bl. 76.
7. SAPMO-BArch, DY 30 IV 2/2.028/90 unpag., Vorsitzender des Staatlichen Rundfunkkomitees, Hermann Ley, an Albert Norden, Betr.: Analyse unserer Musikarbeit, Berlin 3.3.1962. Anlage: Analyse des Musikprogramms des Deutschen Demokratischen Rundfunks, 3.3.1962, S. 1–5, S. 4.
8. DRA, P.-Bblg., Schriftgut Hörfunk, Bestand RIAS, F 504–01–04/0001, RIAS Berlin, Kulturelles Wort , Abt. Jugend und Erziehung, Eckhart Bethke, DT 64. Eine Untersuchung des RIAS-Jugendfunks November 1965, 1–7.
9. BArch B, DR 1/8783 unpag., [Ministerium für Kultur] Abteilung Musik, Vorlage: Die Verbesserung der Lage auf dem Gebiet der Tanzmusik, Schlußfolgerungen für die Leitungstätigkeit und Maßnahmeplan, (3.Entwurf), Berlin 6.12.1965, 1–20, 3.
10. BArch B, DR 1/8783 unpag. [Ministerium für Kultur] Abteilung Musik, Vorlage: Die Verbesserung der Lage auf dem Gebiet der Tanzmusik, Schlußfolgerungen für die Leitungstätigkeit und Maßnahmeplan, (4. Entwurf), Berlin 18.2.1966, 1–26, 4.
11. DRA, P. -Bblg., Schriftgut Hörfunk, Bestand Sender Freies Berlin, Nr. 2016, Protokoll der Sitzung des Programmausschusses des Sender Freies Berlin, Berlin 27.2.1967, 1–4, 2.

Works Cited

Appadurai, Arjun. 2000. *Modernity at Large: Cultural Dimensions of Globalization.* Minneapolis: University of Minnesota Press.
Dussel, Konrad. 2002. *Hörfunk in Deutschland.* Potsdam: Verlag Berlin-Brandenburg.
———. 2004. "Rundfunk in der Bundesrepublik und der DDR. Überlegungen Zum systematischen Vergleich." In *Pop und Propaganda: Radio in der DDR,* ed. Klaus Arnold and Christoph Classen, 301–21. Berlin: Ch. Links.

Fenemore, Mark. 2007. *Sex, Thugs and Rock 'n' Roll: Teenage Rebels in Cold-War East Germany*. New York: Berghahn.
Galle, Petra. 2003. *RIAS Berlin und Berliner Rundfunk 1945–1949*. Münster: Lit.
Gushurst, Wolfgang. 2000. *Popmusik im Radio: Musik-Programmgestaltung und Analysen des Tagesprogramms der deutschen Servicewellen 1975–1995*. Baden-Baden: Nomos.
Heitzer, Enrico. 2008. *Affäre Walter: Die vergessene Verhafttungswelle*. Berlin: Metropol.
Janik, Elizabeth. 2005. *Recomposing German Music: Politics and Musical Tradition in Cold War Berlin*. Leiden: Boston: Brill.
Kursawe, Stefan. 2004. *Vom Leitmedium zum Begleitmedium: Die Radioprogramme des Hessischen Rundfunk 1960–1980*. Cologne: Böhlau.
Lefebvre, Henri. 1996. *Writings on Cities*, ed. and trans. Eleonore Kofman and Elizabeth Lebas. Oxford: Blackwell.
Maase, Kaspar. 1992. *Bravo Amerika: Erkundungen zur Jugendkultur der Bundesrepublik in den fünfziger Jahren*. Hamburg: Junius.
Müller, Andreas, Richard Ortmann, and Uta C. Schmidt, eds. 2004. *Jazz in Dortmund: Hot—Modern—Free—New*. Essen: Klartext.
Poiger, Uta G. 2000. *Jazz, Rock and Rebels: Cold War Politics and American Culture in a Divided Germany*. Berkeley: University of California Press.
Rauhut, Michael. 1993. *Beat in der Grauzone: DDR-Rock 1964 bis 1972—Politik und Alltag*. Berlin: Basisdruck.
Riller, Schanett. 2004. *Funken für die Freiheit: Die U.S.-amerikanische Informationspolitik gegenüber der DDR von 1953 bis 1963*. Trier: Wissenschaftlicher Verlag.
Schaaf, Dierk Ludwig. 1971. "Politik und Proporz: Rundfunkpolitik in Nord- und Westdeutschland 1945–1955." PhD dissertation, Universität Hamburg.
Schafer, Murray R. 1973. "The Music of the Environment." *Cultures* 1, no. 1: 15–52.
Scharlau, Ulf, and Petra Witting-Nöthen, eds. 2006. *"Wenn die Jazzband spielt." Von Schlager, Swing und Operette: Zur Geschichte der leichten Musik im deutschen Rundfunk*. Potsdam: Verlag für Berlin-Brandenburg.
Schwab, Jürgen. 2005. *Der Frankfurt Sound: Eine Stadt und ihre Jazzgeschichte(n)*. Frankfurt am Main: Societäts-Verlag.
Siegfried, Detlef. 2006. *Time Is on My Side: Konsum und Politik in der westdeutschen Jugendkultur der 60er Jahre*. Göttingen: Wallstein.
Stahl, Heiner. 2007. "Youth Radio Programmes in Cold War Berlin. Berlin as a Soundscape of Pop (1962–1973)." DrPhil dissertation, University of Potsdam.
Stanley, Bob. 2008. "We Can't Let You Broadcast that." *The Times Supplement*, 6 July: 2.
Thacker, Toby. 2007. *Music after Hitler, 1945–1955*. Aldershot, UK: Ashgate.
Werner, Michael, and Bénédicte Zimmermann. 2002. "Vergleich, Transfer, Verflechtung. Der Ansatz der Histoire croisée und die Herausforderung des Transnationalen." *Geschichte und Gesellschaft* 28, no. 4: 607–36.

PART TWO

East Berlin, the Socialist Capital

CHAPTER 6

Painting the Berlin Wall in Leipzig
The Politics of Art in 1960s East Germany

April A. Eisman

The Berlin Wall divided Germany for nearly thirty years. In the West, it was viewed with horror and disgust, seen as a symbol of a dictatorship gone wrong, a dictatorship moreover that needed, quite literally, to wall in its own people. In the East, the wall's reception was more complicated. It was neither universally rejected nor condemned. Indeed, many intellectuals saw it as a necessary evil, the only way to save the "better Germany," which had been in danger of collapsing in on itself as a result of the loss of skilled and educated workers across the border (Mittenzwei 2003: 169–72). In the year before the Berlin Wall was built, nearly 200,000 citizens had left the GDR (Mittenzwei 2003: 170). The higher ideals of the self-proclaimed antifascist East were no match for the lure of the materially prosperous West. Something had to be done, and despite Ulbricht's claim in June of that year that no one had the intention of building a wall, that is exactly what began to be built on the morning of 13 August 1961.

In the wake of this event, several artists in East Germany began to create works about the Berlin Wall or its construction. While not a major theme in East German art, a fact lamented later, it was nonetheless addressed in a variety of media in the early 1960s, including prints, tapestries, and at least one painting by the Leipzig artist Klaus Weber.[1] Titled *The Morning of 13 August* (*Der Morgen des 13. August*), it depicts a group of East Germans taking a break from constructing the wall. They gather around a central figure holding open the *Neues Deutschland*, the party newspaper, which reports the events of the previous night. Many of them smile and look proud of their contribution to building the wall, which is located outside the right-hand side of the image.

Figure 6.1 Klaus Weber, *The Morning of 13 August (Der Morgen des 13. August)*, oil on canvas, 1962. Courtesy of Museum der bildenden Künste Leipzig and Klaus Weber.

Praised by the *Leipziger Volkszeitung* as "an important contribution by an artist to our national fight," Weber's painting was quickly purchased by the Leipzig branch of the SED and hung in a prominent place in their building (Unsigned 1962b). Written statements by more than thirty civilians in Leipzig, ranging from chemists to librarians to furniture makers, suggest that many people felt the painting to be a true reflection of the day. As one woman wrote, "The smiles on the face of the fighters says to me that they felt the same as we [did], when we heard that the door to our house is now closed to all troublemakers and parasites" (Unsigned 1962a: 1). Similarly, meeting minutes record an officer from the National People's Army who had been in Berlin on the morning of 13 August as saying, "That's exactly how it was!" when he saw Weber's painting (SED-L 1968: 12).

Notwithstanding such claims, the work was not universally praised but rather polarized opinion throughout much of the 1960s. Interestingly the jury for the German Art Exhibition, the GDR's most important exhibition for contemporary East German art, rejected Weber's painting in the same year that the local SED procured it for their offices in Leipzig. In 1966, there was a competition to replace it with another painting titled *13 August 1961*. Significantly, none of the entries was endorsed, and Weber's painting remained on public display. A final discussion took place in 1968 when members of the Central Committee met with artists in Leipzig to discuss whether it should be included in a major exhibition being planned to celebrate the GDR's twentieth anniversary the following year. After more than four hours, the meeting came to a close without reaching a consensus on Weber's painting. Ten had been in favor of showing the work and five were opposed to the idea. Significantly, opinion split between politicians and lay people on the one side and artists and art theoreticians on the other, a similar division as that which took place in 1962 between the politicians of the SED in Leipzig and the artists on the jury of the German Art Exhibition.

This essay will take a closer look at Weber's painting and the reasons why it divided opinion the way it did. It begins by showing how the painting relates to official press reports about the Berlin Wall from August 1961. It then considers how the painting relates to other works of art on the topic, before looking more closely at the criticism leveled against it. Why did a number of artists in Leipzig not like the work? And why did the competition to replace it fail? Ultimately this painting and the debate around it reflect part of a larger discussion taking place between artists and politicians in the GDR in the 1960s—one strongly felt in Leipzig—about the definition of what art was and should be in East Germany. This larger debate was enabled, in part, by the existence of the Berlin Wall, the building of which sparked a temporary thaw in East German cultural politics.

On the morning of 13 August 1961, the citizens of East Germany woke up to front-page articles in *Neues Deutschland* triumphantly announcing that concrete steps had been taken to secure them from the dangers posed by "West German revanchists and militarists" (Unsigned 1961a). Referred to as taking "control of the border," the building of the Berlin Wall was presented as an important "[measure] to protect the peace and to secure the German Democratic Republic in strength" (Unsigned 1961a; Unsigned 1961b). That it was supposed to be a positive event was further emphasized by a front-page photo on 14 August of two armed soldiers laughing.

Klaus Weber's painting portrays the building of the Berlin Wall in this positive light, illustrating well how the SED saw, or at least publicly presented, this event. It depicts a group of East Germans, mostly police officers (*Volkspolizei*) and soldiers from the National People's Army, taking a break from their long night of putting up barbed wire to secure the border between East and West Berlin. Many of them are smiling, not unlike in the photo that would appear in the next day's newspaper, and appear proud and happy about the work they are doing. They are standing next to the Brandenburg Gate, which is visible in the upper right-hand corner of the work. The depiction of the rising sun behind the two tanks at the left, their cannons pointed toward West Berlin, confirms that the figures are indeed on the eastern side of the border.

The men in the painting gather around a central figure holding up the *Neues Deutschland,* having just received it from the woman at the right who holds several issues in her arms. She is talking to the soldier next to her while he gestures to the wall behind him that he is helping to construct. In the center of the painting, light—the source of which is hidden behind a soldier who has turned to look at us—seems to emanate from the newspaper itself, as if the words of the SED were divine. On the left-hand side of the painting stands a well-dressed couple returning home from a night on the town. Next to them stand two masons, suggesting the existence of the wall, which is not actually depicted.[2]

Whereas Weber's work is fairly conservative in its artistic style, the result of its being a painting and thus at the top of the artistic hierarchy in East Germany, the two works published in *Bildende Kunst,* the GDR's main art magazine, in the months following August 1961 are much looser. The first, *Socialism Wins,* is a four-by-seven-feet tapestry created by a group of lay artists in Altscherbitz, a small town near Leipzig. It appeared in the December 1961 issue. The bottom register of the work shows a mushroom cloud on the far left, thus suggesting a threat of nuclear aggression from the West. In front of this are several armed soldiers advancing to-

Figure 6.2 Collective work of the laymen's circle of Altscherbitz, *Socialism Wins,* tapestry, 1961. Current location unknown. Reproduction from *Bildende Kunst* (Dec. 1961): 833.

ward the wall. On the other side, by contrast, citizens of East Germany rally for peace. A banner states that they are "against nuclear death." Next to these figures, two businessmen come together, shaking hands beneath the triple-M symbol for the international trade fairs that took place in Leipzig.

The second image was published in May 1962, an untitled woodblock print by Gabriele Meyer-Dennewitz. Part of a triptych, it focuses on a stern-looking soldier who is presumably telling someone from the West to stay out of the East. Behind him a line of soldiers stands in front of the Brandenburg Gate upon which the date of "13 August" is written. Between its columns, buildings appear, suggesting that the far side of the gate is the East.

According to Weber, he created *The Morning of 13 August* in response to a suggestion that he address the recent political events in his art (Eisman 2008a and 2008b). Already at work on a multifigure composition, he refashioned the painting into one about the building of the wall. The subsequent work, he states, attracted a great deal of attention, with numerous visits to his studio, including a couple by Alfred Kurella, head of the Cultural Commission of the SED at the time. Overall, the reaction to his work was positive, Weber states, a claim confirmed by an article in the local newspaper and written statements about the painting (Unsigned 1962b; Unsigned 1962a).

Apparently only the Leipzig painter Werner Tübke openly criticized the work, expressing a dislike for the "green tone" of the painting that resulted from the many uniforms depicted and it being a night scene. According to Weber, the other criticisms leveled at the so-called deficiencies in his painting were made behind his back. Several bureaucratic reports from the day, however, allow us to reconstruct the criticisms raised. Essentially the problem for these artists was that Weber's painting reflected an artistic style that was then already in decline in Leipzig.

Although Leipzig had been a center for a conservative type of socialist realism throughout the 1950s, by the early 1960s many artists were beginning to experiment with more modern styles. This was the result, in part, of a new hope among some of them that the Wall would give them more breathing room for their work (Mittenzwei 2003: 171; Damus 1991: 203). Without the immediate threat of the West, perhaps their attempts to formulate a new, more modern type of socialist realism for East German art would not be viewed as subversive by governmental officials the way that similar attempts in Berlin and Halle in the mid-1950s had been. Their desire to create a more complex art was presumably then further encouraged by Ulbricht's calls to create art for an educated nation at the Sixth Party Conference of the SED in 1963.

It is at this point in time that Weber finished his painting, *The Morning of 13 August*. Praised in the local press and by the general public for its content, the painting was criticized by artists for its execution and use of "cheap tricks." Nonetheless, the SED in Leipzig bought the painting and gave it a prominent place for display, much to the chagrin of those artists who thought it a bad work. Indeed, several apparently logged complaints against it, presumably prompting the competition for a replacement work on the same theme four years later (SED-L 1968).

First mention of the competition to create a painting or mural with the title *13 August 1961* for the SED building in Leipzig appears in the meeting minutes of the Regional Council of Leipzig on 11 May 1966 (Wolf 1966a). This competition, together with commissions in general, was intended to help give artists in Leipzig more guidance in the face of the "unclear worldview" and "overemphasis on surface effects" evident in some of their recent work (Wolf 1966a: 5). It was a decision that stemmed from discussions that had taken place in the wake of the controversial Seventh Regional Art Exhibition in Leipzig, which had closed a few months earlier. This exhibition is famous today as marking the emergence of the Leipzig School of modern artists, including Bernhard Heisig, Wolfgang Mattheuer and Tübke, onto the East German art scene. Indeed, it showed that in the years since the Wall had been built, several artists in Leipzig had moved away from a simple realism to develop their own unique styles. In the wake of the Eleventh Plenary in December 1965, however, the cultural thaw of the early 1960s was over and a renewed emphasis was placed on commissions as a useful way to help guide artists toward the proper path.

The details for the *13 August 1961* competition appear several months later in the minutes for a meeting of the Regional Council of Leipzig that took place in November 1966 (Ledwoch 1966: 3). It states that three artists from Leipzig had been invited to contribute a sketch on the theme: Jochen Nusser, Gabriele Meyer-Dennewitz, and Heinz Zander. The final sketches were to be 1:5 in size and delivered to the Regional Council on 15 December, where they would be blind-reviewed by a jury later in the month. Lea Grundig, president of the Association of Visual Artists, was asked to chair the jury, which included Walter Womacka from Berlin and several artists from Leipzig. They met to discuss the works on 21 December 1966.[3]

In comparison to Weber's painting, all three works created for the competition depict the Berlin Wall itself as well as both East and West Germany. Nusser's painting is the most simplistic of the three works in its literally black-and-white portrayal of the two Germanies. As such, it

Figure 6.3 Jochen Nusser, entry for the *13 August 1961* painting competition, 1966. Courtesy of Sächsisches Staatsarchiv, Staatsarchiv Leipzig, SED-BL Leipzig.

best embodies the propagandistic quality that all three entries shared. The Wall appears in the middle of his composition, dividing the two panels of what is presumably a diptych. On the left is West Germany. The color scheme is dominated by black, and the images overlap each other chaotically. On the left-hand side there is a soldier in military uniform with an iron cross on his chest, his hips and legs the bones of a skeleton. Above him, a Guernica-inspired woman screams. Behind her, the outlines of a man with a tie, perhaps Konrad Adenauer, then chancellor of West Germany. Another soldier is a skull in uniform, an "SS" clearly visible on his collar and a swastika on his belt.

On the right is East Germany. The color scheme is dominated by white, and the images, while they overlap, suggest harmony. Indeed, it is an image of the happy life the GDR promises to offer. In the center is a factory worker. Behind him on the right-hand side of the painting is a farmer at work, a pianist, and a dancer. On the left is the Brandenburg Gate guarded by two soldiers and a rocket launcher. A child in a Young Pioneers scarf talks to them. Another throws up its hands in joy, mimicking the wings of a white dove of peace.

In case the meaning was not clear enough from the presentation, Nusser included text, which hangs like a sign in the middle of the painting. It states: "13 August 1961. The antifascist protection wall of the GDR shows the revanchist politicians the borders of their power [and] therewith saves the peace in Europe."

In the jury discussion of these three works, all three artists were judged to have failed to adequately come to terms with the political and ideological content of the theme. The focus was too much on the Wall itself as the problem, and on a simplistic good-versus-evil portrayal of what was actually a complex situation. Moreover, it was presented as if the

East-West conflict was now solved rather than ongoing. It was, to quote one of the jury members in response to Meyer-Dennewitz's work, "too happy ending" (SED-L 1966: 22).

Although all three works are visually quite distinct from each other, the striking similarity between them in terms of the specific content portrayed suggests that they were all responding to the same source. Indeed, Paul Fröhlich, the conservative head of the SED in Leipzig, had been assigned to advise them during the painting process. Presumably he encouraged the simplistic view that emerged. If this is indeed the case, it is yet another example of the division between artists and politicians, with the former advocating for greater complexity in both style and content.

Whereas the artistic style of these works was more challenging than Weber's, they lacked the historical authenticity of his work. As a result, Weber's painting remained in its prestigious place in the SED-Leipzig building. While his colleagues may not have liked his work, finding its style retrograde and unfitting for the GDR, those invited to create a replacement were unable to create a better painting in terms of content. 13 August 1961 was simply too difficult a topic for an oil painting in the wake of the deaths that had taken place at the border and the heartache caused by physically separating East Germans from their friends and relatives in the West.

In 1968, Weber's painting became the center of one final discussion when the question of whether it should be included in a major exhibition honoring the twentieth anniversary of the GDR came up (SED-L 1968; Lauter and Kurella 1968). By this point in time, everyone agreed that the style of the work was dated. Everyone also agreed that as the only major painting on the subject, it was important. The issue at stake was whether it should be included in such an important exhibition. Artists and art theoreticians argued strongly against its inclusion, stating it would lead younger artists astray by suggesting this could be a model for their own work. Politicians and lay people, on the other hand, argued that the work captured the moment and was thus historically valid. In the end, they outnumbered the artists and art theoreticians (Lauter and Kurella 1968: 1).

With Erich Honecker's ascent to power in 1971 and the subsequent relaxation in cultural policy that ensued, the complex, modern painting style that had emerged in Leipzig in the early years after the Berlin Wall was built came to represent the GDR internationally. Significantly it was at this point in time, in 1974, that Weber's painting was finally taken down and put into storage, replaced by a five-panel painting by Heisig about the history of Germany in the twentieth century.

Notes

1. An archival document from 1962 lists a commission for an oil painting by H. Mutterlose titled *13.8.1961*. (Unsigned 1962c). Discussions in 1968, however, indicate that Weber's is the only painting created on the subject (SED-L 1968; Lauter 1968).
2. Weber acknowledges that there would not have been any masons there that night (Eisman 2008a).
3. They also discussed the submissions for a competition titled *Arbeiter-und-Bauernmacht* (The Power of Workers and Farmers). In all the archival documents, these two competitions were always spoken of together.

Works Cited

Damus, Martin. 1991. *Malerei in der DDR*. Reinbek bei Hamburg: Rowohlt.
Eisman, April. 2008a. Letter from Klaus Weber. 9 February.
———. 2008b. Interview with Klaus Weber. 4 July.
Häußler. 1961. Ratsinformation über den Stand der Vorbereitung der 6. Bezirkskunstausstellung (Vertrauliche Dienstsache). 15 September. SächsStAL: BT/RdB-L 1470.
Lauter, Hans, and Alfred Kurella. 1968. Bericht über die Begutachtung des Bildes von Klaus Weber "Am Morgen des 13. August" entsprechend dem Beschluß des Politbüros vom 22.3.1968. 31 May. SächsStAL: SED-L 607.
Ledwoch. 1966. Beschlussprotokoll. 24. Sitzung des RdB-L. 14 November . SächsStAL: BT/RdB 4578.
Lemke, Karl. 1962. "Lieber Kollege Heinrich Witz!" *Das Blatt.* January: 21–22.
Mittenzwei, Werner. 2003. *Die Intellektuellen: Literatur und Politik in Ostdeutschland, 1945–2000*. Berlin: Aufbau Taschenbuch.
Preuß, Heinz. 1961. "Künstler riefen zur Wahl." *Das Blatt.* October: 12.
SED-L. 1966. Stenografisches Protokoll. Tagung der Jury zur Annahme von Bildentwürfen zu den Themen "Arbeiter- und Bauern-Macht" und "13. August 1961." 21 December. SächsStAL: SED-L 362.
———. 1968. Protokoll über die Beratung am 10. Mai 1968 in der Bezirksleitung Leipzig über das Bild "Am Morgen des 13. August 1961." 10 May. SächsStAL: SED-L 607.
Unsigned. 1961a. "Beschluss des Ministerrates der Deutschen Demokratischen Republik." *Neues Deutschland.* 13 August: 1.
———. 1961b. "Maßnahmen zum Schutze des Friedens und zur Sicherung der Deutschen Demokratischen Republik in Kraft." *Neues Deutschland.* 14 August: 1.
———. 1962a. Stellungnahmen und Meinungen zum Ölbild des Malers und Grafikers Genossen Klaus Weber. May. Weber Vorlass.
———. 1962b. "Klaus Weber. Am Morgen des 13. August." *Leipziger Volkszeitung*, 24 June.
———. 1962c. Maßnahmeplan für das Jahr 1962 zwischen dem FDGB Bezirksvorstand und dem VBK-L zur Verwirklichung der Vereinbarung zwischen dem FDGB und dem VBKD. 27 March. SächsStAL: VBK-L 114.
VBKD. 1961. *Sechste Kunstausstellung 1961 des VBKD Bezirk Leipzig*. Leipzig: VBKD Bezirk Leipzig.
Wolf. 1966a. Bericht über die Verwirklichung der Aufgabenstellung des Programms des VI. Parteitages der SED auf dem Gebiet der bildenden Kunst, verbunden mit der Vorbereitung der 6. Deutschen Kunstausstellung 1967. 14 November. SächsStAL: BT/RdB 4578.
———. 1966b. Letter to Bartke. 11 May. SächsStAL: BT/RdB 8062
———. 1966c. Letter to Lea Grundig. 18 November. AdK Archiv: Lea Grundig 409.
———. 1967. Tagesordnung der außerplanmässigen Sitzung des RdB-L am Mittwoch, dem 5. April 1967. 30 March. SächsStAL: BT/RdB 4590.

CHAPTER 7

"You Have to Draw a Line Somewhere"
Tropes of Division in DEFA Films from the Early 1960s

Mariana Ivanova

The year 1961 marked a time of increasing ideological division and competition and brought into sharp contrast the tension between public and private spheres in East and West. Given the fact that nearly 3 million citizens had fled the GDR since 1949, the closure of the East German border signaled the socialist government's attempt to "draw a line" not only in geopolitical terms but first and foremost in private lives. The building of the Berlin Wall, officially to prevent a Western military invasion, nevertheless undermined the socialist project of the 1950s, which was based on the convergence of collective and individual identity. Made of wire, bricks, and cement, the inter-German border had an immediate effect on everyday life in Berlin. Germans who on 13 August 1961 found themselves in East Berlin were not merely deprived of the choice to travel or pursue a career in the West; they also had to face new expectations of ideological compliance and political activism within the socialist state. East Berlin citizens, moreover, encountered the dilemma of either accepting the Wall or attempting to flee and reunify with family and relatives. In order to guarantee political stability and to claim support for their political agenda, East German party officials allowed individual questions and experiences to be addressed in the public realm by artists, as shown by April Eisman in this volume. That was best done by film art, which as Sabine Hake argues, served in the GDR context to "reaffirm the bond between masses and party leadership and to realign public and private fantasies in the interest of the state" (2008: 129). In the 1960s, therefore, the East German DEFA studio commissioned several documentary and feature films focusing on the German division. While some of these films conformed to the official agenda by validating political objectives over personal desires, others explored the Wall's effects on individual lives. This essay will examine this shift in the filmic representation of the division of Germany from the affirmation of official discourse to the focus on personal reactions to the Berlin Wall.

After 1961, the Berlin Wall quickly supplanted the Berlin Blockade of 1948–49 as the premier symbol of the city's contested status between competing ideological systems. On 9 September 1948, West Berlin mayor Ernst Reuter had proclaimed at a rally against the Blockade: "People of the world, look at this city!" This appeal took on symbolic meaning throughout the Cold War: in the West, it served as a premonition of the real and imaginary dangers emanating from the Eastern Bloc, while in GDR political discourse, it stood for western belligerence and revanchism. In 1961, when the Wall's construction drew the world's attention to Berlin, Reuter's words returned in the title of a new documentary film by one of DEFA's most prolific directors, Karl Gass. *Schaut auf diese Stadt* (Look at this City, 1961) revisits pivotal moments in German postwar history and presents Berlin's division as inevitable. In its attitude, Gass's film departs from the representation in two earlier DEFA documentaries from 1959. Helmut Schneider's *Protokoll Westberlin* (West Berlin Report) critiques the recently prescribed role to Berlin as the center of Cold War espionage, while Max Jaap's *Interview mit Berlin* (Interview with Berlin) presents both parts of the city as organically linked by the daily exchange of people and goods. Gass's film invalidates the idea of Berlin's unity by turning Reuter's appeal into a tool for dividing film segments.

Look at This City announces the guaranteeing of world peace as the GDR's historic mission. Gass develops his argument by critically revisiting several events from the immediate postwar history from the Yalta and Potsdam Conferences and General Lucius Clay's negotiations for the city's status to the Sputnik crisis of 1957 and the military showdown at Checkpoint Charlie in 1961. The voiceover instrumentalizes the past, denounces West Germany as the successor of the Third Reich, and equates West Berlin with an island, occupied by imperialist forces. "This border is not new," the narrator concludes toward the end of the film. "We merely built what was devised and designed by others eleven years ago." The building of the Berlin Wall, therefore, appears as dictated by political decisions in the name of the people. Although Gass's state-commissioned documentary lacks an individual perspective and merely advances the official political agenda, DEFA feature films of the 1960s reemploy its imagery, as well as elements of its defensive rhetoric (Allan 2010). Gass's film thus raises important questions: How was the Berlin

Wall viewed in the popular imagination and how can film facilitate our understanding of personal reactions to the Wall? Was the erection of the Wall really a political decision or was it dictated by everyday reality? How did political decisions to "draw the line" translate into individual lives as portrayed in films of the period?

This essay will engage some of these questions by looking at how DEFA feature films from 1961 to 1964 depict the German division before and after the construction of the Berlin Wall while addressing the intersection of private and public discourses, personal and national histories. Like Gass's documentary, earlier feature films openly defend the division, whereas later films treat its reverberations in more ambiguous terms. In order to trace this shift, three films will be compared: Kurt Maetzig's *Septemberliebe* (September Love, 1961), Frank Vogel's *Und deine Liebe auch* (And Your Love Too, 1962), and Konrad Wolf's *Der geteilte Himmel* (The Divided Heaven, 1964). On the one hand, these films reinforce the official rhetoric in the GDR about the Wall's protective function, yet on the other, they underscore the harmful effects of the physical wall upon personal relationships. This double agenda is evident in the discrepancy between rather conventional plots and innovative film aesthetics reflecting the spatial division of the city as well as the experience of confinement. The topography of division will therefore be investigated on two levels: first, on the narrative level, i.e., the introduction of a romantic plot defined by love triangles and crises in gender relationships; second, on the visual level, the employment of spatial metaphors within the mise-en-scène and the filmic organization of public and private spaces. This essay will show how the topography of division is complicated by signifiers of transition on both levels, equally denoting encounter and separation, arrival and departure: for instance, images of bridges, highways, and roads or the motifs of pregnancy and a suicide attempt, loss and mourning, injury and convalescence. The three films represent interpersonal relationships as dependent on political realities; yet they also critically comment on the unwanted and inevitable alteration of everyday life due to the building of the Wall.

Epitomizing DEFA's response to the closure of the border in 1961, the *Mauerfilme* (Wall films) combine aspects of the studio's documentary films and its so-called *Gegenwartsfilme* (films about contemporary society) of the 1960s. The latter usually address struggles of individuals within a collective, which are resolved by their integration into the new society and their commitment to building the socialist state. DEFA Wall films, similarly, seek to guide audiences in coping with the new German-German border, although little space is reserved for the visual representation of the actual Wall. As Sebastian Heiduschke maintains, the absence of the

Wall parallels a strategy to encode it in visual images of fortification and division, which invites various interpretations and allows "alternative views" among audiences (2007: 39). Most Wall film narratives prefer to thematize the act of crossing the border, or the dilemma of choosing between the two Germanies. At the same time, they propose strategies for moving forward and overcoming the quandaries, as implied by their frequent open endings.[1] In other words, even though these films endorse the official propaganda, they also demonstrate the filmmakers' attempt to recognize and attend to an array of individual reactions, including those that do not conform to political myths. Moreover, Wall films express not only resentment or criticism, but also look to restore the utopian project of the 1950s, connecting public aspirations with personal hopes. This is why, according to Daniela Berghahn and Joshua Feinstein, such films should not be reduced to state-commissioned propagandistic affirmations of the Wall (Berghahn 2005: 190; Feinstein 2002: 126). One example for the films' layered structure motivates Berghahn's reading of *The Divided Heaven* as an intertwining of "the personal history of a woman with a momentous historical event," which applies to other Wall films as well (2005: 193). In all three films discussed in this essay, a woman is faced with the dilemma of choosing between following her lover into the West and making the commitment to socialism. With or without the help of the collective, she is led to make the "right choice," usually at the expense of her love relationship. The themes of internal struggles and unresolved desires facilitate a shift in DEFA films of the 1960s from advancing a political agenda to a greater focus on the personal, a trend that continues in films about the Berlin Wall after 1989.[2]

Set in divided Berlin, Maetzig's *September Love* tells the story of the forbidden love between Franka (Doris Abesser) and her sister's fiancé Hans Schramm (Ulrich Thein). Franka's voiceover describes the romance in retrospect: Hans has just received his PhD in chemistry and maintains dubious connections to his uncle in West Berlin who works for IG Farben, a conglomerate once subservient to the Nazi regime. Forced to spy on GDR scientific research, Hans is eventually discovered and becomes the object of investigations by Stasi agents. Despite his refusal to provide his uncle with information, he is now plagued by fears of detention and decides to flee to the West. Unable to convince her lover to trust the GDR's benevolent authorities, Franka reports his plans to a Stasi office. She thus compensates for her lack of morale by performing her duty to the state and preventing her lover from defecting to the capitalist West.

The film premiered at the beginning of 1961, just before the events of 13 August would drive its propaganda message ad absurdum. Director Kurt Maetzig, one of DEFA's most politically active and prolific filmmakers, had already explored the theme of a couple's separation because of Germany's division in an earlier film, *Roman einer jungen Ehe* (Story of a Young Couple, 1952), and continued to engage with the contemporary problem of border crossing in Berlin. *September Love* conspicuously foreshadows the personal conflicts in Vogel's and Wolf's films, thus reinforcing the idea that Germany's division has entered and altered the private sphere. Besides the use of a voiceover and the motif of remembering, Maetzig's film shares basic plot elements with the other two films: the complications of a love triangle, the man's problematic connection to West Berlin, and the woman's decision to remain loyal to the state. Set against the backdrop of the Cold War, the narrative of *September Love* critiques the call for reunification as serving capitalist aspirations to profit from East German labor and know-how. Ironically, Maetzig's film draws on the official rationale behind the Wall's construction, loss of skilled workers to the West, which is replaced in *Look at this City* by a critique of Western authorities rejecting Soviet proposals for reunification. Like Gass's film, however, through Franka's denunciation of her lover, *September Love* privileges official political discourse at the expense of personal desires.

This idea is supported by the visual organization of spaces in *September Love* that significantly differs from the busy urban environment in the later films. Franka and Hans meet and experience intimacy in natural settings, such as the riverbank or the forest, whereas the populated streets of Berlin, still accessible to intruders from the West, are coded as adverse to their happiness. Open and remote spaces provide a shelter for their forbidden love, while Hans's attic room lacks the familiarity and freedom found in nature. The recurring conflicts engendered by Franka's feelings of guilt or disagreement over the trustworthiness of Stasi officials point to the intrusion of public morale and political demands into the private sphere. Though these conflicts are never resolved within the film, they are contained in a fairly partisan narrative that undermines their potential for actual criticism.

Toward the end, Franka succumbs to the idea that the individual good depends on the collective, and in turn attempts to persuade her lover to perform his duty to the state, i.e., to report his correspondence with West Berliners to state security officials. The film includes a rare positive representation of Stasi informants in East German cinema, which was harshly critiqued by West Berlin media. Located at a busy train station, the Stasi office appears as an integral part of everyday life, accessible to East Berliners and at the same time protecting the capital from incoming Westerners. Franka's familiarity with the Stasi office location and the act of recounting her lover's plans are depicted as perfectly acceptable.

Like the other female protagonists in Vogel's and Wolf's films, Franka is plagued by doubts about her relationship, yet her ideological commitment presents her from the onset as a steadfast proponent of the German division.

And Your Love Too is another film that focuses on the dilemma between duty and love, perseverance and hesitancy. The film opens with a playful montage of snapshots of Berlin streets, providing the story's generic character. The camera zooms in on a loft, where Ulrich "Ulli" Settich (Armin Müller-Stahl) follows his daily routine. In a voiceover, he introduces young, vivacious Eva (Kathy Székely), who has just moved from a small town to Berlin. Ulli and Eva alternate in narrating their convoluted love story, which involves a love triangle with Ulli's adoptive brother Klaus. Working in the West while living in the East, Klaus is Ulli's antagonist in terms of political convictions, and his competitor for Eva's attention. On the night of 12/13 August 1961, all three go out dancing, and end up in Ulli's apartment. They wake up in a divided Berlin: Ulli has to guard the construction of the Wall as an armed civilian soldier, Klaus is trapped in the East against his will, and Eva faces the dilemma of choosing between the brothers. Eventually she falls for Klaus, while Ulli is busy performing his duty of protecting the border. Eva's pregnancy soon opens her eyes to Klaus's arrogance and the dangers that remilitarization in the West poses to her unborn child. She thus rejoins Ulli, whose commitment to the socialist project (both at the workplace and at home) embodies the promise of a better, peaceful future.

The working title of the film, *Bei uns,* literally *Among Us* or *On Our Side,* anticipates the theme of division and, similar to *September Love,* suggests the focus on the GDR's demands to consolidate its young socialist society and fight the problem of defection to the West. As its filmmakers maintain, the picture became an "unusual experiment of great political significance to the contemporary situation" (Vogel 1962: 422), since the Berlin Wall was built during the shooting phase, which required alterations in the plot.[3] Even the film's documentary quality benefited from these radical plot changes. As writer Paul Wiens points out in an interview, the film was based on the diary of a woman from Berlin and had no real script, but was largely dependent on the filmmakers' serendipity shooting on Berlin's streets in 1961, as well as on the actors' improvisation in the film studio (Wiens 1962; Vogel 1962).

The film's opening shot shows the people of Berlin from an impersonal perspective in their everyday routines: shopping, chatting, dancing, dining, and roaming the streets. The concreteness of the documentary footage that interrupts the narrative serves to normalize the experiences behind the cemented border. It situates Eva's and Ulli's romance among the daily lives of thousands of other East Berliners in order to facilitate their identification with the lovers. As the film narrative evolves, occasionally documentary shots are introduced and interpreted from Eva's subjective perspective. For instance, the Soviet-American showdown in October 1961 at Checkpoint Charlie and the public celebration of Soviet astronaut Titow on the Marx-Engels-Platz, both familiar already from Gass's documentary, now appear as personalized and motivating factors for Eva's decisions.

Other Cold War themes such as the Soviet Sputnik program and the Cuban Missile Crisis cast the film's agenda as affirmative of the GDR's separation from the West. Ulli's attic room, where he communicates with a Cuban friend via shortwave radio, suggests parallels between the Wall's construction and the Cuban "emancipation from capitalism." The phrase "You need to draw a line" becomes the film's core message, reiterated by Ulli and Eva at key moments to encourage Klaus—and by extension, the viewers—to accept the German division and to actively resist the lure of the West. The verbal admonition translates into the image of a dividing black-and-white line on Warschauer Brücke (allusion to the

Figure 7.1 Film still, *And Your Love, Too*. Courtesy of Deutsche Kinemathek, Filmmuseum Berlin.

Warsaw Pact from 1955) where both brothers meet on the morning of 13 August. Seen through Eva's eyes, the Checkpoint Charlie showdown later alludes to this encounter at the bridge. Both spaces are visually reencoded from signifiers of transition into spaces of decision making and separation.

The motif of transition is reinforced by Eva's pregnancy, which she at first hesitates to accept. After making up her mind at Checkpoint Charlie, she gains back her independence from Klaus and fully commits to the young socialist state. Her unborn child justifies her return to Ulli and her symbolic embrace of the GDR's promise of protection and prosperity. Thus Eva's transition from apolitical young woman eager to experience the big city to a citizen committed to the ideological project of peace through political separation signifies the impact of the public discourse of division on her personal life.

The intrusion of the public into the private sphere is more ambiguously represented in Ulli's uneasy romantic experience. His love song "And Your Love Too" equates the wind on Warschauer Brücke and Eva's love as indispensable for his political decision in the night of 12 August. On the next morning, the stanza acquires a different meaning when Ulli is ordered to guard the Wall during construction. His decision to perform his duty reinforces the interpolation of the private by the political realm. His self-reproaches for initially losing Eva to Klaus point to his struggle in balancing personal desires and public demands. However, can such a balance be achieved? Would it have been possible for Ulli or any GDR citizen to prioritize differently? Rita's story in Konrad Wolf's film *The Divided Heaven* similarly seeks an answer to such questions.

The Divided Heaven (1964) cannot be defined as a Wall film insofar as it never explicitly makes reference to the actual historical event, and is considered by most scholars a *Gegenwartsfilm* (Feinstein 2002: 126; Berghahn 2005: 190). However, the Wall's presence as an imaginary construct is established by the film's title and the recurring visual motifs that divide the screen: bridges, highways, roads, balustrades, staircases, and window grids. These images, indeed, serve to sustain an awareness of physical borders and limitations. Separation comprises the central theme of Christa Wolf's novel of the same title of 1963, which was adapted to the screen by Konrad Wolf. The director chooses to present the love relationship between Rita Seidel (Renate Blume) and Manfred Herrfurth (Eberhard Esche) in a series of flashbacks through Rita's voiceover. The fragmented nature of her reminiscences correlates with the disparate images of a dissected sky and reinforces parallels between the lovers' story and the German division. Like Hans in *September Love,* Manfred receives his PhD in chemistry, yet he is disappointed by the poor career prospects in the GDR. In contrast, Rita commits wholeheartedly to the socialist project. When Manfred decides to flee the GDR only a few days before the border is closed, Rita is left with the dilemma of moving to West Berlin or remaining loyal to her state and renouncing her love. She chooses the latter, which results in her mental and physical breakdown.

Among the three discussed films, *The Divided Heaven* is perhaps most critical of the painful intrusion of the public into the private realm; it employs striking visual tropes to represent it and focuses primarily on subjective experiences. Upon its release, the film stirred heated debates in East and West German media as well as at the GDR's German Academy of Arts in June 1964. Most of the contributors concluded that the highly stylized photography used to dramatize Rita's disorientation and dilemma fits uneasily within a story that should validate the building of the Wall. Already the opening sequence of the film confronts the audience with an unsettling montage of disparate images that divide the sky and suggest a lasting impact on the urban landscape and everyday life. External spaces such as windows and roads, train stations and church towers, bridges and highways constantly split the frame and reflect the separation of the public from the private sphere. Like in Vogel's film, spaces of transition, as well as states of transition, such as Rita's convalescence, are reinterpreted as signifiers of division. Even Manfred's and Rita's attic studio, reminiscent of Hans's and Franka's room, appears visually threatened by an enormous window grid, and becomes cluttered with poisonous chemicals. Whereas public spaces foreshadow the lovers' division, the private spaces similarly translate the visual split into a sense of conflict and disagreement.

Rita's suffering and inability to rejoin Manfred in West Berlin toward the end shows that personal decisions can be hardly reconciled with public demands. While she slowly recuperates under the care of politically engaged mentors, Rita is aware of her own responsibility for, and the repercussions of, sacrificing the relationship. Visually her decision is justified, unsurprisingly, by representing West Berlin as a hostile, cold, confined space, defined by fences, blinds, and grids. Kurfürstendamm as the backdrop of the lovers' final encounter is reduced to empty anonymous facades and window grids looming over the couple. The grid of Manfred's room reappears divided into multiple facets in the West Berliner Café Kranzler, visually amplifying the unbearable experience of division. Sitting alone across each other in a sterile-looking interior, the lovers experience a breakdown in communication. When the love story is over, Rita returns to the busy streets of her town, where she strives for a new beginning among other GDR citizens.

Figure 7.2 Film still, *Divided Heaven.* Courtesy of Deutsche Kinemathek, Filmmuseum Berlin.

The open endings of all three DEFA feature films suggest both the utopian hope for a new beginning and the unresolved conflict between national politics and private lives. In 1961, films still examine the possibilities and positive effects of "drawing a line," yet by 1964 the focus shifts to the painful consequences of political intervention into the private sphere. While DEFA documentary films such as *Look at this City* insist on the necessity of individual lives to fit into grander designs and submit to the imperatives of history, feature films continuously engage with the personal sacrifices brought on by the dramatic transformation of daily life and the demand for compliance with state interests. The shift in filmic representation from the official discourse of division to the personal perspectives on the border closure suggests the new project of DEFA filmmakers from 1964 onward: to critique the growing lack of communication between the GDR state and its citizens.

Notes

1. Other DEFA wall films include *Der Kinnhaken* (The Knock-Out Punch, 1962, Heinz Thiel), *Sonntagsfahrer* (Sunday Drivers, 1963, Gerhard Klein), and the television production *Geschichten jener Nacht* (Stories of that Night, 1967, various directors).

2. Films by former DEFA directors such as Heiner Carow's *Verfehlung* (Misdemeanor, 1992), Frank Beyer's *Der Verdacht* (Suspicion, 1991), and Helmut Dziuba's *Jana und Jan* (1992) as well as Margarethe von Trotta's *Das Versprechen* (The Promise, 1995) and Roland Suso Richter's two-part television production *Der Tunnel* (The Tunnel, 2001) recycle many of the narrative elements familiar from the Wall films, including the motif of unhappy romantic love.

3. *And Your Love Too* was Frank Vogel's first wall film, followed by two other films on the same topic, *Julia lebt* (Julia Lives, 1963) and an episode in *Stories of that Night*.

Works Cited

Allan, Séan. 2010. "Projections of History: East German Film-makers and the Berlin Wall." In *Divided, But Not Disconnected: German Experiences of the Cold War*. Eds. Tobias Hochscherf, Christoph Laucht, and Andrew Plowman. New York and Oxford: Berghahn.

Berghahn, Daniela. 2005. *Hollywood Behind the Wall: The Cinema of East Germany*. Manchester: Manchester University Press.

Feinstein, Joshua. 2002. *The Triumph or the Ordinary: Depictions of Daily Life in East German Cinema 1949–1989*. Chapel Hill: University of North Carolina Press.

Fulbrook, Mary. 2002. *History of Germany 1918–2000: The Divided Nation*. Sec. ed. Oxford: Blackwell.

Hake, Sabine. 2008. *German National Cinema*. Sec. ed. London: Routledge.

Heiduschke, Sebastian. 2007. "'Das ist die Mauer, die quer durchgeht. Dahinter liegt die Stadt und das Glück.' DEFA Directors and Their Criticism of the Berlin Wall." *Colloquia Germanica* 40.1: 37–50.

Maetzig, Kurt. 1987. *Filmarbeit: Gespräche, Reden Schriften*. Ed. Günter Agde. Berlin: Henschel.

Pfelling, Liane, ed. 1964. *Probleme des sozialistischen Realismus in der darstellenden Kunst behandelt am Beispiel des DEFA-Films "Der geteilte Himmel." Referat und Diskussionsbeiträge der II. Plenartagung der Deutschen Akademie der Künste zu Berlin vom 30. Juni 1964*. Berlin: Deutsche Akademie der Künste.

Richter, Erika. 1994. "Zwischen Mauerbau und Kahlschlag: 1961–65." In Schenk and Mückenberger, *Das zweite Leben der Filmstadt Babelsberg*. 164–68.

Schenk, Ralf and Christiane Mückenberger. 1994. *Das zweite Leben der Filmstadt Babelsberg: DEFA-Spielfilme 1946–1992*. Berlin: Henschel.

Schittly, Dagmar. 2002. *Zwischen Regie und Regime*. Berlin: Christoph Links.

Silberman, Marc. 1994. "Post-Wall Documentaries. New Images from a New Germany?," *Cinema Journal* 33: 22–41.

Silbermann, Marc. 1995. *German Cinema: Text in Context*. Detroit: Wayne State University Press.

Vogel, Frank. 1962. ". . . und deine Liebe auch. Notizen zur Entstehungsgeschichte des Films." *Filmwissenschaftliche Mitteilungen* 3: 421–37.

Wien, Paul. 1962. Interview with Heinz Hoffmann. In *Sonntag*, 26 August.

Wolf, Konrad. 1989. *Direkt in Kopf und Herz: Aufzeichnungen. Reden*. Berlin: Henschel.

CHAPTER 8

Constructing a Socialist Landmark: The Berlin Television Tower

Heather Gumbert

In October 1952 representatives of the East German Postal Ministry sought permission to build a television antenna on the rooftop of one of the new apartment buildings that soon would line the premier East German boulevard, Stalinallee. Still under construction, Stalinallee was conceived as the centerpiece of a new, socialist East Berlin. The move was crucial for the Postal Ministry's plans to develop television technology for the German Democratic Republic (GDR): television technicians had been trying to erect a transmitting antenna that would improve transmission and reception of television signals in Berlin for several months. A newly built high-rise apartment building on Stalinallee seemed the perfect location. But East Berlin's Chief Architect Hermann Henselmann rejected the request as "out of the question." The building in question could easily house the equipment, but "the antenna would completely destroy the architectural view and the harmony of the overall view of the Stalinallee" (MPF-BRF 1952). What is more, the antenna would interfere with the reception of radio signals. Unlike radio, television did not yet fit into the socialist master plan.

Almost a decade and several failed attempts later, postal authorities tried again to build a tower in Berlin, but this time their project met with success. By the early 1960s television had emerged as one of the most important political tools of the Socialist Unity Party's campaign to build socialism in the GDR. In 1964 the SED approved plans for an enormous transmission tower that would rival existing towers throughout the world and located it between Alexanderplatz and Marx-Engels-Platz, at the very intersection of East Berlin's cultural, economic, and governmental centers of power. The tower, with its broadcasting transmitters, observation deck, and revolving restaurant, opened to the public to much fanfare in 1969. In his speech inaugurating the tower in October 1969, SED leader Walter Ulbricht celebrated it as an "emblem of Berlin" and, indeed, after five years of well-publicized construction efforts, it had already become one of the most recognizable features of the divided city (Ulbricht 1969).

This essay examines the long and complicated history of the decision to build the tower at Alexanderplatz in the heart of the city. The story of the tower demonstrates the integral role of broadcasting in the Cold War battle between the two German states. Although often narrowly associated with propaganda programming, broadcasting was in fact a much larger battlefield that involved technical, legal, and cultural "fronts." The postwar redistribution of the European airwaves in 1950 pushed states to defend their "air space," for example, so that even before they fought over messages, states fought over airwaves and frequencies. By 1951 officials in East Germany had taken up this challenge, erecting transmitters to expand the broadcasting infrastructure even before there was a program or an audience. Early efforts to "cover" the GDR with television and radio signals were stopgap measures, short-term solutions to an international regulatory framework that forced states to lay claim to the broadcasting frequencies allotted to them (Gumbert 2006). By the early 1960s though, approaches to the television tower had shifted from this kind of technological pragmatism—the drive for "coverage" that reflected an instrumental view of broadcasting—to a greater interest in the television tower as a symbolic monument; no longer "just" an antenna, the tower was rather a cultural symbol of the strength and power of the state itself.

This story also highlights the productive constraints of the GDR and the difficult decisions involved in "socialist planning" during the 1950s and 1960s. Planners had to tackle a wide range of needs, from reconstruction of the war-torn country to ongoing reparation obligations to the Soviet Union, with a finite set of resources, often further limited by Cold War embargoes against the GDR. The nascent East German broadcasting industry faced its own problems: scarce resources, the "brain drain" of educated technicians to the West, and domestic production capacity, given that Soviet contracts took priority in fulfillment of reparations, at least in the 1950s. But this was also a moment of opportunity, when planners had license to reshape the urban space of the *Hauptstadt* (capital). Though this seemingly offered planners a broad mandate to push through the SED's vision for a monumental city center glorifying the power of the state, this story demonstrates, on the one hand, a certain adherence to the architectural history of the city (Tscheschner 1993) and, on the other hand, that architectural conceptions evolved in response to changing patterns of East German social life.

Finally this story reveals the importance of personal interventions in the political culture of the GDR. After nearly a decade of failed attempts to build a TV tower in Berlin, by the early 1960s postal authorities despaired of ever seeing the project to completion. They sought strong advocates within the SED to impress upon the government the increasingly urgent need to improve the broadcasting infrastructure. A direct appeal to Walter Ulbricht ultimately saved the tower and, within a year, it had become an even more monumental project, intended to demonstrate the power and achievements of East German socialism.

In 1951 the Postal Ministry constructed the first postwar television transmitter in the heart of Berlin, signaling the state's intention to enter the Cold War of the airwaves. The Stadthaus transmitter was a provisional solution to the problem of getting a signal out, even before there was a television program to broadcast. The weak transmission reached only a small radius inside Berlin, but it was enough to receive signals from the Television Center at Adlershof in southeast Berlin. It would suffice until authorities could find a location for a new, stronger transmitter to broadcast in Berlin and beyond (MPF-BRF 1956). But advocating for this still-obscure technology was difficult, and postal authorities responsible for television continued to face an uphill battle even within their own Ministry. And, as Henselmann's resistance to placing a permanent antenna above Stalinallee exemplified, they were unsuited to the aesthetic demands of grand urban architecture; they were instead practical, technocratic structures. Shut out of locations that would provide crucial elevation and size, authorities instead erected small-scale transmitters in the city that were prone to interference with industrial radio signals (including diathermic machines, motorized vehicles, and the subway), and would soon have to compete with the new, larger transmitter under construction in West Berlin (MPF-BRF 1954a).

To limit interference and find enough space to build a substantial new tower, postal authorities began to seek locations on the outskirts of the city. In 1953 they settled on a site in the Müggelberge (Müggel hills) southeast of the city center, where a transmitter could be high enough to avoid interference and, potentially, send good signals within a radius of 50 kilometers. In contrast to previous transmitters, they conceived this transmitting "tower" as a massive complex, 130 meters in height, comprised of a sixteen-story building topped by a 40-meter antenna. It would house two new radio transmitters and a television transmitter ten times stronger than the one in the city center. The complex also would become the GDR's broadcasting relay center, coordinating the transmission of radio, television, and other communications signals across the republic (MPF-BRF 1958b). But this grand project soon met difficulties. East German industry scheduled the transmitter for production in 1953, but production difficulties ranging from a lack of materials and funds to an overloaded production schedule pushed the completion date from 1953 into 1954 then 1955, when, finally, the Allied High Commission banned the project to protect air safety around the Schönefeld airport (MPF-BRF 1954b; MPF-BRF 1956). Plans for a central broadcasting tower to serve Berlin languished, while the Postal Ministry continued to battle production difficulties in building the broadcasting infrastructure to provide transmissions elsewhere in the GDR.

In late 1956 the government quite suddenly began to scrutinize more carefully the role of the Postal Ministry in television technology. In November the Hungarian Uprising had become a flashpoint in the Cold War. Hampered by technical limitations and political paralysis, East German television had ignored the revolt, missing what the Central Committee characterized as a good opportunity to disseminate its own interpretation of events (Gumbert 2006: 121–26). The Council of Ministers saw both promise and peril in the state of East German television broadcasting and reorganized the leadership structure of the Postal Ministry to improve the broadcasting infrastructure. A new Radio and Television Section coordinated more closely with East German industry to streamline technical development, eliminate duplication of research into broadcasting technology, and complete existing projects (MPF-BRF 1957b). Such measures raised the Postal Ministry's project completion rate, but at the cost of importing transmitters from the West. Even so, gaps in coverage persisted, especially in western parts of the GDR where East Germans still could receive West German signals much more clearly East German signals, encouraging them to tune in Western broadcasts. Indeed television repair shops there reported that locals serviced their sets to improve their reception of West, not East, German signals (MPF-BRF 1956; MPF-BRF 1957b).

The failure of the Müggelberge project had been a disaster with wide-ranging consequences for the GDR's battle against the West, but renewed emphasis on the Cold War helped to resurrect the project. By 1958 television had begun to take its place in East Germans' everyday lives: viewership was rising just as surely as the program schedule was expanding. At the Fifth Party Congress in July, the SED identified television as a "new, significant political-cultural factor of our lives" (SED 1958) that would take its place in a renewed campaign to build socialism and wage ideological battle with the West. In this context new plans emerged that returned the tower project to the heart of East Berlin. The expectations for the new tower embedded in this conception had been shaped by years of planning. The tower would have to be tall, at least 360 meters from the foot to the tip of the antenna, to improve reception in the dense neighborhoods of Berlin and ensure the most coverage possible in areas to the west and northwest of Berlin. It would have enough space to house the technical equipment of radio, television, and other telecommunications services (Probst 1958; MPF-BRF 1958a). But new ideas emerged as well that were not determined by wholly technological factors. Unexpectedly East Germans had shown great interest in the new, largely rural towers, traveling to visit them on the weekends and clamoring for observation platforms that would offer an outlook on the surrounding countryside: the broadcasting infrastructure had become a network of tourist attractions. Officials concluded that the new tower had to include facilities that would meet this demand, including some kind of observation deck and perhaps even a restaurant (Ministerium für Bauwesen 1959).

Planners began to imagine the tower not simply as a technological challenge, but rather as an indispensable new landmark in the redesign of Berlin's city center. At the Fifth Party Congress in July 1958, the Postal Ministry gave Ulbricht a commemorative set of plans in celebration of their concept for a spectacular new tower (Probst 1958). Contemporary tower design influenced the conception, projected as a circular shaft of reinforced concrete supporting a "basket" located near the top of the tower. The "basket" was envisioned as a half-sphere form with an eight-story structure rising from it that would house technical equipment and tourist amenities. Atop the basket, a 60-meter antenna completed the tower. The Ministry of Architecture lauded the tower's modern design. The reinforced concrete design of the shaft would "satisfy the . . . viewer and reflect the progress of the new construction technology," unlike the old steel framework style, "which seems foreign to a city of concrete, glass, and brick" (Ministerium für Bauwesen 1959). This was more than a broadcasting tower; it was a symbol of the strength and modernity of the GDR.

By 1959 then, the tower project was no longer relegated to the margins of Berlin, but rather poised to become a focal point, perhaps even "part of the architectural ensemble of Stalinallee, Strausbergerplatz, and Alexanderplatz" in the heart of the city (Ministerium für Bauwesen 1959). The city planning authority considered several factors in evaluating possible locations for the tower, including air safety and available space for the tower and associated parking. Yet two additional factors demonstrated how far the project had come since 1952, when a tower built in the city center had to be discreetly hidden in the cityscape. Now authorities sought a location in close proximity to the centers of urban life and clearly visible from neighborhoods around Berlin. They considered five potential locations, including sites near Märkisches Museum, Dimitroffstrasse in Prenzlauer Berg, Kniprodestrasse at the city rail station Greifswalderstrasse, in the Volkspark Friedrichshain between Bunkerberg and Märchenbrunnen (fairytale fountain), and, finally, on the site of the cemetery on Prenzlauer Berg (Stadtbauamt 1959). Of these, only the Friedrichshain and Prenzlauer Berg sites fit the bill.

The advantages of the Prenzlauer Berg and Friedrichshain locations lay in the ease of construction, but also in their potential symbolic value. The city planning office advocated for the Prenzlauer Berg location, which had enough space to build and no obstacles to a quick construction start. Visitors could reach the site quickly by means of two large north-south corridors (Prenzlauer Allee and Greifswalderstrasse); it was a bus service point and, in the future, would also be served by a subway line. Parking would not be a problem. Not least, the elevation would set the tower above the city center, making it easily seen from the center, Friedrichshain, and West Berlin. By contrast, the Postal Ministry favored the Volkspark location, despite city officials' protests that the green space of the park should remain undeveloped. This plan involved the entire western portion of the park, essentially cutting the fountain off from the Bunkerberg (MPF-BRF 1958a; Stadtbauamt 1959). The Ministry of Architecture also supported the park location, where the tower would suit the rolling terrain and draw perhaps thousands of visitors every day. Moreover, people all over Berlin would be able to see the tower, due to the elevation of the location, turning it into a "symbol of unified Berlin" and an example of "the strength of [the GDR's] economy," perhaps even raising the profile of the GDR in the world (Ministerium für Bauwesen 1959).

Between 1959 and 1962 GDR agencies prepared to build the tower in the Friedrichshain Park, even as the heightened tensions of the Berlin Crisis began to redefine the urban space of the city. In 1960 the air safety authority approved the project, and the Postal Ministry received a construction permit to begin work scheduled for completion in 1962. But delays dogged the project. In 1960 site inspections raised questions and construction costs, leading authorities to waver on the exact location. The question of location was still unanswered when the government closed the border to West Berlin on 13 August 1961. The border closure highlighted the significance of the broadcasting infrastructure: in a highly publicized, if short-lived and ineffective campaign, leaders mobilized a state-sponsored youth group to ostracize East Germans who had positioned their antennas to receive West German programming (Gumbert 2006: 194–98). At the same time, the construction of the Berlin Wall created restricted areas that had once been centers of everyday life, transforming urban space and shifting building priorities. Finally the crisis tested the economic resources of the state. In 1962 the municipality of Berlin ran out of money for the project; the planning commission shelved the project twice more (Apel 1963). Fearing for the project's future, the Postal Ministry mobilized the State Broadcasting Committee to advocate for its continuation (Probst 1963).

The Cold War appeared to threaten the project, but it was in fact its *raison d'etre:* the desire to compete with West German broadcasting ultimately saved the Berlin tower. In 1963 GDR authorities learned the West Germans planned to raise the height of their Berlin transmitter to 280 meters, which would decisively improve the reception of West German television in the problematic areas west and northwest of Berlin and in East Berlin. Armed with this knowledge, the head of the Broadcasting Committee, Gerhart Eisler, appealed to Walter Ulbricht directly, arguing that without a new tower the GDR would have no way of countering the stronger signal and lose more ground in the Cold War competition for the airwaves. Ulbricht put Politburo member and Agitation Commission head Albert Norden on the case in November 1963 (Eisler 1963b; Norden 1963).

By year's end in 1963, with the political significance of the tower clear and the Politburo pressing for the project to go forward, it still faltered on the question of location. The Friedrichshain site still proved too expensive and alternate locations in Berlin Weissensee failed to inspire postal officials (MPF-BRF 1964). Then, in 1964 Ulbricht met with state representatives, including members of the Postal Ministry and planning commission, to discuss the future of the center of East Berlin between Marx-Engels-Platz and Alexanderplatz. The basic principles guiding the reconstruction of the city center had been under discussion since the early 1950s and, although consensus on the kinds of buildings that should be included had emerged—including a central monumental government building, a central plaza, a bridge connecting the east and west banks of the Spree, and a monument to Marx and Engels—by 1964 there was still no specific plan for the area (Flierl 1993).[1] Here officials—possibly Ulbricht himself—suggested incorporating the tower into plans for the city center. In July 1964 they decided to build on the site east of Marx-Engels-Platz (now the Marx-Engels-Forum) in the very heart of the city.

With the new location, the technological imperative that had driven the project from the beginning gave way almost entirely to the vision of a mythological symbol in the center of Berlin.[2] Whereas form had followed function in early conceptions of a central tower, this tower would demonstrate the achievements of socialist design, while remaining both visually and physically accessible. Officials redesigned the tower to be more aesthetically pleasing: the shaft of the tower took on a slimmer profile and would now be "crowned by a luminous metallic ball" (Deutsche Bauakademie 1965: 2).[3] They planned more space at the foot of the tower, including a waiting area, catering facilities, and outdoor space dedicated to pedestrian traffic, to encourage people to visit the tower. Planners clearly expected large crowds, including in their design elevators capable of carrying four to five hundred people up the tower every hour. The ball atop the tower shaft now housed six floors, four dedicated to broadcasting services and two that would be open to the public (Deutsche Bauakademie 1965). The observation platform and revolving restaurant on the floor above offered a 360-degree view of Berlin. An impressive modernist monument had emerged that would tower over Berlin, surely to become one the city's most significant landmarks and an important destination for East German and foreign tourists alike (MPF-BRF 1964; Politburo 1964).

Tower construction began in 1965, and authorities expected it to open in 1968 at a cost of slightly less than 40 million Marks. Again the project "exceeded" expectations, opening in what was in any case record time in October 1969 and costing possibly close to 200 million Marks.[4] To achieve this authorities had had to import significant parts of the tower, including the elevators, air conditioning equipment, windows, and "skin" of the ball (Müller 2000: 104). But the results were worth it to the government: the unique architecture of the tower situated it as centerpiece of the newly reconstructed city center, giving "convincing proof of the creativity of our working people" and "the possibilities of our socialist social order" (MPF-BRF 1969). As expected, it quickly became a popular attraction, drawing tourists, appearing in East German television programs and DEFA films, and capturing the attention of the domestic and international press. Writing in 1967, the *Egyptian Gazette* declared that this was a Cold War battle that the East Germans already had won: "People in West Berlin . . . watch (the tower) grow taller wondering when they themselves will have such a tower. . . . 'the sight of it will be a daily shock'" (MPF-BRF 1967).

The tower project *was* a triumph of socialist planning and design, even if behind the scenes it had foundered for a decade on both those fronts, because Cold War battles relied on narratives and symbols of success. By the time that it opened in 1969, the tower had perhaps even managed to eclipse the impact of that other famous, and rather less optimistic, East German building project of the 1960s: the Berlin Wall. Since its conception in 1952, Cold War conflict had shaped the tower project, but increasingly the project also evolved in response to changes in East German

Figure 8.1 Looking south from the 123-meter-tall Interhotel "Stadt Berlin" on the construction sites around the not-yet-completed television tower. 5 March 1969. Bundesarchiv, Bild 183-H0605-0020-001, Photographer: Eva Brüggmann.

social life. Early on, postal authorities had sought to implement simple technical solutions to fulfill a vague mandate to occupy airwaves that could be lost to the West, within a political landscape in which they were relatively powerless. They could not have imagined building such a tower in the heart of Berlin. As the privation of the postwar period was becoming less visible, television broadcasting took on new life, garnering attention and transforming everyday life. Television towers, once little more than large antennae, grew to become objects of East Germans' leisure time. Increasingly the project responsed to such changes in East German social life. But delays threatened the integrity of the system as a whole, a situation made direr during the period of the Berlin Crisis. In 1963, developments in the West German broadcasting system and the intervention of Ulbricht saved the project, ultimately transforming it. Now perceived as a focal point of the city center and a symbol of socialist achievement that would tower over the West, aesthetic imperatives trumped the technical imperatives that had driven the project from the beginning. Architects redesigned the tower, transforming it into one of the best known and visually most compelling examples of the political and economic power of the socialist state. With that the transition from technical pragmatism to symbolic monumentalism was complete.

Notes

1. Hermann Henselmann drafted a plan for the city center in 1958 that included a 300-meter-high tower similar in form to the one that exists today, but conceived explicitly as a monument to Marx and Engels that would include a sort of museum dedicated to preserving their written works (Flierl 1993). It was however, purely monumental and not conceived as a telecommunications tower (Müller 2000).
2. Peter Müller wrote his book on the tower in part to "dispel the myth" surrounding the tower.
3. It is still unclear exactly who can claim to have designed the tower. The principle of the socialist collective meant that it was understood that a group of unnamed architects had designed the tower: no single architect was named as its progenitor. Perhaps it was the notoriety of the tower that precipitated the ensuing battle over intellectual property rights to the tower design. In 1969 Hermann Henselmann claimed the tower as his own, as did another group of architects, including Fritz Dieter, Günter Franke, and Werner Neumann. Neither party was conclusively able to make its case and, in 1989, Gerhard Kosel, the former president of the Deutsche Bauakademie, also claimed the tower as his own intellectual property (Müller 2000: 128ff).
4. According to Peter Müller the tower cost *at least* 132 million Marks, but we may never know the final total due to creative bookkeeping methods used to keep costs in check.

Works Cited

Apel, Eric. 1963. Letter to Albert Norden. Bundesarchiv Berlin. DY 20 IV A 2/2.028 121.

Deutsche Bauakademie. 1965. "Erläuterungsbericht zur Konzeption für die Ergänzung des Projektes 'Fernseh-UKW-Turm Berlin.'" Bundesarchiv Berlin Dahlwitz-Hoppegarten (DH). DM 3 BRF II 6339.

Eisler, Gerhart. 1963a. "Fernseh- und UKW-Turm Berlin-Friedrichshain." Bundesarchiv Berlin (DH). DM 3 BRF II 2962b.
——. 1963b. "Kurzbegründung zum Bau des Fernseh- und UKW-Turmes Berlin . . ." Bundesarchiv Berlin. DY 20 IV A 2/2.028 121.
Flierl, Bruno. 1993. "Rund um Marx und Engels: Berlins 'sozialistische' Mitte." In *Hauptstadt Berlin: Wohin mit der Mitte?* ed. Helmut Engel und Wolfgang Ribbe. Berlin: Akademie.
Gumbert, Heather. 2006. "East German Television and the Unmaking of the Socialist Project, 1952–65." PhD dissertation, University of Texas at Austin.
Ministerium für Bauwesen. 1959. "Fernsehturm." Bundesarchiv Berlin (DH). DM 3 BRF II 2962a.
MPF-BRF (Ministerium für Post und Fernmeldewesen, Bereich Rundfunk und Fernsehen). 1952. "Abschrift." Bundesarchiv Berlin (DH). DM 3 BRF II 637.
MPF-BRF. 1954a. Postal Ministry letter to Council of Ministers, Bundesarchiv Berlin (DH). DM 3 BRF II 637.
MPF-BRF. 1954b. 'Bericht über Schwierigkeiten im Fernsehsenderbau im Planjahr 1954,' Bundesarchiv Berlin (DH). DM 3 BRF II 74.
MPF-BRF. 1955. "Bericht und Stellungnahme zu einer Anzahl des Fernsehen und UKW-Funk betreffender Fragen." Bundesarchiv Berlin (DH). DM 3 BRF II 633.
MPF-BRF. 1956. "Beschluss." Bundesarchiv Berlin (DH). DM 3 BRF II 724.
MPF-BRF. 1957a. "Die Entwicklung der Technik im Funkwesen seit 1950." Bundesarchiv Berlin (DH). DM 3 BRF II 1786.
MPF-BRF. 1957b. "Bericht über den Stand der Entwicklung der Technik auf dem Gebiete des Rundfunks . . ." Bundesarchiv Berlin (DH). DM 3 BRF II 6341.
MPF-BRF. 1958a. "Welche technische Möglichkeiten bietet der Turm." Bundesarchiv Berlin (DH). DM 3 BRF II 2962a.
MPF-BRF. 1958b. "Der Fernsehsender F4." Bundesarchiv Berlin (DH). DM 3 BRF II 6341.
MPF-BRF. 1963. "Gliederung." Bundesarchiv Berlin (DH). DM 3 BRF II 2962b.
MPF-BRF. 1964. "Beschluss über die Zustimmung zur Errichtung des bis 1968 in Betrieb zu nehmenden Fernseh-, UKW- und Richtfunkturmes Berlin im Zentrum der Hauptstadt der DDR." Bundesarchiv Berlin (DH). DM 3 BRF II 2962b.
MPF-BRF. 1967. "East Berlin Tower Triumph" from the *Egyptian Gazette*. Bundesarchiv Berlin (DH). DM 3 BRF II 2962b.
MPF-BRF. 1969. "Thesen zum FS-UKW-Turm Berlin." Bundesarchiv Berlin (DH). DM 3 BRF II 3834.
Müller, Peter. 2000. *Symbol mit Aussicht*. Berlin: Verlag Bauwesen.
Norden, Albert. 1963. Letter to Erich Apel. Bundesarchiv Berlin. DY 30 IV A 2/2.028 121.
Politburo. 1964. "Anlage Nr. 4 zum Protokoll Nr. 23 vom 14.7.1964." Bundesarchiv Berlin (DH). DM 3 BRF II 6339.
Probst, Gerhard. 1958. Letter to Winkler. Bundesarchiv Berlin (DH). DM 3 BRF II 2962a.
Probst, Gerhard. 1963. Bundesarchiv Berlin (DH). DM 3 BRF II 2962b.
SED. 1958. *Bericht des Zentralkomitees an dem V. Parteitag der SED*. Berlin: Dietz.
Stadtbauamt. 1959. "Standortvorschläge für das Bauvorhaben XYZ." Bundesarchiv Berlin (DH). DM 3 BRF II 2962a.
Tscheschner, Dorothea. 1993. "Der 'Ideenwettbewerb zur sozialistischen Umgestaltung des Zentrums der Hauptstadt der Deutschen Demokratischen Republik, Berlin." In *Hauptstadt Berlin: Wohin mit der Mitte?* ed. Helmut Engel und Wolfgang Ribbe. Berlin: Akademie.
Ulbricht, Walter. 1969. "Rede des Ersten Sekretärs . . . zur Eröffnung des II. Fernsehprogramms." Deutsches Rundfunkarchiv. Sammlung Glatzer: Geschichte des Fernsehens 1966–1971.

CHAPTER 9

Transparency in Divided Berlin
The Palace of the Republic

Deborah Ascher Barnstone

>The very same land too long observed
>The very same language too long heard
>too long awaited, too long desired
>Too long the same old men admired
>(Rockband Pankow 1997: 9)

The use of transparency ideology to explain the glass facades and open spatial planning at the GDR's Palast der Republik (Palace of the Republic) underscores the complex double history of the division of Germany after 1945. Konrad Jarausch describes this history as replete with "surprising parallels, multiple interactions, and mutual projections" (Jarausch 1999: 10; Lemke 2006). The parallels belie Cold War–era propaganda from both East and West about a radical difference between the two political systems and societies (Butter and Hartung 2004; Ladd 2002: 91–92; Strobel 1994: 25). In the limited realm of state architecture, the debates over the appropriate architectural styles and urban planning strategies for the postwar period, the stylistic and aesthetic choices made for state buildings, and the public rhetoric supporting these choices were often astonishingly alike in spite of the very different political systems the architecture was designed to represent. The similarities underscore the lack of a meaningful and clear visual identity for either state but especially for the East (Ladd 2002: 92). They are important because each side of Berlin was considered a *Schaufenster* ("shop window," but literally "show window") to the other side and the rest of the world. As Greg Castillo points out, the parallels largely date to the post-Stalinist period of the late 1950s when the Soviet influence on East German aesthetic policies diminished and modernism was rehabilitated. The use of transparency as a motif to symbolize the "democratic" state was one trope adopted by East and West. In the West, the architect Hans Schwippert first equated transparency with democracy, namely, openness, accessibility, and honesty in government. In the East, Heinz Graffunder used similar language to describe his Berlin Palace of the Republic for the German Democratic Republic (Graffunder 1976a). Jarausch's assertion implies that competition was a motivating factor, rather than confrontation or the development of unique, representative aesthetic systems, across the divide marked by the Berlin Wall. In the case of state architecture, transparency was one concept over which Eastern and Western notions of modernity and self-image converged and diverged.

The competition for state legitimacy between the two Germanies is well known. Each vied for international recognition and for status as the true Germany; each believed, at least in the immediate postwar era, that unification was imminent and hoped to impose its political and social system on the other half. Both East and West German officials believed that culture would serve as the foundation for a united Germany and both pursued cultural policies with this in mind (Palutzki 2000: 57). If competition was fairly explicit in these areas, it was implicit in the aesthetic arena. But architects designing for the state clearly articulated the importance of aesthetics as a political symbol. In the East, the first party chairman, Walter Ulbricht, architects Kurt Liebknecht and Hans

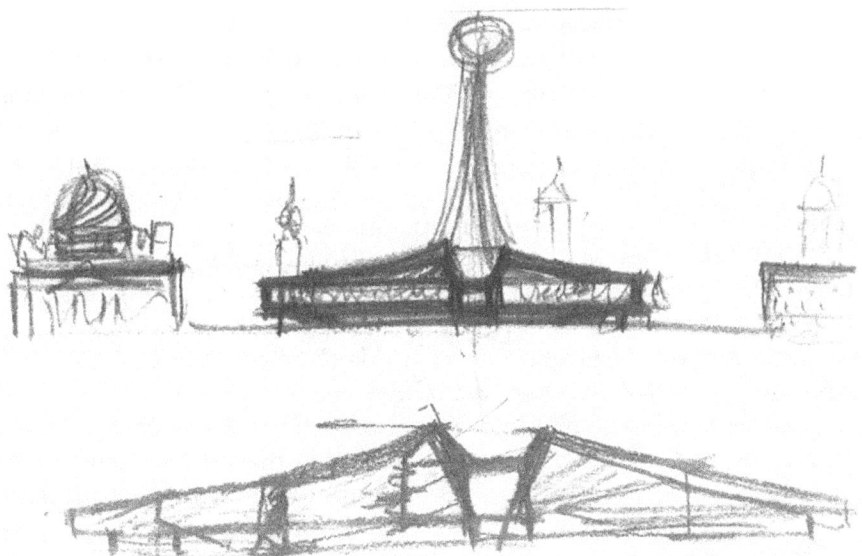

Figure 9.1 Sketch of the Palast der Republik as a suspended structure. Courtesy of The Getty Foundation.

Figure 9.2 Palast der Republik seen from the Karl-Marx-Platz with the Fernsehturm in the background. Courtesy of Bundesbildstelle.

Hoppe, and the director of the Ministry of Building, Lothar Bolz, were early spokesmen demanding a distinct style for East German architecture. When Minister President Otto Grotewohl declared that "the idea in art must follow the marching direction of the political struggle," he probably stated the case for the inextricable connection between politics and art in the most explicit terms possible (Jäger 1995: 35–36). "How should art be? Socialist in content, nationalist in form!" (Durth, Düwel, and Gutschow 1998: 71) Of course these pronouncements do not articulate a style, only intent. In the 1970s, Graffunder and then–party chairman Erich Honecker repeatedly underscored the aim of the Palace of the Republic to be a symbol of the "worker's state" (Honecker 1974). It was Graffunder who defined an aesthetic for this symbol.

West German parliamentarians wrangled for decades with the question of the proper style for representative buildings in their democracy. Unlike in the East, there was never an official approach to architectural symbolism, a sanctioned style, or an explicit aim to marry political beliefs with aesthetics. Nevertheless, the question of the symbolic representation of the state was the subject of parliamentary meetings, competition briefs for government buildings, meetings of the parliament's Building

Committee, and government publications like *Bauen in der Demokratie* (Building in Democracy). Underlying all these endeavors was the question, what style and symbolic content will differentiate state buildings for a democracy from those for other political systems, especially in East Germany?

Transparency was not the obvious choice for democratic architecture. Although German fascination with transparent construction dates to the nineteenth century, to the greenhouses and exhibition pavilions constructed out of glass and steel, transparency as a *concept* developed later. From the start, glass architecture was layered with associations: utopian aspirations, progressive ideals, even futuristic ones. In 1914 the mystical poet Paul Scheerbart published *Glasarchitektur* (Glass Architecture), extolling the potential of glass architecture to change the world. Other tracts soon followed, like Bruno Taut's imaginary *Alpine Architektur* (Alpine Architecture, 1919) in which crystalline glass structures are tied to social utopia. In 1929 Arthur Korn published *Glas im Bau als Gebrauchsgegenstand* (Glass as Commodity in Building), which provided a catalog of built and unbuilt glass architecture alongside a practical guide to glass applications in construction. These writings contributed to the growing interest in transparency, as did explorations by artists such as László Moholy-Nagy who made transparency the central theme in his photography, drawing, painting, and sculpture during the interwar period.

By 1927 the German architectural critic and philosopher Walter Benjamin could write that "the twentieth century, with its porosity and transparency, its longing for tendency toward the well-lit, light and airy, putting an end to dwelling in the old sense [of the word]" (1999: 221). The architectural historian Sigfried Giedion tied transparency to new conceptions of space/time, arguing that "the essence of space as it is conceived today is its many-sidedness, the infinite potentiality for relations within it" (1982: 430). The physical and spatial transparency that Benjamin and Giedion wrote about was a key element in many Weimar-era *Neues Bauen* (New Building) projects.

After 1945, transparency assumed other dimensions of meaning. The utopian notions of Scheerbart and Taut joined with the material and spatial ones and new models for democratic institutions in the West. The distinguished lawyer and parliamentarian Adolf Arndt was the first political thinker to articulate a connection between transparency and democratic state architecture in a speech he delivered at the opening of the Berlin Building Week in 1960. Arndt's influential logic tied the concept of transparency—understood as accessibility, openness, honesty, and clarity—to democratic government. He contended that because the ideal democracy should be transparent, so too should its most representative buildings. Interestingly Schwippert had made similar points in his 1949 defense of his aesthetic choices for the first Bonn Bundeshaus (Parliament House). His rationale pitted temporary, fragile, antimonumental, transparent architecture against permanent, monumental, opaque structures (Schwippert 1951). Implicit in his argument was the rejection of neoclassical models for contemporary ones (Barnstone 2005). Again and again, Schwippert, and the critics writing about his building, pointed to the "lightness" it achieved, by which they meant how flooded with natural light the Bundeshaus was (Blomeier 1949: 466; Schwippert 1951). Schwippert argued for a "house of openness, an architecture of encounters and discussions" designed to counter the contemporary perception that the National Socialists had duped common Germans by conducting government in secret, behind closed doors, away from public view (Blomeier 1949; Schwippert 1951). Finally Schwippert presented transparency as the logical choice for a democracy because he claimed that it suggested openness, accessibility, and honesty as opposed to the "dark powers" lurking in other political systems. The GDR of course was one of the "others" (Barnstone 2005: 240–42).

Documents from East and West Germany are rife with evidence of mutual awareness of post-1945 developments in architectural design. Although the West is more unambiguously present in Eastern discourse because of the anxieties about submitting to a capitalist Western culture, the East was just as present in Western discourse, albeit often in more subtle ways. West Germany is regularly referred to in East German writing as a negative example to be avoided, where "cosmopolitanism" and "Americanism" were the dangerous results of capitalist expression in the built environment (Liebknecht 1952: 6). The West is also present in more veiled ways such as in the adoption of modern aesthetics for buildings and product design, the desire to compete internationally, and the almost obsessive interest in modernization after 1957. Much of the mass-produced East German objects of the late 1950s onward could have been designed in either country, although as the decades progressed, East German modern design seems to remain frozen in the 1950s, unaware or unable technically to keep up with Western developments.

By 1961, East German architects had adopted the glass aesthetic, promoting it in pamphlets like *Guten Morgen Berlin* (Good Morning Berlin) as modern and therefore desirable. A project for a Marx-Engels-Forum (1961) on the Spree Island site of the future Palace of the Republic featured a transparent Plexiglas model of a glass tower. Hermann Henselmann's 1961 Haus des Lehrers (Teacher's House) on Alexanderplatz is likewise a glass-clad steel structure (*Guten Morgen Berlin* 1961). According to *Good Morning Berlin,* these projects were intended to embody the "spirit of our free, socialist, future-oriented time" and "will give the old plaza on the Spree Island, once the form of monarchical and imperialistic control over Germany, its new countenance." Although transparency is not specifically mentioned, the image is up-to-date, constructed of transparent glass and steel. The intended message is clear: East Germany is as modern as West Germany.

Conversely East Germany was a frequent presence in West German political and cultural discourse. Adolf Arndt chose to stage his famous speech, *Demokratie als Bauherr* (Democracy as Building Client), in Berlin where the East served as a backdrop for his commentary, rather than in Bonn, the seat of West German government. In the speech Arndt asked, "Should not there be a connection between the public principles of democracy and an outer and inner transparency and accessibility of her public buildings?" (1996: 52–65) Although the speech presented a highly original argument, over time West German architects and politicians almost universally adopted its ideas. The 1955 decision to renovate the Reichstag in Berlin was undoubtedly a deliberate provocation. The Bundestag (parliament) planned to hold occasional meetings in the former government seat located at the very edge of the Wall. Renovation did not actually begin until 1961 and lasted until 1971. The architect Paul Baumgarten worked with visual and spatial transparency for the Plenary Chamber and argued in similar terms to Schwippert. Interestingly, the Four Power Agreement of 1971 included a provision barring any West German Bundestag meetings in Berlin. The Baumgarten project must have been viewed as a threat; otherwise the East Germans would not have insisted that it not be used.

In the years immediately following the end of World War II, architects in both East and West grappled with similar questions: How should Germany rebuild? What was the proper stylistic expression of the post-Nazi state—A Marxist/Leninist regime? A democratic regime? In both countries, a faction favoring the reconstruction of destroyed cities as they had been before 1940 and the reinstatement of traditional German architecture battled with others who saw the destruction of the urban fabric as an opportunity to rebuild Germany in the most modern way possible. In a strange twist, those advocating a modern style in the East and West used similar arguments. They pointed to the interwar *Neues Bauen* as the most important German contribution to twentieth-century architecture. They asserted that *Neues Bauen* best represented democratic principles since it was the product of the democratic Weimar Republic. In the East, architects argued that Bauhaus aesthetics mirrored the progressive Marxist/Leninist state's politics; in the West, architects argued that the *Neues Bauen* style reflected the progressiveness of democracy! Transparent glass architecture was considered desirable precisely because it was closely tied to *Neues Bauen* aesthetics.

During the 1940s and early 1950s both the Soviet and East German regimes embraced socialist realism and rejected modernism. They termed avant-garde and modern art "decadent" forms of expression because they were supposedly closely tied to capitalist cultures and therefore inappropriate for a worker's state. This view ignored the social program associated with much of the modern movement, and was highly reductive, throwing together under the label "modern" aesthetic and ideological approaches to art that were very different in their aims and forms. At the same time that Schwippert advocated pristine modernism, for example, East Germany was engaged in a strident antimodern struggle. Oddly both Soviet and East German antimodern sentiment ignored the pioneering Soviet work of 1917–1932 that explicitly tied new architectural forms to revolutionary government.

After Stalin's death in 1953, and Khrushchev's assumption of the party leadership, cultural policy in the Soviet Union, and ultimately in the GDR, shifted from socialist realism to an industrial modernism (Duwel 1995). Official reasons for the shift cited the tremendous need for affordable housing and the efficacy industrial production methods provided. But the move toward such technologically advanced systems does not fully explain the aesthetic change that accompanied the new policy. After all, it is possible to build neoclassical buildings using industrial systems. One plausible explanation for the stylistic change is the increasing concern party officials had for making East Germany an attractive place for people to live and work. There was a constant drain of population to the West from 1945 onward partly because the economy was better there: people had more material wealth and the latest in household electronic gadgets, automobiles, and contemporary furniture and other goods. In the 1950s alone, two million people "voted with their feet" by moving West. Adopting modern aesthetics allowed East Germany to claim to be the same as the West. Conversely, although the West might be able to claim that its citizens were generally better off than in the East, it needed to be able to claim political, ethical, and social superiority as well. Adopting an aesthetic associated with progress and using the metaphor of transparency associated with good democratic government served this end (Barnstone 2005).

By 1971, when the SED decided to commission a Palace of the Republic for East Berlin, the party was ready to sanction a modern approach to the design, even for its most publicly representative state building. Of course, the Palace was never as politically important as the Bonn Bundeshaus since the government functions it was to house were those designed for public consumption: the national parliament and periodic party congresses (Ladd 2002: 93). The commission for the Palace followed the 1961 modern addition to the Kremlin, a project Graffunder studied. The Palace project coincided with the West German decision to rebuild its parliament in Bonn in a decidedly modern idiom. It came as Baumgarten's Reichstag renovation was winding down. In the West, competition briefs called for using transparency as an analogy for democratic, open, and accessible government. By the time the Palace of the Republic was completed in 1976, Graffunder would defend his glass building in strikingly similar, though not identical, terms.

From the start, Graffunder hoped to embody the cultural, social, and political aspirations of the East German state in the Palace. He wanted the East German government to be housed in a building that average citizens used daily, rather than in a separate and protected one as was usual in most countries (Graffunder n.d. 63/5). He wrote, "The people of our Republic come into possession of a truly meaningful object of cultural and social politics . . . in the heart of the capital city of the first socialist German state, with a building that is suitable to represent it" (Graffunder 1976a: 9). Furthermore the Palace had the "forms of a democracy" (Staufenbiel 1967: 62/11). Honecker called the Palace the "sociopolitical high point" of East Germany (1973 63/5). But it was equally the high point of architecture for the new socialist mass consumer Castillo addresses. The site was chosen for its symbolic importance to East German history. The Hohenzollern Palace occupied the site until it was bombed in World War II; Karl Liebknecht proclaimed a communist state from one balcony on 9 November 1918; and the square witnessed several important workers' demonstrations in the 1920s (Graffunder, "Inbesitznahme" 63/5). Placing the seat of the workers' state where the monarchy used to reside had particularly strong appeal since it suggested the triumph of socialism over monarchism. Graffunder modeled the Palace partly after Soviet people's palaces to accommodate government functions together with a cultural center comprised of more commercial than cultural functions. The Palace included a plenary chamber, party meeting rooms, and conference rooms, as well as public theaters, exhibition spaces, restaurants, cafes, bars, a newsstand, a youth center, and a bowling alley. The combination of seemingly unrelated functions in the building's program epitomized the fusion of political and cultural realms in the GDR (Graffunder 1976a: 22–23). Many of Graffunder's claims for the architecture are in keeping with typical East German cultural propaganda of his day but with new dimensions.

The most unusual claims appear when he describes the building's aesthetic. The Palace had a steel reinforced concrete frame clad in reflective bronze-tinted glass. It was unapologetically monumental in scale; an approach that fit the size of the public space it bordered and the programmatic burdens placed on the building. Graffunder wanted the Palace to fuse symbolic and urban planning goals (Graffunder 1973: 63/5). He therefore designed it to frame views of the *Fernsehturm* (television tower) on Alexanderplatz and as a backdrop for party demonstrations on Marx-Engels-Platz. The iconic images of the Palace show the television tower on-center flanked by the two glazed wings. The building was designed with spatial penetration between interior and exterior as well as individual interior spaces in mind. Early sketch studies experiment with a suspended structure that appears to be completely clad in transparent glass. A later series of drafted studies renders the building lighter and more transparent than the actual built object. The glass cladding, Graffunder wrote, was "an essential condition for the unity of outer and inner architectural openness" ("Inbesitznahme" 63/13). Yet the building appeared opaque most of the time from the outside because both the transparent glass at street level and the bronze-tinted glass above were opaque in typical daylight conditions. The building was see-through only at night when it was lit from inside. Sketch perspective studies of the foyer and entry show spatial connections across the horizontal plan and through the vertical dimension of the section. According to Graffunder, "the vision of progressive German architects at the beginning of the century, of the workers' self-expression in light-suffused people's houses has been realized in the Palace of the Republic" (Graffunder and Beerbaum 1976: 15). Here he clearly associates his glass construction with the visionary architecture of Taut and others in the 1920s and 1930s (Graffunder 1973 63/5; Honecker 1973 63/5).

Equally interesting, Graffunder used many of the same terms to describe his palace for the Marxist/Leninist state that Hans Schwippert, Paul Baumgarten, and later, Günter Behnisch used for their West German projects. Graffunder cited the "festiveness," "lightness," "openness," and "optical transparency" in this "light," "inviting," "representative" building. He penned several essays and speeches on the building as an example of Light Architecture, even calling it a Cathedral of Light. By this Graffunder meant that the building used natural, reflected, and artificial light as principal aesthetic components (Graffunder, "Inbesitznahme" 63/16). He chose the primary materials, bronze-colored and see-through glass and white marble, because of how they responded to light.

Schwippert famously tied his light aesthetic to democratic expression while Graffunder merely asserts the use of light in his architecture as a means of making the building see-through but without a conceptual rationale. Schwippert's building used a *Neues Bauen*–style white stucco modernism with transparent glass walls flanking the plenary chamber and open spatial planning.

On the first day of parliament in 1949, bleachers were assembled in the courtyard in front of the glass facades whose operable windows were open to the plenary chamber so that citizens could listen to, and participate in, the proceedings inside. But openness was largely symbolic because the building was designed as a traditional parliament. After the first day, the bleachers were disassembled and the public permitted inside only after careful vetting. Although Graffunder's project was far more accessible to the public, the real workings of the GDR government did not take place there. Thus while the building was open, government was not. Ironically, transparency failed at both buildings. Visual transparency was occasional but not constant because of the optical properties of glass that made it reflective and opaque during the day and transparent only at night. Physical transparency failed in Bonn because of the exigencies of modern-day security and in Berlin because of the realities of GDR government.

East Germans certainly knew the Schwippert building. It was published in *Deutsche Architektur* (German Architecture) in 1951 with a tiny image of the courtyard view, and biting criticism directed at the foundation of an independent state rather than at the building's design. It was also widely published in the West German press, architectural and nonprofessional, beginning on 7 September 1949. We know that many West German publications made their way to the East, so it is likely that these did. It is hard to say for certain whether Schwippert's aesthetic aims were known, but interwar glass architecture and its aspirations were. At a minimum, the images of the Bundeshaus show a modernist glass structure aligning the project with *Neues Bauen* work. There is one significant difference in the rhetoric used by Graffunder and Western architects, however. Western architects were clear about the conceptual meaning of transparency in relationship to democracy; Graffunder was not.

In spite of rhetorical similarities, Graffunder never explained transparency in the conceptual terms used in the West. He saw transparency as a means to realize "visionary architecture" akin to that imagined in the 1920s for "light-filled people's houses," as a way to make the "social meaning of the building" apparent to the people, and as a mode to make the inner functions of the building visible to the outside (Graffunder 1976b 63/15; *Objecta* 1976 63/15). He repeatedly discussed the light qualities and the ways transparency and reflectivity related the Palace to its context. However, Graffunder did not associate his transparent architecture with political accessibility, openness, or honest government. The closest he came was to proclaim the Palace the representative building for East German socialism (Graffunder n.d.: 63/16). Ironically, it was representative of the GDR in ways other than those Graffunder intended. In many ways the Palace was a palliative for the East German people, offering them leisure-time activities in place of real political empowerment.

It is important to remember that Graffunder's project began twenty-two years after the completion of the Schwippert building. By that time, transparency ideology was firmly entrenched in West German thinking, so much so that the briefs for the 1971 competition to design a new parliament building mandated transparency (Deutscher Bundestag 1971). Was the use of similar rhetoric in the East coincidental? Transparency was not an ideology yet adopted anywhere else in the Western world; it was particular to West German thinking. One can only speculate, but Graffunder's use of transparency ideology may have been a direct response to the West, an attempt to equate architecture in the GDR with that of its sister state. Alternatively, the adoption of transparency may have made sense to Graffunder as a way of connecting present-day East Germany with the heroic architectural fantasies of the 1920s. Or, Graffunder may have wanted to show the West that the East was *more* democratic, *more* modern, and perhaps *more* utopian; he might have hoped to beat the West at its own game.

Works Cited

Arndt, Adolf. 1996. "*Bauen für die Demokratie.*" In *Architektur und Demokratie: Bauen für die Politik von der amerikanischen Revolution bis zur Gegenwart,* ed. Ingeborg Flagge and Wolfgang Jean Stock, 52–65. Stuttgart: Hatje.

Barnstone, Deborah Ascher. 2005. *The Transparent State: Architecture and Politics in Postwar Germany.* London: Routledge.

Benjamin, Walter. 1999. "The Interior, the Trace." *The Arcades Project,* trans. Howard Eiland and Kevin McLaughlin, 212–28. Cambridge, MA: Harvard University Press.

Blomeier, Hermann. 1949. "Das Bundeshaus in Bonn." *Bauen und Wohnen* 4, no. 10: 466–70.

Butter, Andreas, and Ulrich Hartung. 2004. *Ostmoderne: Architektur in Berlin 1945–1965.* Berlin: Jovis.

Deutsche Bundestag. 1971. "Auszug aus dem Wettbewerbs-Program." Behnisch Archiv, SAAI. Karlsruhe.

Durth, Werner, Jörn Düwel, and Niels Gutschow. 1998. *Architektur und Städtebau der DDR,* vol. 2. Frankfurt am Main: Campus.

Duwel, Jörn. 1995. *Baukunst voran! Architektur und Städtebau in der SBZ/DDR.* Berlin: Schelsky & Jeep.

Giedion, Sigfried. 1982. *Space, Time and Architecture: The Growth of a New Tradition.* Cambridge, MA: Harvard University Press.

Graffunder. Heinz. 1976a. *Der Palast der Republik.* Leipzig: Seemann.

———. 1976b. "Zur Gesamtkonzeption des Palasts der Republik." DDR Collections, Getty, 63/15.

———. 1977. "Thema Lichtarchitektur." DDR Collections, Getty, 63/16.

———. n.d. "Die Inbesitznahme." DDR Collections, Getty, 63/5.

———. n.d. "Der Palast der Republik." DDR Collections, Getty, 63/13.

———. n.d. "Palast der Republik." Druckschrift. DDR Collections, Getty, 63/16.
Graffunder, Heinz and Martin Beerbaum. 1976. *Der Palast der Republik: Architektur und Bildende Künste.* Leipzig: Seemann.
Guten Morgen Berlin. 1961. "Hier schlägt das Herz Deutschlands." Sonderillustrierte Aufbau Stadtzentrum. Berlin.
Honecker, Erich. 1973. "Gesellschaftliche Zielstellung." Grundsteinlegung. DDR Collections, Getty, 63/5.
———. 1974. Speech at the Richtfest. In *Palast der Republik, Berlin, Hauptstadt der DDR.* Berlin.
Jäger, Manfred. 1995. *Kultur und Politik in der DDR: 1945–1990.* Cologne: Edition Deutschland Archiv.
Jarausch, Konrad. 1999. *Dictatorship as Experience: Towards a Socio-Cultural History of the GDR.* New York: Berghahn.
Ladd, Brian. 2002. "East Berlin Political Monuments in the German Democratic Republic." *Journal of Contemporary History* 37: 91–92.
Lemke, Michael. 2006. *Schaufenster der Systemkonkurrenz: Die Region Berlin-Brandenburg im Kalten Krieg.* Cologne: Böhlau.
Liebknecht, Kurt. 1952. "*Deutsche Architektur.*" In *Deutsche Architektur* 1: 6.
Objecta Magazin. 1976. "Der 'Palast der Republik,' Ein Veranstaltungsgebäude besonderer Art," DDR Collections, Getty, 63/15.
Palutzki, Joachim. 2000. *Architektur in der DDR.* Berlin: Dietrich Reimer.
Rockband Pankow. 1997. In *DDR-Geschichte in Dokumenten: Beschlüsse, Berichte, interne Materialien und Alltagszeugnisse,* ed. Matthias Judt. Berlin: Christian Links.
Schwippert, Hans. 1951. "Das Bonner Bundeshaus." *Neue Bauwelt* 17: 65–72.
———. 2005. "Glück und Glas." In Barnstone, *The Transparent State,* 240–42.
Staufenbiel, Dr. 1967. "Probleme des Verhältnisses von Kultursoziologie und Architektur." Vorbereitung IX. UIA-Kongress v. 23.5.67. DDR Collections, Getty 62/11.
Strobel, Roland. 1994. "Before the Wall Came Tumbling Down." *Journal of Architectural Education* 48, no. 1: 25–37.

PART THREE

West Berlin, Showcase of the West

Chapter 10

The Woman Between
Hildegard Knef's Movies in Cold War Berlin

Ulrich Bach

"I know of no town, no city, that has been besieged for eighteen years that still lives with the vitality and the force, and the hope and the determination of the city of West Berlin" (Safire 2004: 559). This resolute statement, taken from John F. Kennedy's famous speech in front of the Schöneberger Rathaus on 26 June 1963, demonstrates the interminable American commitment to the city in precarious times. For Kennedy and the Western Allies, West Berlin was an island of liberty in the midst of a red flood. This special position of West Berlin was the result of rapid political and economic developments in the aftermath of the Second World War. Soon after the fall of Berlin in May 1945, a functioning public transport system once again traversed the various occupied zones and connected eastern and western parts of the city. Most importantly, West Berlin hosted the only open transit route from Eastern Europe into the West. No less than 3 million refugees and young professionals fled East Germany to West Berlin between 1949 and 1961. With an open border between the socialist and capitalist blocs, "the city had become the primary listening post and spy center of the Cold War" (Judt 2005: 250).

The lure of adventure, human drama, and the heightened political importance of Berlin also inspired the national and international film industry. Hildegard Knef became West Germany's first postwar movie star for her role in *Die Mörder sind unter uns* (The Murderers Are Among Us, 1946) and continued to play a pivotal role in Berlin movie productions throughout the 1950s. After her initial success in Germany, Knef received, like Marlene Dietrich twenty years earlier, a contract from Twentieth Century Fox in Hollywood. But once the film offers turned out to be less attractive, she became a chansonneuse in the 1960s, and a successful author in the 1970s. Her live performances were loved and admired because of her affinity to, and identification with, West Berlin. Knef's chansons about the city, "I Still Have a Suitcase in Berlin" or "Berlin, Your Face Has Freckles," became hits that reached the top of the charts. At the same time, Knef's activism for gay and lesbian rights rendered the star a beloved icon for the gay community.

In what follows, I discuss Knef's symbolic function within Berlin's visual imaginary. From the end of the Second World War to the height of the Cold War conflict in 1961, the actress became a celebrity if only by transgressing the moral norms of the German zeitgeist.[1] Berlin, the former metropolis, was the urban space in which the contemporary political and cultural climate of divided Germany was most evidently symbolized and politically negotiated by the chess-like moves of the Allies. It is therefore not surprising that Berlin should be the setting for the majority of Knef's films of this era. From the moment of Susanne's arrival at a ruined train station in *The Murderers Are Among Us* to Lilli's chic apartment in the hypermodern Hansaviertel (Hansa Quarter) in *Subway in the Sky* (1959), the city repeatedly acts as the backdrop for the larger moral questions pertaining to the Nazi legacy. As Berlin rose to geopolitical significance in the Cold War confrontation, Knef's onstage and offstage stardom personified the shifting identities of West Berlin and the rapid reorientation of its image from enemy to cherished friend of the Western Allies. These changing configurations raise the question about how the Cold War is featured in these films: through the narratives, national stereotypes, or as political rhetoric? The French philosopher Jean Baudrillard, alluding to a dialectical relation between city and cinema, argues that "you should begin with the screen and move outwards to the city. It is there that cinema does not assume an exceptional form, but simply invests the streets and the entire town with a mythical atmosphere" (1988: 56). In other words, the reframing of the urban imagery produces an altered perception of the city, and eventually transforms the city itself and those who view it through the filmmaker's lens. This observation raises the question whether Knef's films also invested West Berlin "with a mythical atmosphere" and fostered a similar transformation in her fellow Berlin citizens.

Hildegard Knef (born 1925) grew up in Berlin, where as a teenager during the war she worked as a graphic designer in UFA's special effects department while taking acting lessons. A love affair with Ewald von Demandowsky, director of Tobis-Film, helped her to find her way through the Nazi studio system, a relationship that later compromised

Figure 10.1 Hildegard Knef in front of the Brandenburg Gate. Courtesy of The Granger Collection.

her career.[2] In fact, the teenage actress had several short parts in UFA films; most notably in Helmut Käutner's neorealist *Unter den Brücken* (Under the Bridges, 1944). The film features a strangely well-preserved and peaceful Berlin. This filmic denial of the ominous "total war" in and around Berlin fostered a poetic utopia and sought to provide hope for a better future. Sabine Hake sees Käutner's study of Berlin's canals and bridges alternatively as "moral defeatism, individual resignation, or passive resistance—all qualities that made Käutner well suited for postwar cinema" (2002: 71). Tellingly, the film was not released in Germany until after the war.[3] Knef's reputation began to gain luster, however, in 1946 when she received critical acclaim for her stage performance in Marcel Pagnol's *The Golden Anchor* in the Schloßpark Theater in Berlin-Steglitz. Her breakthrough came with a stellar performance as Susanne in Wolfgang Staudte's *The Murderers Are Among Us*. The film, a Soviet-licensed DEFA production, was the first German rubble film. As I will show, Staudte's film resonated with the public, and overnight rendered Knef an allegory of hope for a new democratic beginning in Berlin.

The reestablishment of the German film industry was a process of differentiation. While Soviet authorities rapidly implemented measures to jump start movie production as part of the larger cultural sphere, the Western Allies decentralized the film industry from the beginning. This differentiation, combined with the escalating ideological competition of the Cold War, led to a bourgeoning film industry in all four Allied sectors with rubble movies made in the West and *Aufbau* (construction) movies in the East. Rubble films, according to Robert Shandley, address the problem of "the long shadow cast by the legacy of the Third Reich" and "share the fundamental mise-en-scène of destroyed and defeated Germany" (2001: 3). The genre served a brief but important societal function. In fact, Shandley lists seventeen films released between 1946 and 1948, the majority of which are set in Berlin. Their overarching moral message not only called on the German movie-going public to accept responsibility for the Nazi atrocities, but also provided models to help Germans to recognize and cope with their dire living circumstances. In *The Murderers Are Among Us,* Knef's character, Susanne, is a young woman who returns from a concentration camp only to find a stranger now living in her apartment. They decide to share the flat, and before long Susanne begins to care for the stranger, a war-damaged and guilt-ridden surgeon, Dr. Hans Mertens. The main part of the story deals with the resolution of his trauma, and throughout the movie the spectator catches glimpses of Mertens's wartime ordeal in various flashbacks. However, the spectator never learns anything about Susanne's past in the concentration camp; instead, she is shrouded in mystery. This is also expressed visually through the many mystifying close-ups of her radiant face. As Susanne Marshall points out: "The human physiognomy becomes part of the landscape of ruins; the realistic scene comments inevitably on the moral, spiritual and physical constitution of postwar society" (Mennel 2008: 114). It is Susanne's appearance that predestines her for the paradoxical role of Nazi victim and savior of her lover. In the establishing shot, as Susanne arrives in Berlin, she passes endless rows of ruins on her way toward the home she left when taken to the camp. Suddenly a perfectly preserved Pietà statue appears in the midst of debris. With this simple rendition of redemption the viewer's perception of the ruins as destruction, decay, and loss is transformed—through an image of motherly love—into a reconstructive vision for the future.

Knef assumed prominence in the bourgeoning West German movie industry through her appearances in two other major rubble films. One of these was Rudolf Jugert's much-acclaimed *Film ohne Titel* (Film Without a Title, 1947), a subtle satire of the genre. Shortly after the end of the Second World War, a director, screenwriter, and actor discuss the form and topic of a proposed film project. Two acquaintances of the screenwriter, a country girl (Knef) and a Berlin art dealer (Hans Söhnker), enter the scene and propose a film based on their lives. Toward the end of the war, Knef's character had worked as a housekeeper in Söhnker's Grunewald villa and amidst the heightened tensions of an Allied air raid began a love affair with her employer. The protagonists' passionate response to the destruction of the city perhaps distracted postwar filmgoers from their dire contemporary living conditions in Berlin, but it also served to swiftly eclipse the recent German atrocities. Above all, the movie captures the spiritual vacuity of an emotionally starved audience through an open narrative, while Knef's character acts as an attractive projection for the viewer's desires. This emplotment of Berlin's fall and destruction raises questions about Germans coming to terms with the past. How much of the recent past needs to be forgotten by a defeated nation struggling toward reconstruction in order to meet present challenges? The self-reflective narrative of *Film Without a Title*, and the ensuing demise of the rubble movie genre, is as indicative of West Germany's desire to move on as quickly as possible from a traumatic past as it is a testimony to the rapidly changing Cold War politics.

On the eve of the premiere of *Film Without a Title*, Knef left West Berlin for New York and Los Angeles as a veritable war bride. Needless to say, her departure sparked the imagination of many German women who saw in her example a way out of their precarious situation. But the "Hilde goes to Hollywood" fairytale also raised concerns among the conservative echelons of German society about family values and the status of men and masculinity.[4] Ironically the actress left West Berlin just as she was finding success, only to discover that her German identity was a problem for Hollywood. Eventually she was offered the female lead role in George Seaton's semidocumentary *The Big Lift* (1950) about the Berlin Airlift undertaken by the Western Allies for the relief of the recently blockaded city. Since the topic of fraternization with American servicemen in occupied Germany is at the heart of the story, Knef seemed destined for the part. But at the last minute, the novice actress Cornell Borchers supplanted Knef. By 1949, the political landscape in Europe had changed, and with it the aesthetic opportunities for filmmakers. Instead of producing rubble films depicting the lingering shadow of the Nazi past, films on both sides of the Iron Curtain focused on the present and thereby discursively created an image of the enemy along the new political fault lines. West Berlin is depicted as a site of profound ideological and cultural competition, and the conversations in the film incessantly circle around the relative merits of democracy and communism.

While *The Big Lift* was caught between the restoration of normalcy and the increase in ideological confrontation, Knef became entangled with her own political past: "A folder with interrogation protocols of her former lover—Ewald von Demandowsky—had surfaced, who allegedly claimed having married Knef as a Soviet POW" (Schröder 2005: 121). Apparently director George Seaton and producer William Perlberg were concerned about possible repercussions of this discovery, since the semidocumentary was coproduced with the US Army. Her past could adversely impact the film if she were retained in a leading role. Annette Brauerhoch, who discusses *The Big Lift* extensively in her recent book, '*Fräuleins*' *und G.I's*, explains Knef's substitution differently: "Hildegard Knef exudes in her rubble movies not only cosmopolitan femininity but also vulgar sensuality—and thus corresponds too closely to the existing stereotype of the frivolous German *Fräulein*. . . . Apparently, *The Big Lift* wanted to alert to the dangers of fraternization, without showing the underlying sexual allure" (2006: 364–65). In Brauerhoch's reading, Knef's individual past was not the problem, but rather her representation of the seductive German Fräulein and the US Army's reluctance to release such an image while American servicemen were stationed in West Berlin in great numbers. After all, in order to conform to the logic of the Cold War, it was required that the film simultaneously portrays Germans as former enemies *and* future partners in crime.

In the wake of the Korean War and the further escalation of the political tension between East and West, Knef was cast to play an alluring double agent from Eastern Europe, who ends up on the "right" side. To be precise, in Henry Hathaway's *Diplomatic Courier* (1952), starring Tyrone

Powers and Patricia Neal, Knef stars as Janine Betki, a latter-day Mata Hari. Interestingly enough, by 1952, she was no longer cast as a German with a Nazi past, but as a victim of communism. The color of the enemy has suddenly changed. Staying with the genre, Knef appeared next in another Cold War drama *The Man Between* (1953), a British production by Carol Reed, the director of *The Third Man* (1949). True to the force of circumstance, Knef's character Bettina, a well-dressed West Berliner, resists the vicious communist threat emanating from the East. Married to a British officer, Bettina mysteriously suffers from bouts of headache and depression. Secretly implicated in human trafficking, she embodies the difficult past of war-torn Berlin and is emblematic of Germany's difficult transition from enemy to friend of the Western Allies. The film is set in snow-covered Berlin, with all its potential for East-West tensions following the Berlin airlift in 1948, and amidst the growing confrontation between the Allied powers. The Berlin setting makes for an enthralling thriller in the heated climate of the Cold War, against a backdrop of espionage, suspicion, and propaganda on both sides. And the city's topography plays an integral part of the drama; Desmond Dickinson's cinematography surveys calm and composed the decay of bombed-out buildings, the vacant lots, and the omnipresent rubble of Berlin. Bowing to the political realities, the filmmaker had to recreate all East Berlin settings at Potsdamer Platz in West Berlin. Given the economic situation at the time, corruption is a fundamental feature of the city's filmic representation, and the plot deals with human trafficking by mean-spirited agents who kidnap people from the eastern to the western zone. Suzanne (Claire Bloom) represents the audience's point of view; she is a naive English girl whose visit to her brother and sister-in-law, Bettina, sets the story in motion. In his recent biography on Carol Reed, Peter W. Evans describes the relation between the female protagonists: "Through these two women the film measures the innocence of the British against the experience of the European. Claire Bloom's fresh English rose plucked from the sheltered environment of the Home Countries is, though, clearly unsuited to the climate of the continent in which Bettina, her more hardened sister-in-law, survives" (2005: 129).

Knef is not only hardened by Berlin's omnipresent political corruption, she has also lost her filmic persona as duplicitous foreign spy, femme fatale, or prostitute. Instead, the actress has become an ally in the Western coalition against communism. While kidnapping, espionage, and prostitution were a reality in Berlin at the beginning of the 1950s, the ideological tilt of *The Man Between*'s winter landscape becomes evident when one considers what Reed omitted. The then highly visible commercial reconstruction in West Berlin, which was concentrated in the area around

Kurfürstendamm (Kudamm) and Gedächtniskirche, only appears in one scene at the beginning of the film. The historian David Clay Large illustrates the early effects of the Marshall Plan on West Berlin: "The most impressive new building on the avenue was the rebuilt Hotel Kempinski, which opened in 1952 on the site of the original hotel, destroyed in 1945. Erected with the money from the Marshall Plan, the new hotel was, as the *Tagesspiegel* wrote, a prime symbol for 'the faith that's being shown in our city'" (2000: 424).

In 1953, the Kudamm was not yet the center of West Berlin's consumerism and glitzy entertainment, but for the inhabitants it was in this part of town where they could feel like Berliners again. Toward the end of the 1950s, Knef shot another British production in this part of town with the director Muriel Box.[5] Like many of Box's films, *Subway in the Sky* (1959) has a stage-bound feel, and unfortunately rarely ventures out on location. Accordingly, most of the film unfolds in a luxury penthouse in the Hansaviertel. The establishing shot, however, features a slice of the West German Economic Miracle, when the camera pans over the Tiergarten to the Siegessäule to the new high-rises of the Hansaviertel. The film's setting displays West Berlin's innovation and prosperity, as if the director were seeking to underscore the city's prominent role within the Cold War from a Western perspective. In *Subway to the Sky,* Knef is cast in the role of Lilli Hoffman, an extravagantly clad nightclub singer who hides in her luxurious penthouse an American military doctor (Van Johnson), who is falsely accused of being a drug dealer. Knef sings in two nightclub scenes, but otherwise "she does not have to do much, apart from looking pretty for the American officer" (Sannwald, Jaspers, and Mänz 2005: 17), as Daniela Sannwald notes. Knef wears see-through blouses, shoulder-free dresses, and naughty nightgowns: not surprisingly, *Subway in the Sky* provoked a scandal. Muriel Box allegedly shot the shower scene, which features Lilli half-naked, without Knef's consent. But this time, instead of motivating millions of moviegoers to go to the theaters to see what the ruckus was about, this scandal had no impact on the cultural climate of Berlin, and London's *Daily Mail* rightfully suspects: "Miss Neff is obviously after publicity" (Sannwald, Jaspers, and Mänz 200518). *Subway in the Sky* was a failed version of a Berlin style "kitchen sink drama" and marked a caesura in Knef's international career during the 1950s.

As a film star and trendsetter, Hildegard Knef attracted the attention of the audience and consistently managed to transgress societal norms or expectations. If *The Murderers Are Among Us* was intended to reeducate Germans after the Nazi defeat, *Subway in the Sky* sought to entertain the audience in the consolidated climate of late 1950s West Berlin. In her films made before 1959, she transgressed various female role models: a motherly girlfriend/wife who seeks an independent existence in *The Murderers Are Among Us*, a countryside naive who has an affair in *Film Without a Title*, a scandalous "Maria Magdalene" prostitute in *The Sinner*, a Nazi prostitute who sympathizes with the enemy in *Decision before Dawn*, a duplicitous Eastern European double agent in *Diplomatic Courier*, a West-Berliner polygamist in *The Man Between*, and an attractive nightclub singer who hides a criminal in *Subway to the Sky*. In only twelve years, the actress had come full circle. She began as the quintessential rubble woman Susanne (*The Murderers Are Among Us*), who cares for a guilt-ridden German veteran and former doctor in a dilapidated Berlin apartment. And she ended the circle as Lilli, a nightclub singer and resident of a Berlin penthouse, who also looks after a desperate officer, this time an American physician who is falsely accused of illegal drug deals. If the rubble was already cleared from Susanne's face and demeanor in the 1940s *The Murderers Are Among Us*, then the elegance of Lilli's wardrobe, combined with her indifferent demeanor, point to West Berlin in the 1960s. But at each time, Knef's acting was contingent on the recognition of the audience, and her performances helped to alter the perception of West Berlin's cultural life through her interpretation of social figurations. Movingly, in his homage to Knef, Hans Helmut Prinzler, the former director of the Deutsche Kinemathek in Berlin, portrays the German actress as a symbol of transience: "She embodied something like an airlift between Germany and America. At the end her terminal was Berlin" (in Sannwald, Jaspers, and Mänz 2005: 7). Like no other German actress—perhaps with the exception of Marlene Dietrich—Knef has captured the imagination of West Berlin, and no other city captured her like Berlin.

Notes

1. In 1950, Knef appeared in a film noir called *Die Sünderin* (The Sinner, 1950). *The Sinner* negotiates the immediate postwar configuration of independent female and weak male characters prevalent in rubble movies. For an extensive discussion of the scandal surrounding the film, see Fehrenbach (1995: 92–118 [Section III]).
2. See Moeller (in Sannwald, Jaspers, and Mänz 2005: 83–90) for more information regarding Knef's relationship with Ewald von Demandowsky.
3. The German premiere was on 18 May 1950 in Göttingen.
4. Tellingly, in Jugert's next film *Hallo Fräulein!* (Hello Fraulein! 1949), the sexuality of the Fräulein is carefully coded; her appearance is testimony to a filmic determination to ennoble young German women by desexualizing them. On the film, see Brauerhoch (2006: 391–417 [Section XVIII]).
5. Between 1953 and 1959, Knef appeared in *Eine Liebesgeschichte* (A Love Story, 1954), *Geständnis unter vier Augen* (Confession under Four Eyes, 1954), *Svengali* (1954), *Madeleine und der Legionär* (Escape from Sahara, 1957), and *La fille de Hambourg* (The Daughter from Hamburg, 1958); none of the films referred to Berlin.

Works Cited

Baudrillard, Jean. 1989. *America*. London: Verso.
Brauerhoch, Annette. 2006. *'Fräuleins' und GIs: Geschichte und Filmgeschichte*. Frankfurt am Main: Stroemfeld/Nexus.
Evans, Peter William. 2005. *Carol Reed*. Manchester, UK: Manchester University Press.
Fehrenbach, Heide. 1995. *Cinema in Democratizing Germany: Reconstructing National Identity after Hitler*. Chapel Hill: University of North Carolina Press.
Hake, Sabine. 2002. *German National Cinema*. London: Routledge.
Judt, Tony. 2005. *Postwar: A History of Europe Since 1945*. London: Penguin.
Large, David Clay. 2000. *Berlin*. New York: Basic Books.
Mennel, Barbara. 2008. *Cities and Cinema*. London: Routledge.
Safire, William. 2004. *Lend Me Your Ears: Great Speeches in History*. New York: W.W. Norton.
Sannwald, Daniela, Kristina Jaspers, and Peter Mänz, eds. 2005. *Hildegard Knef: Eine Künstlerin aus Deutschland*. Berlin: Bertz + Fischer.
Schröder, Christian. 2005. *Hildegard Knef: Mir sollen sämtliche Wunder begegnen*. Berlin: Aufbau.
Shandley, Robert. 2001. *Rubble Films: German Cinema in the Shadow of the Third Reich*. Philadelphia: Temple University Press.

CHAPTER 11

Benno Ohnesorg, Rudi Dutschke, and the Student Movement in West Berlin
Critical Reflections after Forty Years

David E. Barclay

At 4:30 p.m. in the afternoon of 11 April 1968, a twenty-four-year-old casual laborer named Josef Bachmann waited on the sidewalk in front of the headquarters of the Sozialistische Deutsche Studentenbund (Socialist German Student Federation, SDS) at Kurfürstendamm 140 in West Berlin. He had arrived that morning on a train from West Germany armed with two pistols. At 4:35 p.m. he recognized another young man on a bicycle. Bachmann asked the young man if he were Rudi Dutschke, the most charismatic and "visible" representative of the radical student movement in West Berlin. When Dutschke affirmed his identity, Bachmann replied, "You filthy communist pig," and shot him three times, once in the cheek, once in the head, and once in the shoulder. Miraculously Dutschke survived, but he was—obviously—never the same again and died eleven years later in Denmark as a result of the long-term consequences of Bachmann's attempted assassination (Ulrich Enzensberger 2004: 272–75).

A little more than ten months earlier, on 2 June 1967, another young man, Benno Ohnesorg, a twenty-six-year-old student of Romance languages at the Free University of Berlin, had been shot and killed in a courtyard in the Krumme Strasse near the Deutsche Oper during a demonstration against a visit of the Shah of Iran. In this case, the man who pulled the trigger was a plainclothes West Berlin policeman—and, as we know now, Stasi agent—named Karl-Heinz Kurras (Soukup 2007: 79–144). By every eyewitness account—and those accounts are substantial—Ohnesorg was innocent of any kind of aggressive or hostile behavior, while

Kurras seems to have "snapped" and shot. Ohnesorg's death helped accelerate a sequence of events that, according to many observers, were not only dramatic but indeed decisive in the history of West Berlin, among them the rapid growth of the student movement with which Dutschke was so closely identified. In view of these historical consequences, it is more than a little ironic that Kurras turned out to have been a long-time agent of the East German Stasi (Müller-Enbergs and Jabs 2009).

Fortieth anniversaries seem to have become occasions for very serious stock taking, and certainly the events of 1968 in Germany are no exception. It should be emphasized at this point that the term *1968* has become a kind of shorthand for a whole series of events between roughly 1966 and 1970 or 1972. To be sure, 1968 and its long-term consequences, including the emergence of the terrorist "Red Army Faction" or RAF, are not exactly new themes, and have attracted a rather substantial literature (Aust 1998; Koenen 2004; Berman 2007; Peters 2007; Suri 2009; Brown 2009). Indeed, what has sometimes been called "*Faszination RAF*" is still very much with us too. New monographs and new memoirs rolled off the presses in 2008, including several that have attracted a great deal of critical discussion, perhaps most notably and certainly most controversially Götz Aly's 2008 memoir on 1968, of which more will be said below.

These remarks are not intended as a critical review of recent literature on 1968 or as a reassessment of its global significance. Rather, they shall focus on the significance of events between 1966 and 1972 for an understanding of the cultural and political history of West Berlin itself, reflecting among other things on the issues of turning points in history: in this case an important caesura that has to be dated somewhere between 1966 and 1972, because it is quite clear that pre-1966 West Berlin and post-1972 West Berlin were, in many respects, very different places.

The remarks in this chapter are grouped under six headings, some of which will be rather obvious and not all that original, but which nevertheless bear emphasizing.

First: The events connected with the emergence of the student movement and the Außerparlamentarische Opposition (Extraparliamentary Opposition, or APO) in West Berlin still stir controversy, four decades later. To a certain extent this reflects the prominent role played at that time by a charismatic personality like Dutschke, supported by a cast of characters that can only be described as colorful, like the residents of Kommune I, and the fact that a lot of them, like the Enzensbergers or Peter Schneider, were good writers and very good at self-representation. Moreover, many of the characters involved in the SDS, APO, and the West Berlin student movement more generally have had complex and in some cases extremely fraught and controversial careers. Some, like Walter Momper or Christian Ströbele, have moved into the political mainstream. Others continue to advocate for alternative lifestyles, like Uschi Obermaier, who now lives in California, or Rainer Langhans, who now lives in a commune in Munich. And then there are the more controversial cases of people like Bernd Rabehl and especially Horst Mahler, who have moved to the opposite side of the political spectrum. Mahler's career is certainly the most extreme. He first became famous as a radical lawyer who undertook a separate investigation of the Ohnesorg shooting on behalf of the student government at the Free University of Berlin. Then he quickly became a defendant himself, with close connections to the terrorist RAF, and a legal defense in the famous Springer trial headed by the subsequent Interior Minister Otto Schily. Thereafter his connections with Gerhard Schröder were helpful when he applied to resume his legal practice. And now, as we know, Mahler has become a convinced Nazi, as evidenced among other things by his very controversial 2007 interview with Michel Friedman in the German edition of *Vanity Fair* (Friedman 2007). Was Mahler's an individual case, or an extreme example of something more generalizable and problematic? For example, what about the relationship of other prominent 68ers to violence? Wolfgang Kraushaar has consistently argued, for example, that Rudi Dutschke was himself far more willing to entertain the idea of violence than a number of Dutschke's erstwhile friends and comrades are prepared to admit (Kraushaar et al. 2005; Kraushaar 2006).

In addition, a number of critics assail the 68ers, especially those from the old West Berlin, for their relative lack of interest in what was going on across the wall in the GDR and Czechoslovakia, and indeed some contend that, as a consequence, they were particularly ill prepared to deal with what happened in 1989. Even if this were true, Rudi Dutschke would probably have been an exception. Having been brought up in the GDR, like his friend Bernd Rabehl, he demonstrated considerable interest in the question of German reunification, and indeed thought that West Berlin could be a bridgehead for such a reunification (Kraushaar 2000).

And then there are more general and generic criticisms of the 68ers forty years on. For example, in the spring of 2008 a Christian Democrat politician, Jörg Schönbohm, published a long article in the Berlin *Tagesspiegel* in which he blamed the 68ers for a colossal act of generational "self-betrayal" which has led to a "process of erosion in our society" (Schönbohm 2008). Götz Aly suggests that the students of the late 1960s shared a number of frightening similarities with the parents they had supposedly rejected, which leads him to conclude, "Thank God their children foundered on the firmness of the second German republic" (Aly

2008). And of course there is the question of the role of women—or the relative absence of such a role—in the West Berlin student movement of the late 1960s. So the controversies continue to swirl, and feelings remain strong. Not long ago Klaus Schütz, the Social Democratic governing mayor of West Berlin from 1967 to 1977, was asked to comment on the long-term historical significance of the late sixties, and his response was emphatic: "It is interesting to me that in all those forty years I have been unable to discern any great change in my assessment. I regarded it as nonsense and hogwash (*ein Unsinn und ein Quatsch*)" (Schütz 2007). Schütz insists that the student movement, specifically in West Berlin, fed on a number of myths and illusions, one of them being the notion that they were revolting against their Nazi parents. But in fact, Schütz contends, they were revolting against a system in West Berlin that had largely been shaped by people like Ernst Reuter and Willy Brandt, who were anything but Nazis.

Of course, Schütz has reason still to be bitter after forty years. His attempt to reach out to students at the Free University was essentially shouted down when he appeared there. He well remembers the untranslatable slogan that was so often chanted during those years: "*Brecht dem Schütz die Gräten, alle Macht den Räten!*" ("Break Schütz's bones, all power to the councils!") (Schütz 2007). And, finally, as governing mayor of Berlin he was directly confronted with the terrorist violence that was certainly one byproduct of the student revolt of the late sixties, most notably the 1970 killing of the innocent archivist Georg Linke during the armed escape of Andreas Baader from his incarceration, the 1974 murder in Berlin of the judge Günter von Drenkmann, and the 1975 kidnapping of the Christian Democratic mayoral candidate Peter Lorenz by the Bewegung 2. Juni (2 June Movement) named, of course, after the day on which Benno Ohnesorg was killed. This leads to the second major point of these remarks.

Second: West Berlin itself is critically important for an understanding of the events of 1968. In his recently published memoir of 1968, Peter Schneider recalls the impressions that West Berlin made on him when he first arrived there from his native Freiburg: "the absence of a sense of beauty, the lack of a context or of an architectural order." Still, "Berlin's ugliness was just right for me. ... Here I would have to invent myself anew" (2008: 51). And so it was for an entire generation of students—and, for that matter, dropouts and nonstudents—from West Germany. West Berlin was always different, Western but not the Federal Republic, Eastern but certainly not GDR, a unique, insular *Biotop,* as Olaf Leitner and many others have described it (2002). In the words of Wolfgang Kraushaar: "Because of its geopolitically conditioned isolation, entire branches of industry and the economy were languishing, while since the end of the war and the beginning of Germany's division its occupational and social structures had been significantly transformed. Social niches emerged in the shadow of economically underdeveloped parts of the city. . . . These were especially concentrated in districts like Kreuzberg, Schöneberg, and Wilmersdorf " (2008: 216–17).

As Peter Schneider observes of the mid-1960s, there were two West Berlins, one the Berlin of war widows and traditional *Hausmeister* (apartment-house maintenance men), and the West Berlin that was an "experimental stage for new forms of art and new styles of writing" (2008: 56). The West Berlin that was attractive to people like him was precisely the emerging, alternative Berlin, a Berlin that also was a haven—and this is a point that everyone makes—for young males seeking to avoid military service in the West German Bundeswehr.

Ultimately this Berlin was an artificial entity that, in the end, could only be sustained by artificial means. But more than any other German city, perhaps even more than in the world of the Spontis in Frankfurt am Main or, in later years, the Hamburg Hafenstrasse, it offered a rich palette of political and lifestyle possibilities, especially to students, with its unique mix of gurus ranging from Herbert Marcuse and Hellmut Gollwitzer to Wilhelm Reich and Jimi Hendrix and David Bowie.

Third: When one reviews the chronology of the student movement in West Berlin from 1965 to 1969 or 1970, there can be no doubt that the killing of Ohnesorg and the shooting of Dutschke had dramatic multiplier effects that extended far beyond the SDS and APO, and in many ways transformed the structure and character of West Berlin politics and culture more generally. The culture of student protest in Berlin can perhaps be dated to as early as 1961, when the SDS lost its affiliation with the SPD, or perhaps to the protests in 1965 over the visit of the Katanga secessionist leader Moïse Tshombe in West Berlin, or to the first significant protests against the Vietnam War in front of the Amerika Haus in 1966, or to the creation of Kommune I in early 1967, or to the famous flour and pudding attack, a sort of pie-in-the-face gambit, on US vice president Hubert Humphrey in the spring of that year. In these connections one need simply allude to the important work on the Free University of Berlin by James Tent and Siegward Lönnendonker, as well as the extraordinary holdings of the APO-Archiv in Berlin, a gold mine that has scarcely been explored so far (Tent 1988; Lönnendonker and Kubicki 2001; Lönnendonker and Kubicki 2008).

But there can be no doubt whatsoever that the Ohnesorg shooting represented a radicalizing moment that dramatically concentrated and intensified a spirit of almost apocalyptic expectation and fear among the students of West Berlin, at the Free University, the Technical University, and elsewhere. A primary target of the fear and loathing was the Springer press, more powerfully represented in West Berlin than in any other German city (Schwarz 2008: 470–83). Contemporaries like the journalist Manfred Rexin, who was involved with coordinating the details of the famous funeral cortege for Ohnesorg, consistently emphasize the real sense of isolation and fear among Berlin student leaders in the days and weeks after 2 June, a fear that became focused on the Springer press, from the *Berliner Morgenpost* to the *BZ* and, above all, the *Bild Zeitung* (Rexin 2007). Added to that was the fundamental mistrust of the police and of existing political institutions, and one result was the independent investigation launched by the student government at the Free University and coordinated by Horst Mahler.

And the chronology continues from there, from the Springer tribunal in late 1967, the anti-Vietnam demonstrations at a US troop parade in Neukölln, the arrest and imprisonment of the Kommune I activist Fritz Teufel, the intensification of campaigns for the creation of a "critical university," or the Vietnam Congress in February 1968, up to the shooting of Dutschke on Shrove Thursday in April 1968. This in turn unleashed violent attacks on Springer property and large-scale demonstrations throughout Germany. One consequence of all this was the now almost legendary "battle of Tegeler Weg" in November 1968, in which demonstrators clashed with police near the courthouse building where charges against Horst Mahler were being heard, charges based on his alleged support for the violence of the spring demonstrations. With 130 injured police officers and 14 injured students, the confrontation on the Tegeler Weg represented the worst incident of civil violence that West Berlin had experienced since the Second World War (Müller 2008: 287–303). Together with the violence of the spring, the battle of the Tegeler Weg really does represent the beginnings of a culture of alternative-movement violence, largely focused on Berlin, which continues to this day.

In focusing on the post-1967 radicalization of the SDS and APO, however, and their ultimate fragmentation after 1969 into a dizzying array of factions and quarreling sects like the Tupamaros Westberlin or the Schwarze Ratten (Black Rats), not to mention the RAF, it is all too easy to overlook the effects of these events on the larger structure and character of West Berlin politics. The governing mayor at the time of the Ohnesorg shooting, the Social Democratic theologian Heinrich Albertz, had to leave office under a cloud; the historian Uwe Soukup argues that, unloved as Albertz was within the Berlin SPD—Klaus Schütz calls him "a curiously difficult figure"—the events of 2 June offered an excellent opportunity for his comrades to get rid of him and replace him with Willy

Brandt's confidant Schütz, who served in office for a decade (Soukup 2007: 180–209; Schütz 2007; Müller 2008: 156–61). These events also led to a significant, long-term modernization and reorganization of the West Berlin police, spearheaded largely by the Social Democratic police president Klaus Hübner. Whether the events of these years contributed to significant and enduring university reforms in West Berlin is, of course, an entirely different matter, and one about which a certain amount of skepticism is justified.

Fourth: Again, it may seem obvious, but one must never overlook the utopian and, in many ways, quite fantastic quality of the discussions within the radical West Berlin opposition between 1967 and 1969, a utopianism that is all the more startling in terms of the visible realities of the Cold War. Among the classic examples of this utopian thinking, especially as it affected West Berlin, were a now-famous meeting involving Dutschke in Berlin-Pichelsdorf in late June 1967, an article by Dutschke that same month in the publication *Oberbaumblatt,* and a conversation in October 1967 among Dutschke, Bernd Rabehl, Hans Magnus Enzensberger, and Christian Semler. It concerned the prospects for creating a grassroots *Rätedemokratie* (council democracy) specifically in West Berlin that could in turn serve as a catalyst for similar efforts elsewhere. Among other things, Dutschke stressed at the June meeting that it would be possible, within five to ten years, to transform West Berlin radically, and perhaps even to separate West Berlin from the Federal Republic while abolishing the existing city government and all its structures in their entirety. The October discussants called for the elimination of all bureaucracies—indeed, all the structures of the existing state, including the police, who would no longer be necessary—in West Berlin and the creation of what Dutschke described as "associations of free individuals." Because many West Berlin bureaucrats could not be reeducated, Rabehl contended, they would have to emigrate to West Germany. Ultimately the new West Berlin would serve as a kind of transmission belt that would transform both the Federal Republic and the GDR.

The discussants did not anticipate that either the Western Allies or the Soviets and the GDR would have a problem with this. The Western Allies would be unwilling to risk a reverse Budapest à la 1956 and so would not intervene except to provide planes to fly the unwanted bureaucrats to the West, while the GDR would use the proximity of a radicalized West Berlin to renew and humanize the bureaucratic socialism under which it suffered (H. M. Enzensberger 1968; Aly 2008: 89–103; Schneider 2008: 208–18). Jeremi Suri has shown how the events in West Berlin were part of a global nexus of protest that in turn has to be understood in terms of larger geopolitical shifts during the middle decades of the Cold War (Suri

2003: 172–81). But it is fairly obvious that, at least in 1967–68, Dutschke and his allies were remarkably unaware of the realities of global power relationships, despite their embrace of Mao Zedong, Fidel Castro, Ho Chi Minh, Che Guevara, and Frantz Fanon. This leads to the fifth point, in the form of two questions.

Fifth: How significant were the events of 1967–1969 for an understanding of significant turning points in the history of West Berlin from 1948 to 1990? To what extent did they in fact constitute a turning point? When one considers the history of West Berlin, from its more or less official creation in 1948 to the withdrawal of Allied troops in 1994, it is evident that, both synchronically and diachronically, we are speaking of at least two and probably several distinctive yet overlapping histories. Klaus Schütz contends that those former West Berliners who were born before and after 1961 experienced two very different places. The writer Kerstin Schilling, who was born in 1962, echoes Schütz's view in an insightful autobiography that describes an idyllic Reinickendorf youth far removed from the battles of APO and Springer and all the rest of it (2004). These kinds of arguments suggest that, recognizing the obvious artificiality of such divisions, the most profound caesura in the history of West Berlin can be dated to some point between 1966 and 1972. But, in reviewing the history of West Berlin in its totality, it seems that the radical activism of 1966–1970 and thereafter is, for all its cultural importance, a less significant marker in that history, or those histories, than the Four Power Agreement of 1971 and the Berlin agreements that followed upon it. The Four Power Agreement had the effect of creating what Ann Tusa has called a condition of "abnormal normality" in West Berlin (1996: chap. 2). Its effects not only upon the lives of ordinary West Berliners but also the geopolitical situation of the city were profound, and they lasted far beyond the end of the era of détente and the new Cold War of the late 1970s and early 1980s. Moreover, that agreement helped make it possible for West Berlin to continue to be hospitable to the kinds of alternative cultures that the student movement and APO helped to spawn in the 1960s. This leads to the sixth and final point.

Sixth: There can be no doubt that the student movement and APO did have long-term consequences for the history of West Berlin and, indeed, for the history of reunified Berlin after 1990. One might simply mention four closely overlapping "cultures" that significantly shaped the experience of the city after the 1970s: a) the alternative culture generally speaking, a culture that came to be reflected in everything ranging from eco-shops to kindergartens to the emergence of the Alternative Liste (Alternative List) as a significant political force in the 1980s; b) the niche culture, a Kreuzberg variation on the old Prussian motto that everyone can be "happy in his own way;" c) a culture of violence that reached considerable dimensions in the 1980s and has persisted in the postunification period, as witnessed by the Mainzer Strasse episode in 1991 or the continued presence in Berlin of antiglobalization radicals; d) a subvention culture, a reflection of the fact that West Berlin always depended on artificial respiration from the outside. This culture of subvention persisted all the way down to the 1980s, and has left an enduring, if ironic, legacy. In the spring of 2008, for example, just in time for the fortieth anniversary of 1968, Berliners were treated to the bizarre sight of a transport workers' strike being denounced by the SED successor party, the Linke (Left Party), as evidence of the old West Berlin subvention mentality!

And one last observation by way of conclusion: Those who describe 1968 after forty years have to avoid the baby-boomer sin of narcissism and self-importance. In his recent book, Götz Aly describes the controversy about the possible renaming of a Berlin street after Rudi Dutschke, a street that would actually and symbolically intersect with the already existing Axel-Springer-Strasse. Aly's hero from 1968 is the late Richard Löwenthal, who was indeed a great man in many ways; and Aly suggests that, in all justice, the Axel-Springer-Strasse should be connected to the Rudi-Dutschke-Strasse by a Richard-Löwenthal-Promenade (Aly 2008: 210). Interestingly, though, throughout this whole discussion it became evident that lots and lots of younger Berliners, including natives and recent arrivals, had no idea who these people were. Nor did they care. For them, it was all water over the dam, *Schnee von gestern.*

Works Cited

Aly, Götz. 2008. *Unser Kampf: 1968–ein irritierter Blick zurück*. Frankfurt am Main: Fischer.
Aust, Stefan. 1998. *Der Baader Meinhof Komplex*. Rev. ed. Hamburg: Goldmann.
Berman, Paul. 2007. *Power and the Idealists: Or, the Passion of Joschka Fischer and Its Aftermath*. New York: Norton.
Brown, Timothy S. 2009. "'1968' East and West: Divided Germany as a Case Study in Transnational History." *American Historical Review* 114, no. 1: 69–96.
Carini, Marco. 2008. *Fritz Teufel–Wenn's der Wahrheitsfindung dient: Eine Biografie*. Hamburg: Konkret Literatur.
Enzensberger, Hans Magnus. 1968. "Ein Gespräch über die Zukunft mit Rudi Dutschke, Bernd Rabehl und Christian Semler." *Kursbuch* 14: 146–74.
Enzensberger, Ulrich. 2004. *Die Jahre der Kommune I: Berlin 1967–1969*. Cologne: Kiepenheuer & Witsch.
Frei, Norbert. 2008. *1968: Jugendrevolte und globaler Protest*. Munich: dtv.
Friedman, Michel. 2007. "So spricht man mit Nazis." *Vanity Fair* (German edition). 1 November. http://www.vanityfair.de/articles/agenda/horst-mahler/2007/11/01/04423/.
Hockenos, Paul. 2008. *Joschka Fischer and the Making of the Berlin Republic: An Alternative History of Postwar Germany*. New York: Oxford University Press.

Koenen, Gerd. 2004. *Das rote Jahrzehnt: Unsere kleine deutsche Kulturrevolution 1967–1977.* Frankfurt am Main: Fischer.
Kraemer, Olaf, and Uschi Obermaier. 2007. *High Times: Mein wildes Leben.* Munich: Heyne.
Kraushaar, Wolfgang. 2000. "Rudi Dutschke und die Wiedervereinigung. Zur heimlichen Dialektik von Nationalismus und Internationalismus." In *1968 als Mythos, Chiffre und Zäsur.* Ed. Wolfgang Kraushaar. Hamburg: Hamburger Edition. 89–129.
———. 2006. *Die RAF und der linke Terrorismus.* 2 vols. Hamburg: Hamburger Edition.
———. 2008. *Achtundsechzig: Eine Bilanz.* Berlin: Propyläen.
Kraushaar, Wolfgang, Jan Phillip Reemtsa, and Karin Wieland. 2005. *Rudi Dutschke, Andreas Baader und die RAF.* Hamburg: Hamburger Edition.
Langhans, Rainer. 2008. *Ich bin's: Die ersten 68 Jahre.* Munich: Blumenbär.
Leitner, Olaf. 2002. *West-Berlin! Westberlin! Berlin (West)! Die Kultur–die Szene–die Politik: Erinnerungen an eine Teilstadt der 70er und 80er Jahre.* Berlin: Schwarzkopf & Schwarzkopf.
Lönnendonker, Siegward, and Karol Kubicki. 2001. *50 Jahre Freie Universität Berlin aus der Sicht von Zeitgenosssen.* Berlin: Freie Universität Berlin.
———. 2008. *Die Freie Universität Berlin 1948–2007: Von der Gründung bis zum Exzellenzwettbewerb. Beiträge zur Wissenschaftsgeschichte der Freien Universität Berlin 1.* Berlin: V&R Unipress.
Mohr, Reinhard. 2008. *Der diskrete Charme der Rebellion: Ein Leben mit den 68ern.* Berlin: WJS.
Müller, Michael L. 2008. *Berlin 1968: Die andere Perspektive.* Berlin: Berlin Story.
Müller-Enbergs, Helmut, and Cornelia Jabs. 2009. "Der 2. Juni 1967 und die Staatssicherheit." *Deutschland Archiv* 42, no. 3: 395–400.
Peters, Butz. 2007. *Tödlicher Irrtum: Die Geschichte der RAF.* Frankfurt am Main: Fischer.
Rexin, Manfred. 2007. Unpublished interview with author. 20 April: Berlin.
Schilling, Kerstin. 2004. *Insel der Glücklichen: Die Generation West-Berlin.* Berlin: Parthas.
Schneider, Peter. 2008. *Rebellion und Wahn. Mein 68: Eine autobiographische Erzählung.* Cologne: Kiepenheuer & Witsch.
Schönbohm, Jörg. 2008. "1968–Selbstbetrug einer Generation." *Der Tagesspiegel,* 9 March.
Schütz, Klaus. 2007. Unpublished interview with author, 7 March, Berlin.
Schwarz, Hans-Peter. 2008. *Axel Springer: Die Biografie.* Berlin: Propyläen.
Soukup, Uwe. 2007. *Wie starb Benno Ohnesorg? Der 2. Juni 1967.* Berlin: Verlag 1900.
Suri, Jeremi. 2003. *Power and Protest: Global Revolution and the Rise of Détente.* Cambridge MA: Harvard University Press.
———. 2009. "The Rise and Fall of an International Counterculture, 1960–1975." *American Historical Review* 114, no. 1: 45–68.
Tent, James F. 1988. *The Free University of Berlin: A Political History.* Bloomington: Indiana University Press.
Tusa, Ann. 1996. *The Last Division: Berlin and the Wall.* London: Hodder & Stoughton.

CHAPTER 12

Berlin and Post-Meinhof Feminism
Yvonne Rainer's *Journeys from Berlin/1971*

Claudia Mesch

During the 1970s, the final decades of the Cold War, feminist or "women's cinema" flowered in West Germany. Most often the canon of German feminist film does not include the work of visiting artists and filmmakers to West Germany. These "guest workers" were carefully recruited and cultivated through cultural programs such as the Deutsche Akademischer Austauschdienst (German Academic Exchange Service, DAAD). Established in 1925 in order to enable Germans to study abroad, mostly in the US, the DAAD preceded the Cold War. In 1965 the exchange program expanded to channel foreign artists and filmmakers into West Berlin through the DAAD's Artists-in-Berlin Program, first set in place by the Ford Foundation in the year that the Berlin Wall was erected. The DAAD served the FRG well in mobilizing a critical mass of advanced artists on the borderland of divided Berlin as part of the culture war against its Cold War opponents in the GDR. Like later government-sponsored cultural programs such as the National Endowment for the Arts (NEA) in New York, the DAAD gave structure to the culture-war dimension of the Cold War in West Germany and West Berlin. These artists clearly exercised freedom of expression in their work, which the state sought to link to its own American-style brand of capitalist democracy. The artists, however, oftentimes turned a critical eye on their hosts. Many artists found material traces of history and political violence to be the most striking characteristic of the city of West Berlin. Particularly in the late 1970s, in the wake of the FRG's prosecution of the Red Army Faction, artists began to link the traces of historical violence and fascism they found in West Berlin to more recent episodes of state repression.

The American dancer and filmmaker Yvonne Rainer traveled to West Berlin as part of the DAAD program in 1979. As B. Ruby Rich recounts, Rainer learned that her Berlin landlord had left the country to seek employment after she had been dismissed from her position as part of the 1972 *Radikalenerlass* that banned "radicals" from public service, a ruling the state claimed to be precipitated by the violent events staged by the RAF (Rainer 1989: 20). The drama around the RAF and its media icon Ulrike Meinhof still had direct implications for the West German intellectuals whom Rainer met and possibly "identified with" during her residency in West Berlin, even as late as 1979. The work she produced there, the powerful avant-garde feminist film *Journeys from Berlin/1971*, continues the critique of narrative and the concern with the issue of (female) identification that had animated Rainer's earlier work in dance. Relentlessly critical and objectivist, *Journeys* references certain conventions of women's film and even melodrama in its careful psychoanalysis of Meinhof. Rainer also uses Meinhof as a foil for ruminations on the artist's own identity and on the possibilities, personal risks, and limits of political engagement. It remains for cultural and art historians to investigate why Gerhard Richter's painting series, *October 18, 1977*, now in the collections of the Museum of Modern Art in New York, has been defined as the definitive cultural icon of the historical moment of the RAF in West Germany, while Rainer's film has been largely forgotten. Almost everything in the film works against the impulse to freeze the female image, one that Richter arguably flirts with across his paintings.

Rainer's film examines the crisis of identity and identification that has also been attributed to the bifurcation of the student movement into more and less radicalized camps, as David Barclay discusses in his essay in this volume. Petra Rethmann has pointed to a "disjunction in student identity due to political awakening" in West Germany in the late 1960s (2006: 71). She argues that this shift in student identity toward "something larger" resulted in "militancy," or the use of political violence by students after 1967. In fact, Meinhof herself used the term *urban guerilla*—drawing from statements by Mao and insisting vaguely that the term came from "Latin America"—to describe a vision of RAF revolution in her manifesto "The Urban Guerilla Concept." Because it lies outside the focus of this essay, I will not comment on the implications of Rethmann's argument that the student movement became "militant" or violent long before the formation of the RAF, whom she then declines to categorize as a terrorist group. More generally, Rethmann's tracking of West German students' turn to violence as a tool in political struggle parallels Rainer's earlier filmic investigation of the psychic shifts in Meinhof's identity as she embraced political violence.

Rainer's film instead situates Meinhof's radicalization within the context of communist anarchism and political violence practiced by women since the nineteenth century. *Journeys from Berlin/1971* also marks Rainer's shift from an exclusive concern with the crisis of the (female) self to consider how the self forges connections with "social formations" in times of severe state repression. In *Journeys* Rainer analyzes the complex process of identification, or even transference, between herself and Meinhof-as-subject. Rainer remains ambivalent about the case and figure of Meinhof throughout most of the film, but she makes clear that she shares with Meinhof, and with many feminists of the late 1970s, a distrust of the abuse of power that is inherent to the analytic situation, or to the relation of analyst to analysand, within psychotherapy. Meinhof was forced to meet with psychotherapists against her will during her incarceration beginning in 1974.

Journeys is then anchored, albeit loosely, in the persona of Ulrike Meinhof and the location of West Berlin. Rainer makes the Berlin Wall the film's primary visual metaphor for the opening of the self to the linear flow of history, or to social and political concerns. She ties the film to Berlin's topography, although only in an abstract manner. It was the site where Meinhof began her early RAF activities, and where she is buried. Meinhof moved to West Berlin from Hamburg with her twin daughters after her divorce in 1967. A regular contributor to the leftist journal *konkret,* even after she had stepped down as chief editor, she produced articles and radio segments from West Berlin on social issues, the student movement, and related developments like the Benno Ohnesorg and Rudi Dutschke shootings in 1967 and 1968. She lived in upscale Dahlem, and moved in 1970 to an apartment in Schöneberg. Based in part on the life stories of girls she met at the Eichenhof Youth Custody Home in West Berlin, she shot a film for television, *Bambule,* about the problems and ultimate revolt of female juvenile delinquents in detention in late 1969 and early 1970. Around this time she met Andreas Baader and Gudrun Ensslin, who had connections with Kommune 1 and were wanted for the bombing of two department stores in Frankfurt. She resigned from *konkret,* and served as an accessory in Baader's escape from Tegel prison. Meinhof then went underground, producing the "guerilla" manifesto that named the Rote Armee Fraktion (RAF, Red Army Faction) in 1971. She was apprehended near Hannover on 15 June 1972. Like Meinhof—and curiously around the same time, 1970–71—Rainer also turned rather suddenly to film as a medium for her work and as a framework for a developing sense of feminist political engagement. But after this initial similarity, the two women clearly chose widely diverging paths to realize their respective notions of feminist activism.

Journeys from Berlin/1971 is in part an autobiographical film about Rainer's development as a feminist artist. It is also an extended formalist reflection on the psychic mechanism of identification within cinema, and on the specific dynamic of (ambivalent) identification between the artist and Meinhof. Rainer addresses the ethics of identification as it is staged within cinema and the ego ideals it holds out for its viewers, feminist and otherwise. Theorists Laura Mulvey and Teresa de Lauretis have pointed to the psychic mechanism of identification as the major preoccupation of feminist film theory of the 1970s. They understand the process of identification in two ways: within cinema as the female spectator's identification with an onscreen female image, in conjunction with psychoanalysis, but also as "the operation itself whereby the human subject is constituted" (de Lauretis 1987: 130) on an ideological level, drawing upon Althusser's notion of the ideological function of the process of identification within bourgeois representations of the subject (Mulvey 1989: 115). Through the lens of psychoanalysis, a motif that she literally foregrounds in the film, Rainer scrutinizes Meinhof's anarchistic activism as a violent "renunciation of the ego" and questions the relation between a sometimes unstable (female) subjectivity and women's social and political agency.

Other West German filmmakers, many of them women, also responded to women's increasing involvement in the violent actions of the RAF: Margarethe von Trotta, in *Die bleierne Zeit* (Marianne and Juliane, 1981); *Die Stille nach den Schuss* (The Legend of Rita, 2000) by Volker Schlöndorff; and most recently Uli Edel's *Der Baader Meinhof Komplex* (2008), based on Stefan Aust's 1985 bestseller. Helke Sander and Ulrike Ottinger used the Meinhof tragedy to frame sustained investigations of the situation of West German feminism. In contrast to these narrative-based feminist films, *Journeys* foregoes traditional relations between sound and image as well as traditional editing and framing in order to analyze the process of identification and explore the stability of female and artistic identity, and that of Rainer herself. It is difficult to describe the film given its disparate quality, most notably in terms of its disjunction between sound and image. In line with the cultural critique offered by other counter cinema filmmakers, Rainer formally negates the conventions of patriarchical cinema that package visual pleasure into filmic images of woman in favor of a critical, non-imagistic presentation of (violent) feminine/feminist resistance (Johnston 1973).

Rainer makes clear that her own presence in West Berlin coincided with historical events, and conversely that historical events that took place in that city resonated with her own life. In the first minutes of the film, three of the film's major and recurring textual "voices" are introduced: one is a visual crawl script oriented like a newspaper column that scrolls upward (moving vertically), and presents historical and personal information about West Germany. Two soundtrack elements are juxtaposed over this text, which is interrupted by cuts to an aerial and rather illegible image of Stonehenge: the first is a conversation between two New Yorkers, a man and a woman, who argue about political consciousness, political anarchism, and the events around the RAF, also detailed by the scrolling text, while they prepare dinner. The second is a mostly unrelated monologue, a young woman reading from what appears to be her diary, which Rainer has identified as passages from her own diary.

The written visual text outlines several events and conditions that speak to, or took place in, West Berlin, such as the attempted assassination of German Socialist Student Union (SDS) leader Rudi Dutschke and the increasing number of bombings and shootings by the Red Army Faction in the spring of 1972. The scrolling text remarks, "You were surrounded by police as your lover cut your hair by a country road near Cologne. Your activity—along with the sticks of rhubarb lying on the back seat of your car—marked you both as suspicious characters" (Rainer 1989: 141). As Rainer inserts the first person "I" earlier in the scrolling text, in using the second person here, she suggests that she herself—or any other woman finding herself in West Germany in these years—may have been mistaken for one of the female members of the RAF. At the conclusion of the film, when Rainer faces the camera and gives a (feigned) or faux "emotional" address to her own mother, the sequence is intercut with a female voiceover that reads a letter by Meinhof to fellow inmate Hanna Krabbe.

An association between Rainer and Meinhof is therefore consistent in the film. It does, however, alternate between a number of locations outside Berlin. As script cues tell us, the camera cuts to different locations both visually and aurally: to the Bowery in New York, coinciding with the New Yorkers' conversation; to London as the setting for the therapy session; and to Berkeley. The one repeated visual sequence that is filmed in West Berlin features the entrance to Ernst Paulus's Asian-inspired expressionist building, the Kreuzkirche in Berlin-Schmargendorf, built from 1927 to 1929. The sculptor Felix Kupsch completed the striking entrance to the church.

In the film sequence two figures, a man and a woman, walk back and forth in front of it (referred to as the actors "Cynthia and Antonio" in the script). Britain and Germany are recapitulated in two other recurring aerial shots: one of Stonehenge, which becomes increasingly legible, and the other an almost unrecognizable view of the Berlin Wall, slightly out of focus and difficult to make out or place. These landmarks become punctuating metaphors for the tensions Rainer stages in the film

Figure 12.1 Film Still, Yvonne Rainer, *Journeys from Berlin/1971* (1979). Courtesy of Yvonne Rainer.

between the interiorized self—by means of the young woman's voiceover and the therapy sessions featuring the analysand, played by art critic Annette Michelson—and an "exteriorized" one, the self in relation to historical events, by means of the couple's conversation and their reading of the writings of various nineteenth-century anarchists.

In addition to the scrolling vertical script, Rainer uses an audio text, the voiceover of the New Yorkers' domestic conversation, as another point of historical and political orientation. Their conversation presents a short history of anarchism by means of a series of first-person texts that are read over the course of the film. The two are never seen but their conversation mirrors the intense exchanges of the psychotherapy session. The couple's conversation has to do with the issue of social responsibility, and the extent to which the female voice identifies herself with the words and actions of anarchists. In the course of the film she alternatively talks about and reads first person texts by Vera Figner, Sofia Berdina, Angelica Balabanoff, Emma Goldman, Rosa Luxemburg, and in an extended sequence, Vera Zasulich's 1877 account of her attempted assassination of a St. Petersburg magistrate to avenge a savage prison beating: she was later acquitted. Part of the so-called nihilists, these socialist activists emerged from the generation around 1850 in Tsarist Russia. In the late nineteenth century some, like Goldman and Alexander Berkman, emigrated for a time to New York City.

The male voice reads a long passage from Berkman's account of his 1892 attack on Henry Clay Frick. Rainer thereby underscores the gendered aspect of identification with these historical figures that takes place in their conversation. These long voiceovers are punctuated by static views out of an upper-story window onto the Bowery and a Berlin street, and finally by the silent filmic wanderings of "Cynthia and Antonio" in front of Paulus's church. Rainer leaves it to the viewer to forge possible connections between sound and image—for example, are the views out the windows point-of-view shots from the couple, or are these images of two people the two who are conversing in the soundtrack?—but none are made explicit.

In the voiceover the New York couple compares the actions of the RAF to these Russian predecessors and argues over the ethics of violent resistance. "She" concludes that whereas the Russians were justifiably motivated by gross social injustice and inequality, Meinhof and the others "show(s) a muddled vindictive streak in her nature that got in the way of her social thinking. A lot of their violent acts were carried out in a spirit of personal revenge rather than social justice. . . . The little I've read [of Meinhof's writings] sounds like hysterical rhetoric" (Rainer 1989: 148). Finally and in a self-reflecting turn, "she" confesses her difficulty in accepting "political imperatives" because she cannot, as a habit, empathize with others. It remains to the viewer to decide as to whether in this quality "she," for better or for worse, is similar to Meinhof. After this point her voice is intercut with that of the analysand or "patient" played by Michelson, and her voice is accompanied by the static shot of the ongoing therapy session. "She" begins to merge with the "interiorized" voice of the female subject of psychoanalysis. Rainer intercuts images of the therapy session with the voiceover of another young American woman reading from her diary.

The therapy session is visualized throughout the film and must be considered central to the its content. Rainer uses it to examine the relations of power and identification inherent in the analytic situation as it is constructed by various schools, and also to empathize with Meinhof's turn to self-destruction and her refusal of psychoanalysis and compassion, or "humanity" as the patient puts it, when it is appropriated as a means of repression by the state. In the film the therapy session is intercut with the voiceover of the young American woman reading from her diary, which Rainer identifies as her own. The young woman often discusses her parents: a forceful and politicized anarchist father, and her alternating shame and compassion for her overly emotional (or possibly prefeminist) mother; this voice then represents the Oedipal situation, arguably Rainer's own.

Rainer visualizes the therapy sequences in contrast to this soundtrack. In the therapy sequence she presents the Oedipal relation as an interiorized space where female subjectivity is negotiated. At various points a small group or chorus moves behind the analysand in a manner that recalls Rainer's earlier choreography, perhaps tying the exploration of the psyche that goes on in this space to Rainer herself. The therapist is alternatively played by a man, a woman (Rainer), and a male child, and is positioned very close to the camera with his/her back to it. Throughout the film a table separates the analyst and the analysand who sits behind it. This suggests that the camera, and by extension the viewer, takes up the authoritative position of the therapist, whose reactions to the patient's monologues go from silence to ridicule, but who finally urges empathy and "mutual respect" as the means to counter the patient's—and possibly Meinhof's—self-destruction and violence. The patient signals the realm of psychoanalysis in her first monologue about a dream, the traditional subject matter of analysis; she recounts other dreams over the course of the film. She discusses her sexual fantasies and experience, including her fear of the erect phallus when she was "young and innocent." At one point she addresses the therapist/camera as "a properly constituted authority," but she also takes on a mocking tone to lessen that authority, as when she babbles in baby talk. She thereby feigns to infantilize herself, an insincerity that would make true psychotherapy impossible. Several of her monologues debate the measure of equality that exists or not between herself and the faceless therapist. It is clear that, on the one hand, the patient is testing the power relations inherent to therapy and perhaps by the figure of Meinhof on the other. In another test, the patient refuses Freud's views of female identity in declaring, "my cunt is not a castrated cock. If anything it's a heartless asshole!" (Rainer 1989: 153). The patient states that psychotherapy has failed her in the past despite its best efforts. Rainer then shares a feminist awareness of the pitfalls of the talking cure.

The patient relates a "search for a final exit" and a "decision" that she repeatedly links to the site of the Mariannenplatz in Berlin's Kreuzberg district and the year 1971, a year when Meinhof may still have lived in Berlin. Perhaps this decision means suicide, but as "she" announces in voiceover moments later, it is more likely the conscious choice to "renounce egoism" in taking on a mission for others to "gain justice" that might erase or destroy the self. It is the choice of historical political anarchists whose voices "she" has read aloud from the beginning of the film. But the patient repeats, almost in unison with "she," that she has little or none of the empathy required for such sacrifice in the name of social justice—"people *still* exist *for* me rather than *with* me" (Rainer 1989: 151)—and that her choice may result only in her own death or madness. Rainer suggests that in contrast to the Russian anarchists who preceded her, Meinhof shares this patient's pathological frame of mind.

During the film Rainer introduces the subject of object relations, a body of psychoanalytic theory that became key to understanding the dynamics of psychic identification beyond transference, or the dynamic between analysand and analyst. In one sequence, the therapist turns from ridiculing the patient to reading a passage on object relations from Freud's "Mourning and Melancholia." He discusses object cathexis that might occur for the subject either in love or in the opposing process of the "suicide of the ego." In each case, Freud explains, the "ego is overwhelmed by the object, though in totally different ways" (Rainer 1989: 163). According to Freud, if the ego can rechannel hostility against an earlier object against itself, it initiates its own destruction; this analysis seems to deliver a blow to the patient in that it confirms her worst suspicions about her own disintegration. The therapist also cues the patient to articulate the emotion she finds most foreign, compassion; when she manages to say the word, the therapist quotes D. W. Winnicott on compassion as a "natural virtue . . . a disposition suitable to creatures so weak and subject to so many evils as we certainly are" (Rainer 1989: 165). Winnicott insists that compassion exists before reflection, ego formation, and identification can take place. Winnicott envisions an ego that forms within a positive and "nurturing" relation with others and is not reliant solely on notions of the narcissistically generated self. The patient's breakthrough follows when she states: "Suicide then can be seen as a failure of imagination . . . a failure to imagine a world where conscious choice and effort might produce mutual respect between you and me." Her words are intercut on the soundtrack with those of "she," who comes to a similar conclusion.

The final sequence of the film presents the image of Rainer and a long voiceover, the voice of Meinhof raging shortly before her death against the "psychiatrification" that was turned on her and an imprisoned RAF colleague. In contrast to the enlightening passages about analysis that Rainer has just staged in the film, Meinhof understands analysis as a repressive weapon used to break the will of those who resist the state's authority, or those who "den[y] the state's monopoly of force"—a quote from the West German Federal Criminal Investigation Bureau (BKA). But as Rainer presents it, Meinhof's motivation for "fighting against them" remains unclear at best and at its worst has to do with a rage she has rechanneled and turned upon herself. Rainer implies that Meinhof's object cathexis originates in the excesses of state repression; she therefore condemns the Federal Republic and in some measure holds it responsible for the violence and self-destruction it set into motion. Rainer's message seems to be that while feminists can learn from the image and case of Ulrike Meinhof, the political violence she pursued was pathological. Her case is therefore in strong contrast to earlier feminist and anarchist precedents. Meinhof reacted against the injustices of capitalism and patriarchy but did so in way that refused compassion. Rainer suggests that feminists think compassionately about the legacy Meinhof left behind, and view it more with pity than as an ideal for the feminist struggle toward equality.

Works Cited

de Lauretis, Teresa. 1987. "Rethinking Women's Cinema: Aesthetics and Feminist Theory." (1985). Reprinted in *Technologies of Gender: Essays on Theory, Film and Fiction*, 127–48. Bloomington: Indiana University Press.
Johnston, Claire. 1973. "Women's Cinema as Counter-Cinema." In *Notes on Women's Cinema*, ed. Claire Johnston, n. p. London: Society for Education in Film and Television.
Mulvey, Laura. 1989. "Film, Feminism and the Avant-Garde." (1978). Reprinted in *Visual and Other Pleasures*, 111–26. Bloomington: Indiana University Press.
Rainer, Yvonne. 1989. "Journeys from Berlin/1971" Film script. In *The Films of Yvonne Rainer*, 133–72. Bloomington: Indiana University Press.
Rethmann, Petra. 2006. "On Militancy, Sort Of." *Cultural Critique* 62: 67–91.

CHAPTER 13

Daniel Libeskind's Jewish Museum in Berlin as a Cold War Project

Paul B. Jaskot

Perhaps no contemporary German building has been so thoroughly discussed as Daniel Libeskind's Jewish Museum in Berlin. From the competition design in 1989 to the opening of the permanent exhibition in 2001, Libeskind's project has generated endless public debate, architectural criticism, and philosophical speculation. Art and cultural historians have naturally focused on one of the most unique aspects of the plan, its central void, a space that can be seen but not entered, the absent axis to the zigzag structure. Libeskind's decision to center the Jewish Museum on the void has led to extensive analysis of its potential meaning and philosophical import.[1] Yet, concomitant to a scholarly focus on the void is, typically, a decided tendency to isolate the building from its historical process of conception, financing, and production. Explorations of the metaphoric or phenomenological significance of form have outweighed a rigorous and more sober understanding of its cultural function.

As a result, what has gone unremarked by scholars is that the Jewish Museum within the Berlin Museum began not as a symbolic manifestation but rather as a building that engaged very pragmatic goals of the Cold War. First planned as an extension of the existing museum facility, it resulted from interests that marked local Berlin politics as well as the developing relationship between West and East Germany since the 1960s up to the competition in 1989, completed before the Wall fell. As Deborah Ascher Barnstone and Greg Castillo highlight elsewhere in this volume, that relationship was anything but static. It included important political clashes concerning the use of space and specific building projects. In the last decade of the Cold War, the Jewish Museum was an even hotter example of these charged debates across the Wall. The relative isolation of the building from this history in the historiography removes it from the specific political and architectural variability of its site. This removal tends to promote the slippery interpretive abstraction that tells us little about the kinds of choices made by the patrons in formulating the building's program or the architect's response. The architect worked within the strictures set up by decades of previous debates and his decisions were quickly absorbed into the specific political economic conditions of Berlin. Reestablishing the political and architectural terms of the Jewish Museum's development before the fall of the Wall must be the foundation from which any philosophical or historical argument on the structure can be built.

In particular, outlining the precompetition history of the project and its genesis within the physical and conceptual parameters of the Internationale Bauausstellung (International Building Exhibition, IBA) will be crucial for understanding the changing function of the building during the Cold War. Indeed one important aspect of the following will be to argue more generally that regional variation endemic to Cold War policy and ideology on the ground is too often sacrificed in cultural studies of the period. Such has been the case, I would argue, for the analysis of the particular and peculiar circumstances of Cold War Berlin, including its architectural developments, whose international and local valences are in obvious tension with one another. In this regard, my work is in particular dialogue with Emily Pugh's contribution to this volume. The museum extension is thoroughly integrated with the local architectural debates in West Berlin as well as its developing competition with East Berlin. Reintegrating the Jewish Museum with a more concrete understanding of politics clarifies key aspects of the design itself as well as its social significance. Before reunification, the unstable and ever-changing history of the project reveals the uneven and strategic use of architecture and urban planning that characterizes in particular the last decade of Berlin during the Cold War.

Plans for a Jewish Museum in Berlin go back to the art collection left to the Jewish community in 1907 by Albert Wohl, a Dresden jeweler. During the Nazi period, the museum initially remained open and functioned as an important site for attempts by the community to continue its cultural existence. Exhibitions included a retrospective of Max Liebermann after his death in 1936. The museum was closed on 10 November 1938, after the so-called *Kristallnacht* pogrom, and the collection confiscated by the Reichskulturkammer (Steinweis 1993: 123–24; Weinland and Winkler 1997: 7–10).[2] After the war, it was not until 1971 that city museum officials began discussing with the remnants of the Jewish community in West Berlin the plans for opening a department within the municipal museum that combined Jewish history with that of the city as a whole. On 4 February 1975, the Berlin Senate approved a plan for the Jewish Department within the Berlin Municipal Museum (Bussenius 2006: 345–48; Weinland and Winkler 1997: 104–5).

But difficulty with financing and planning delayed further work on the project until the 1980s. By then, naturally, architecture in Berlin had already been well established on the center stage of Cold War policy, for the city was, after all, the symbolic outpost of the West in the face of the communist GDR centered in East Berlin (Pugh 2008). In the 1980s, architecturally speaking, funding concerns focused on reinvigorating residential construction as a means of reviving local economies (Strom 2001: 79–87). In 1979, the Social Democratic (SPD) administration in West Berlin appointed Josef Paul Kleihues to lead this architectural effort through the IBA. With a keen eye on local and international implications, as Pugh shows in this volume, the goal of the IBA was twofold: to restore usable turn-of-the century residential buildings and to create mixed-use residential structures in poorer parts of West Berlin to stimulate growth and provide needed housing. With competitions beginning in 1980 and construction in 1984, the IBA brought together well-known architects such as Peter Eisenman and Zaha Hadid to create attention-grabbing structures that nevertheless blended with the character of specific parts of the city, particularly the three designated areas of the southern Tiergarten, the Prager Platz, and the Friedrichstadt south of the Berlin Wall (part of Kreuzberg). The completion date was rescheduled to 1987 in order to align the project with the 750-year celebration of Berlin. The resulting new buildings showcased through their formal innovation the supposed glamour and success of Cold War West Berlin (Kleihues 1986; Ladd 1997: 106–7, 228–35).

In relation to the Jewish Museum, the IBA was more than mere architectural context. Rather the IBA had targeted the Berlin Museum and many of its surrounding plots for a coordinated building campaign to restore the area. Since 1969, the Berlin Municipal Museum had been located in the baroque Kollegienhaus (Collegiate House), built in 1735 by the architect Philipp Gerlach in the southern Friedrichstadt on the Lindenstrasse. Gerlach's building was part of his eighteenth-century extension of the city, which included the formal street grid and the laying out of geometric plazas such as the Mehringplatz, the former Belle-Alliance-Platz, just south of the Kollegienhaus. Notably Gerlach's early plans emphasized visual continuity and standardization of scales and spatial units. During the Nazi period, this area contained many headquarters for the National Socialist bureaucracies, including the notorious SS; today it houses the Topography of Terror outdoor museum. As a result of this concentration of political power, it was thoroughly bombed by the Allies and, with the exception of the Kollegienhaus, few elements of the eighteenth-century city remained after the war (Biller and Schäche 1981; Ladd 1997: 127–73; Spode 1994; Till 2005: 120–52).

For this particular site, the arrival of the Wall in 1961 to the north and the focus on housing and building at the Mehringplatz to the south cut off north-south communication and left it bereft of little active planning or coordination of building. In accordance with the 1965 *Flächenbenutzungsplan* (Ground Utilization Plan), Lindenstrasse was curved in 1965 in order to speed the movement of traffic through the area, and a proposal was made by the city to develop an east-west autobahn corridor here since it appeared that, given the Wall, there was not to be any north-south development. Obviously this proposal was not completed, but it left traces behind. When it was given up, the local community officials pushed to substitute an east-west green belt for the autobahn project (Biller and Schäche 1981: 249–51).[3]

But with the founding of the IBA in 1978 and Kleihues's subsequent appointment, these concerns and previous proposals were subordinated to the IBA's wish to plan more systematically to create an area of mixed uses, including housing, cultural institutions, and work. In addition to reemphasizing the north-south orientation of the original eighteenth-century plan, the IBA proposed establishing institutions that had a larger regional importance, restoring the historic height of the neighborhood fixed at a maximum of six stories and the creation of a variety of visually differentiated spaces of parks, alleys, semiprivate courtyards, and the like. The IBA set the important criteria of formal orientation but also the functional variability that engaged the history of the site.[4] The planners attempted to balance the visual continuity and scale evident in the baroque origins of the area with the flexibility and semiotic diversity characteristic of a successful capitalist development. The extension to the museum and its grounds were meant to fit within these criteria of form and economic stimulation.

Due to the decision to locate the museum extension south of the Kollegienhaus, the project came within the purview of the IBA. Hence the planning for the Jewish Museum leading up to the competition included working with the IBA and called for the political support of Kleihues (Weinland and Winkler 1997: 137–38, 153–57, 262–63). Kleihues and the IBA had a significant amount of authority over the many projects in the Friedrichstadt that fell under their auspices. For the area around the museum, they had proposals for several housing complexes, a number of gardens, and a school for the speech impaired. So, for example, with the massive housing project just to the north of the museum known as Wohnpark, the architectural team of Kreis, Schaad, and Schaad turned to Kleihues and his staff for design approval as well as practical help with the necessary zoning variances and other bureaucratic issues. The IBA planners were in turn supported by city officials who endorsed the general goals but also specific interests in reasserting the historic north-south orientation of the district.[5]

Tying the proposal of the Jewish Museum extension to the IBA secured the integration of local governmental planning and a new architectural project. But the Jewish extension was also not outside of the Cold War political competition between East and West that supported the IBA in the first place. Most directly, the planning for the extension to the museum went in tandem and referenced East Berlin's actions to commemorate the former Jewish community. Historically speaking, part of the founding mythology of East Germany had been that, as a socialist state, it had taken up the mantel of antifascism and resistance to National Socialism. Yet, coupled with the continued support of the Western bloc for Israel in the postwar period as well as Stalin's anti-Semitic campaign in 1952, relatively little had been done at the official level in terms of acknowledging the culpability of perpetrators still living in the GDR or in recognizing any remnant of the Jewish community (Cohn 1994). In East Berlin, this situation changed in 1981. As part of the plan to rebuild the medieval Nikolai Quarter in preparation for the city's 750-year anniversary celebration, the government announced that it was also going to rebuild the eighteenth-century Jewish residence of the Ephraim Palais as a symbol of the Jewish contribution to the city's history. Furthermore, Peter Kirchner, head of the Jewish Community in East Berlin, revealed in 1987 that the state had dedicated funds to rebuild the Oranienburgerstrasse synagogue, the heart of the pre-Nazi community (cf. Meng 2008; Vees-Gulani 2008). An official decree was issued in July 1988 that named the establishment of a foundation for the "New Synagogue Berlin-Centrum Judaicum" (Weinland and Winkler 1997: 21, 27–20, 36).

In West Berlin, these initiatives became a leitmotif in the documents and meetings surrounding the Jewish extension to the Berlin Museum and spurred the West Berliners to action. So, for example, developments in East Berlin became of interest to the participants at the Aspen Institute meeting of 15 March 1988. At that meeting, discussion of the new museum extension referenced the plans in the East and how they must provide a point of departure for key aspects of Western decision making (Bussenius 2006: 350–52; Weinland and Winkler 1997: 226–52). Within the city government, Eastern developments were carefully monitored, particularly in the jubilee year, for example, with a clippings file in the

Jewish division of the museum containing news of any exhibitions or plans for commemorating the Jewish community in East Berlin that might require an appropriate West Berlin response. Most specifically, as the CDU senator for culture Volker Hassemer prepared the announcement for the architectural competition, he emphasized how important it was to have a big public statement concerning commemoration on the date of the fiftieth anniversary of the 9 November 1938 pogrom. Naturally, this was an important historical moment, but West Berlin officials were also concerned about having an appropriate event to compete with its neighbor, as East Berlin city officials were to announce plans to lay the cornerstone for the Centrum Judaicum on that same date.[6] This indicates the balancing act of local West Berlin Cold War thinking that also spurred on the development of the Jewish Museum.

Crucial for the competition jury deliberations that began in June 1989 were, naturally, the interests and local criteria that had conditioned the development of the idea for a Jewish Museum in the first place. City officials, under the SPD and Green/Alternative List coalition since early 1989, had approved the program for the extension, which was to include the "Integrative Model" of the history of the Jews intersecting with the broader history of Berlin. In addition, any entry had to conform to IBA housing policy standards and incorporate the significance of the structure into the terms of the Cold War politics, of which many of the architectural decisions continued to be a flashpoint. As the overwhelming favorite with the jury, Libeskind's proposal addressed the concerns of the city administrators and urban politics particularly well.[7]

Libeskind's proposal attempted to spatialize the integrative model by generating the form out of a complex geographic, historical, and conceptual matrix that combined rational criteria with seemingly random or irrational choices. Briefly, the project was set within the larger urban and historical context of Berlin, best exemplified by the intersecting lines he drew to connect the former residences of famous cultural and intellectual Jews and gentiles. By triangulating these lines, he formed the side of a kind of compressed star to make up the zigzag of the museum's walls, a form he related to the Berlin Jews being forced to wear the yellow star during World War Two. The zigzag symbolizes the torturous but continuous history of the city that has no real beginning or end. This form is interrupted by the simple but broken element of the famous void, commemorating the disruption of history created by the genocide.[8]

But the building's success with a jury depended on making the connection between the concept and the local conditions of Cold War West Berlin, which had engendered the planning and development of the competition. Libeskind's plan not only inscribed the building within the

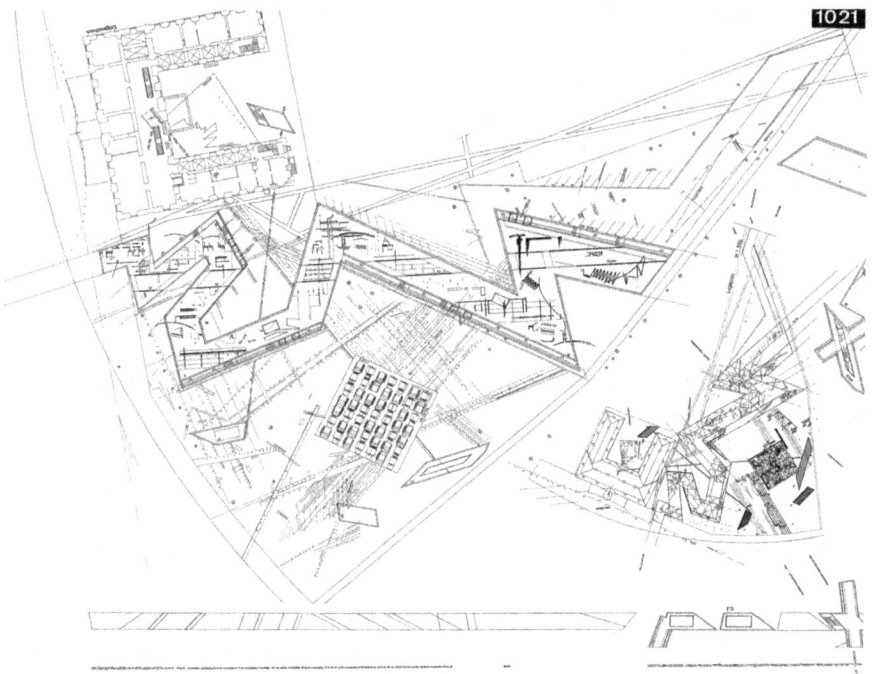

Figure 13.1 Daniel Libeskind, The Jewish Museum within the Berlin Municipal Museum, Competition Entry, ground floor plan (1989). Courtesy of Studio Daniel Libeskind.

specific geographies of German Jewish cultural and intellectual life in Berlin, but also, in specific details, it related to the site more broadly. While the zigzag contrasts strongly with the staid plan of the older structures in the neighborhood, the line of the interior void is approximately aligned with the neighboring Gerlach building and maintains the underlying integrity of the grid, something evident in the idealized proposal if hard to experience in the final building. Nevertheless, this contrasting and complementary form connects the building to other IBA projects, which equally attempted to play off of local buildings but also to create dynamic sculptural facades that enlivened the streetscape. As put by the architect himself in his first statement on the building: "In terms of the city, the idea is to give a new value to the existing context, the historical context, by transforming the urban field into an open and what I would call a hope-oriented matrix. ... The compactness of traditional street patterns is gradually dissolved from baroque origins and then related diagonally across to the 1960s housing development and the new IBA projects" (Libeskind 1997: 63).[9]

The connection of the plan to its site and the city is more explicit in the discussions the architect and his team had with the museum and the city bureaucracy. In an unpublished interview from 26 July 1989, Libeskind emphasized the continuity of his cornice line with Gerlach's building. As the front section of the building goes beyond the current property line of the Lindenstrasse, he thought it acted like a city gate, emphasizing the local interest in an east-west orientation while not hindering further designs for a stronger north-south linkage with the Mehringplatz. Such claims and connections were further elaborated in a discussion of museum personnel and city landscape planners with the architect and his staff on 22 January 1990. The report summarizing the conversation noted that the plan incorporated not only the historic eighteenth-century city but also the plans of the 1960s as well as the new needs such as those articulated in the IBA. So, for example, the facade's visibility to the north-south traffic along Lindenstrasse would emphasize the older axis even while the east-west greenbelt proposed by the local officials to replace the autobahn idea in the 1960s would be signaled with the orientation of the main body of the building and its accompanying green space. Such accents connected the building to the model of city planning from the IBA in the 1980s, with its emphasis on dramatic buildings to pump up the profile of West Berlin that were nevertheless tied in terms of scale to their communities. In sum, "the architect suggested . . . that the emphasis in this part of the city should be as a connecting point of three centuries of building traditions."[10]

Such a balancing act integrated the building with the local and ideological goals of the IBA, as the building was thoroughly tied to the environment around it. Libeskind's design connected with its site and the city and, in formal terms, also radically broke with previous built environments. With its spectacular form, it was also an effective response to anything the East Berlin government would do to commemorate its Jewish community, as I have attempted to show. The IBA context as well as the specific, local Cold War dynamics concerning commemorating the Jewish heritage of Berlin on both sides of the Wall during the 1980s spurred the planners to coordinate the timing of specific developments of the building. It further thoroughly connected the project to the West German goal of presenting the city as vibrant and stable. Libeskind's own designs incorporated that history of building, and the architect himself responded to these specific demands of the site and its postwar history through his attempts to articulate a relation of the building to its north-south and east-west precedents. By looking at the specific history of the political development of the site, this Cold War context of the building comes more clearly into focus, above all the competition

Figure 13.2 View along the Lindenstrasse, showing from left to right: Kreis, Schad and Schad, Wohnpark am Berlin Museum (1986), Gerlach, Kollegienhaus (1735), and Libeskind, Jewish Museum (1989). Photograph by the author.

to establish a connection to pre-Holocaust Jewish culture with building projects on each side of the Wall. As a result, it pushes us to reconsider other buildings, other sites, in more lucid and materialist ways, rather than emphasizing only the phenomenological or semiotic interpretation of form in the abstract. With such a reorientation, the importance of the Cold War in Berlin can be most effectively reassessed in terms of both its built environment and its political significance.

Notes

1. The literature on Libeskind's design is vast. One of the most influential interpretations, with its introduction of Heidegger's concept of the uncanny, remains Anthony Vidler (2001), 235–42. For a historical account that has expanded on the concept of the uncanny and become standard, see James E. Young (2000), 152–83. Andreas Huyssen discusses more historical and literary contexts for the void itself (1997). Katrin Pieper's recent sustained analysis in *Die Musealisierung des Holocaust* (2006) is an excellent consolidation of historical information and interpretation of the building as well as the curatorial choices in the permanent installation. However, the give and take of Berlin politics as well as the Cold War history of the project is outside of the focus of her work.

2. Weinland and Winkler is the most comprehensive published collection of documents relating to the Jewish Museum and is the starting point for most scholars.
3. See also the very useful IBA chronology of this site and others in Lampugnani 1981: 225–66. As Pugh notes in her contribution to this volume, the IBA put great stress on its own publications and message.
4. Wolfgang Engel, "Berlin-Südliche Friedrichstadt," preparatory report, 15 March 1989, in Landesarchiv Berlin (LA Berlin), B Rep 009 Nr. 4577. For debates about green space, see, e.g., the 1989 exchange of Bezirksstadträtin Franziska Eichstädt-Bohlig with the office of Bausenator Wolfgang Nagel in Senatsverwaltung für Wissenschaft, Forschung und Kultur, Berlin Museum Documents (SenKult), File Nr. 327: Berlin Museum, Erweiterungsbau, 2/88–90.
5. Kreis, Schaad, and Schaad in LA Berlin, B Rep 009 Nr. 4576, Südliche Friedrichstadt. This file also contains a report from Wolfgang Engel, Senator für Stadtentwicklung und Umweltschutz, from 21 June 1982 stating that he thought the overall plan by Hans Kollhoff and Arthur Ovaska for the housing complex was too starkly oriented to the east-west.
6. Clippings file concerning East Berlin, in SenKult, File Nr. 331, Berlin-Museum, Jüdische Abteilung, Sonderakte, 9/88–12/90; Hassemer and plans for the announcement of the competition in SenKult, File Nr. 329, folder 19, Berlin-Museum, Erweiterungsbau.
7. Press release from 26 June 1989, Senator für Bau- und Wohnungswesen, Pressestelle, announcing results of competition in SenKult, File Nr. 329, folder 20, Berlin-Museum, Erweiterungsbau. See, also, Senatsverwaltung für Bau- und Wohnungswesen 1990. For an excellent overview of the dynamics of the Red/Green coalition, see Raschke 1993.
8. Libeskind articulated the goals of his design in a lecture first given in Hannover, December 1989, entitled "Between the Lines," his preferred title for the proposal. Reprinted in a variety of publications ever since, the talk has become his most well-known statement on the building (Libeskind 1997).
9. See, also, selective jurors' comments reprinted in Weinland and Winkler 1997: 43–45.
10. Meeting report, 22 January 1990, in SenKult, File Nr. 327, Berlin-Museum, Erweiterungsbau, 2/88–90.

Works Cited

Biller, Thomas, and Wolfgang Schäche. 1981. "The Development of South Friedrichstadt." In *Internationale Bauausstellung Berlin 1984: Die Neubaugebiete. Dokumente. Projekte,* vol. 2, *Erste Projekte,* ed. Josef Paul Kleihues, 240–51. Berlin: Quadriga Verlag.

Bussenius, Daniel. 2006. "Die Anfänge des Jüdischen Museums Berlin. Zur Entstehung des "integrativen Konzepts" vor der Wiedervereinigung." *Mitteilungen des Vereins für die Geschichte Berlins* 102, no. 2 (April): 345–52.

Cohn, Michael. 1994. *The Jews in Germany 1945–1993.* Westport, CT: Praeger.

Huyssen, Andreas. 1997. "The Voids of Berlin." *Critical Inquiry* 24, no. 1: 57–81.

Kleihues, Josef Paul. 1986. "Von Großstadtträumen zur Stadterneuerung. Architektur und Städtebau in Berlin." In *750 Jahre Berlin: Stadt der Gegenwart,* ed. Ulrich Eckhardt, 170–79. Frankfurt am Main: Ullstein.

Ladd, Brian. 1997. *The Ghosts of Berlin: Confronting German History in the Urban Landscape.* Chicago: University of Chicago Press.

Lampugnani, Vittorio Magnago, ed. 1981. *Internationale Bauausstellung Berlin 1984: Die Neubaugebiete. Dokumente. Projekte,* vol. 1, *Modelle für eine Stadt.* Berlin: Quadriga Verlag.

Libeskind, Daniel. 1997. "Between the Lines." *Architectural Design* 67, no. 9/10 (September/October): 58–63.

Meng, Michael. 2008. "The Politics of Antifascism: Historic Preservation, Jewish Sites, and the Rebuilding of Potsdam's Altstadt." In *Beyond Berlin: Twelve German Cities Confront the Nazi Past,* ed. Gavriel D. Rosenfeld and Paul B. Jaskot, 231–50. Ann Arbor: University of Michigan Press.

Pieper, Katrin. 2006. *Die Musealisierung des Holocaust: Das Jüdische Museum Berlin und das U.S. Holocaust Memorial Museum in Washington D.C.* Cologne: Böhlau.

Pugh, Emily. 2008. "The Berlin Wall and the Urban Space and Experience of East and West Berlin, 1961–1989." PhD dissertation, City University of New York.

Raschke, Joachim. 1993. *Die Grünen: Wie sie wurden, was sie sind.* Cologne: Büchergilde Gutenberg.

Senatsverwaltung für Bau- und Wohnungswesen, ed. 1990. *Realisierungswettbewerb Erweiterung Berlin Museum mit Abteilung Jüdisches Museum: Voraussetzungen, Verfahren, Ergebnisse.* Berlin: Senatsverwaltung für Bau- und Wohnungswesen.

Spode, Hasso. 1994. "Das Kammergericht." In *Geschichtslandschaft Berlin*, vol. 5, *Kreuzberg*, ed. Helmut Engel, Stefi Jersch-Wenzel, and Wilhelm Treue, 235–50. Berlin: Nikolai.

Steinweis, Alan. 1993. *Art, Ideology and Economics in Nazi Germany: The Reich Chambers of Music, Theater, and the Visual Arts.* Chapel Hill: University of North Carolina Press.

Strom, Elizabeth A. 2001. *Building the New Berlin: The Politics of Urban Development in Germany's Central City.* Lanham, MD: Lexington Books.

Till, Karen E. 2005. *The New Berlin: Memory, Politics, Place.* Minneapolis: University of Minnesota Press.

Vees-Gulani, Suzanne. 2008. "The Politics of New Beginnings: The Continued Exclusion of the Nazi Past in Dresden's Cityscape." In *Beyond Berlin: Twelve German Cities Confront the Nazi Past,* ed. Gavriel D. Rosenfeld and Paul B. Jaskot, 25–47. Ann Arbor: University of Michigan Press.

Vidler, Anthony. 2001. *Warped Space.* Cambridge, MA: The MIT Press.

Weinland Martina, and Kurt Winkler. 1997. *The Jewish Museum in the Berlin Municipal Museum: A Record.* Berlin: Nikolai.

Young, James E. 2000. *At Memory's Edge: After-Images of the Holocaust in Contemporary Art and Architecture.* New Haven, CT: Yale University Press.

Chapter 14

Beyond the Berlin Myth
The Local, the Global and the IBA 87

Emily Pugh

In a 1994 article entitled "Berlin: Once and Future Capital," urban sociologist Hartmut Häußermann and political scientist Elizabeth Strom discuss the importance of a country's capital city, calling it the place where "national identity in its most tangible form is rooted." They note, however, that if the capital is a "symbolic space, it is also an ordinary town in which rubbish must be collected" (1994: 335). What Häußermann and Strom are alluding to are two interrelated aspects of any city, but particularly a capital city: its image, both figurative and literal, in the public imagination, as well as the more mundane side of the city that is often left out of nationalist and/or heroic visions of it, such as the workaday tasks that are a necessary part of urban living.

Perhaps nowhere have these two facets of the capital city stood in such sharp relief as in West Berlin, where the effort to construct the city in international terms as the "capital of the free world" was complicated by the city's own social and economic problems, many of which were ironically endemic to its unique position at the center of the Cold War. With this essay, I will explore what might be characterized as the push-pull relationship between global and local demands placed on West Berlin, particularly in the 1970s and 1980s, through an examination of the squatter movement and the 1987 International Building Exhibition or IBA. In particular, I will examine the latter as a response to the former, and in doing so, consider the ways West Berlin's local politics often conflicted with the more lofty goals related to the construction of its global image. An assessment of the IBA's impact on West Berlin's global image is particularly relevant in this postunification era, given the influence that the exhibition had on the architecture and development of post-1989 Berlin, a topic explored in detail by Paul Jaskot in his essay on the Jewish Museum in this volume.

Since the end of World War II, governments in the West had gone to great lengths to define West Berlin in international terms, to cast it as a bastion of freedom, democracy, and capitalism: the so-called show (or shop) window (*Schaufenster*) of the West. However, while there was truth to this image, it was also somewhat exaggerated. For example, though West Berliners did enjoy civil liberties that those in East Germany did not, to speak of freedom in a city that was cut off from the West and, after 1961, barricaded by the Berlin Wall was somewhat ironic. Moreover, the economy of a city that was supposed to be the shop window of the West was from the start heavily subsidized by the West German government, and as a result West Berlin never had an independent economy (Ribbe 2002: 132). Though defined as a symbol of the West overall, West Berlin was in many ways a special case, subject to a set of political, economic, and social circumstances that were specific to it.

As an attempt to reconcile the local and global demands placed on West Berlin, the 1987 International Building Exhibition ended up being caught between them. Staged as part of the larger celebration of the city's 750-year jubilee, the exhibition featured built architectural projects along with historical exhibitions, and exhibits of drawings, designs, and models, all of which were supposed to encourage discussion about city planning and housing policy on a global scale. However, the IBA was also an attempt to address West Berlin's housing shortage and, in so doing, to respond to the critiques of the city's squatters, who in the 1970s had joined together as part of a broad-based social protest movement.

While other West German cities were also experiencing housing crises, the situation was more dire in West Berlin, partly because of the city's limited amount of space, and was more visible, given the city's symbolic role. The squatter movement had emerged in the 1970s, spurred by a severe shortage of particularly lower-income housing but also by widespread and widely publicized corruption in West Berlin's city government and building industry. The squatters were in fact one group within a set of sociopolitical activist groups that had grown out of the student protests of the 1960s. Groups of activists espousing a variety of related concerns, from nuclear arms proliferation to women's rights, were linked by communal and/or cooperative "projects" such as bookstores, cafés, and organic food markets. The largest of these alternative communities was in West Berlin where by 1981 a large network of around 1,500 cooperative projects had been established, collectively known as the *alternative Szene* (Görtemaker 2004: 644–45; Mayer 2000: 132).

The alternative scene generally, and the squatter movement specifically, were centered primarily in the neighborhood of Kreuzberg where, starting in the 1960s, university students and foreign laborers from countries like Turkey and Yugoslavia had moved in search of increasingly scarce affordable housing. The scarcity of low-income housing was a result of the building policies that had guided redevelopment in West Berlin following World War II. These policies were designed to correct what were seen as the mistakes of prewar urban development in Berlin, mistakes that had produced the widely reviled building-type known as the "rental barrack" or *Mietskaserne*. Comprised of multistory housing blocks centered on comparatively small, linked courtyards, *Mietskasernen* would in the late nineteenth and early twentieth centuries help to create in Berlin the densely built, "stony" urban landscape for which the city became notorious. Thus in the postwar period, reconstruction generally focused not on renovating such buildings, but on replacing them with large, high-rise housing developments. These developments, one example of which is Gropiusstadt in Neukölln, were for the most part built in the outlying districts of West Berlin, leaving inner-city districts like Kreuzberg largely untouched either by urban redevelopment or renovation.

As a result of such policies, there was a decrease in the overall number of new housing units constructed in the 1960s and 1970s, at the same time that government subsidies and other economic incentives encouraged landlords to leave existing buildings unoccupied and/or unrenovated. By 1982, at the height of West Berlin's housing crisis, almost 10,000 housing units were in empty or partially empty buildings despite the fact that 70,000 applications for housing were languishing in the offices of the city's Housing Authority (Bodenschatz, Heise, and Korfmacher 1983: 47; Mulhak 1983: 205). This shortage of particularly lower-income housing disproportionately affected the city's foreign worker and student populations, many of whom began illegally squatting in the unoccupied buildings as well as organizing protests against the city's housing construction and urban development policies.

As the squatter movement grew, images of West Berlin's squatters and the members of other, related protest groups began increasingly to replace the images of prosperity and rebirth that had predominated in the 1950s and 1960s. Instead of, for example, photos of the pristine, newly rebuilt Hansaviertel or of the sleek, modernist Europa-Center rising behind the reconstructed ruins of Kaiser Wilhelm Memorial Church, the images of the city that filled the West German and international press in the 1970s and 1980s were of West Berlin's immigrant population, of long-haired squatters protesting in the streets or of crumbling tenements festooned with graffiti and antigovernment slogans. And, in contrast to the photos of modernist buildings or shops on the Kurfürstendamm, which had helped to convey the idea that West Berlin was a cosmopolitan city of international importance, the images of the 1970s and 1980s

Figure 14.1 View of squat in Kreuzberg in 1980. Photo by Jochen Moll. Courtesy of Bildarchiv Preussischer Kulturbesitz.

were informed by the local politics and conflicts that seemed to have overwhelmed the city's grander, globally oriented pretensions. Indeed, images of protesters and immigrant residents encouraged the perception that West Berlin was populated with outsiders, a center not of mainstream, Western values, but of aberration, difference, and the critique of such values. As filmmaker Rosa von Praunheim put it in 1983, West Berlin had become the "mecca for all that is extreme and flipped-out" (Krüger 1983: 40).

West Berlin's unrenovated inner-city districts, above all Kreuzberg, featured prominently in such press reports, and, as the center of West Berlin's counterculture, were viewed as the source of the city's problems by many in the press and in the West Berlin and West German governments. For example, because of the high number of immigrant residents in these neighborhoods, journalists worried that the city was no longer truly German, but was becoming what one called a "Turkish city" (Nawrocki 1976; cf. Engert 1981). Protest groups in West Berlin were, according to a 1981 article in *Newsweek,* clearly concerned with "self, not society," happy to spend their days out of work and on the dole (Bruning 1981). As a result of such "problems," West Berlin was said to be suffering from what was called an "identity crisis," having lost its function and relevance vis-à-vis West Germany and indeed the entire Western world. Moreover, the city, argued many, was diseased and dying, kept alive only by the constant transfusion of West German funds.[1] In a 1983 article in the news magazine *Der Spiegel,* journalist Karl-Heinz Krüger did not mince words: "The city is—sad but true—kaput" (Krüger 1983: 40).

Those who regretted West Berlin's "lost identity" saw it as a grave problem primarily in relation to the city's Cold War importance. The fact that the most notorious venue of squatters' and other groups' critique of Western ideals and values was the "shop window of the West" was for many difficult to countenance. Indeed, though the media's dire pronouncements regarding West Berlin were no doubt exaggerated, the negative press was clearly viewed as a liability, in particular by the city's government. The approach of Berlin's 750-year celebration in 1987 was therefore greeted as an opportunity to restore West Berlin's "lost identity," to resuscitate the postwar image of West Berlin as a glamorous European metropolis of international importance, and, in doing both, to reassert the city's association with mainstream values. The IBA 87 was a major part of this effort, designed not only to provide much-needed lower-income housing, but also, according to the West Berlin Senate, to "work against the widely criticized, inhospitable modern city" and to reestablish "Berlin's preeminence as a cultural metropolis" on a global scale (LArch; B Rep 150/416, Mitteilung Nr 105).

The IBA was originally planned for 1984, but debates about the feasibility and expense of the exhibition delayed plans until 1987, at which time the IBA was integrated into the larger, government-organized celebration of Berlin's 750-year jubilee. Formally opened in May 1987, the architectural exhibition was divided into two sections: the IBA-*Neubau* or new construction, which focused on new buildings constructed as "infill" at various points throughout the city, and the IBA-*Altbau* or old construction, which focused on the refurbishment of existing buildings. This two-pronged approach, along with the exhibition's two themes, "Saving the Ruined City" and "The Inner-City as a Place to Live," reflected the planners' goals of revitalizing the supposedly "dead" city with new construction but also by paying attention to previously neglected areas. At the same time, drawings and sketches for planned projects were supposed to spark a global debate about contemporary planning and architecture, and built projects were to make West Berlin a "model city," serving as an urban development blueprint for other cities to follow.

In terms of approach, the IBA represented a snapshot of theoretical as well as stylistic trends of the late 1970s and 1980s, especially postmodernism and the style that would later be called deconstructivism, and this remains the exhibition's best-known attribute.[2] IBA projects communicated an overall rejection of modernism, an approach that had influenced the design of developments like Gropiusstadt, and were therefore presented as a repudiation of West Berlin's earlier municipal housing policies. Rather than zoning areas of the city according to their use, for example, IBA projects often repurposed spaces and/or united residential with commercial and institutional facilities. Architect Abel Volkmann, for example, created designs for a kindergarten and residential building that was to be installed in a former factory (Naunynstrasse 69, 1985), while Gino Valle designed a building intended to house both an elementary school and a wholesale flower market (Block 606, Bessel Park; 1983).[3]

Other projects adhered to the postmodern approach by incorporating historical decorative motifs or referencing past uses of a particular site through layout or design. The plan for Peter Eisenman's apartment and office building, built near Checkpoint Charlie, was an elaborate reference to the city's grid system (1985–1988) (Eisenman 1987). Indeed, the grid, a major leitmotif of postmodern architecture, appears and reappears throughout IBA designs—in Eisenman's building but also in Stanley Tigerman's design for Tegel Docks housing (1985), Oswald Mathias Unger's design for an apartment complex on Lützowplatz (1979–1981), and the IBA-*Altbau* scheme for "Residential Shelving" built in Kreuzberg and designed by Kjell Nylund, Cristof Puttfarke, and Peter Stürzebecher (1986).

Figure 14.2 O. M. Ungers, apartment complex on Lützowplatz (1979–1981). Photo by author.

In addition to built projects like these, the IBA sponsored conferences, a major historical exhibition entitled "750 Years of Architecture and Urban Planning in Berlin," and the publication of numerous books, essays, pamphlets, and other literature both in and outside of West Berlin and West Germany. Moreover, the IBA's planners wanted the exhibition itself to embody architecture/urban-planning discourse and thus used different styles and approaches to stage a kind of physical "debate" and to encourage discussion around the various proposed urban visions. To help achieve this goal, 20 percent of the exhibition budget was given to bringing the IBA's various urban planning and design ideas to an "intensive confrontation with the public" in the form of books, pamphlets, maps, guides, official tours, and architecture and urban planning conferences (Parliament of West Berlin, Section A.3.5 cited in Miller 1993: 205).

As a result of such initiatives, the IBA's visibility on an international scale was undeniable, but its reception, both in the popular and professional press, was—and is—decidedly mixed. Politicians and the public balked at the exhibition's bloated price tag, and architecture critics charged that its mix of different styles and approaches had turned West Berlin into a postmodern Disneyland (see Guratzsch 1987: 7). However, despite such criticisms, most architecture critics agreed that the IBA marked an important moment for West Berlin in terms of its role as a center of culture. In a more recent assessment of the exhibition, for example, published in *Metropolis* magazine, critic Max Page argues that the IBA "produced no great works of architecture," but that it was nonetheless significant in that it sparked important debates about design and planning and because it gave architects like Peter Eisenman, Zaha Hadid, and John Hejduk their first major commissions (2005: 133, 108).

Indeed, whether one considers the IBA 87 a success or failure depends largely on what one considers its central goal: Was it an attempt to create long-term, practical solutions to housing in West Berlin and throughout the Western world? Or was it primarily an attempt to restore some of the cultural cachet that West Berlin had lost in the 1970s and early 1980s? If one accepts the former as the IBA's goal, the exhibition was undoubtedly a failure. One reason for this was that the IBA and the buildings it produced were a product of West Berlin's heavily subsidized and uniquely structured construction industry. Planned and executed under rarefied circumstances, the IBA projects were not ones that could be reproduced either in West Germany, or in the West generally on a large scale. In addition, IBA projects were often granted additional dispensations because of their role in the 750-year celebration, meaning that, because of their scale and expense, they were not even reproducible in West Berlin outside the confines of the exhibition (Hoffmann 1985; Schonlau 1987).

In addition, though the effort to incorporate many different voices and perspectives was appealing in theory, it had proved difficult in practice. Specifically the inclusion of so many different groups in the planning and construction processes—from residents to local administrations to credit institutes to property owners and speculators—resulted in what was characterized as a "small war." Even within the IBA's administration, disagreements between the head of the *Neu-* and *Altbau* divisions eventually led to a split between the two so that in the end they functioned as more or less separate exhibitions (Krüger 1987). As architecture critic Colin Rowe famously put it, the goals of the exhibition were simply too ambitious and resulted only in a "hostile examination of details" (1984: 93) rather than any real, workable solutions.

If one considers the goal of the IBA not in terms of architectural solutions, however, but primarily in terms of raising West Berlin's international profile, the exhibition was a resounding success. It brought much-needed positive attention to the city, along with an international roster of top-tier architectural talent. Every major Western architectural publication featured articles on the IBA and some did so twice, in the early 1980s when the exhibition was scheduled for 1984 and again in 1986–87. By virtue of the IBA as well as the 750-year celebration as a whole, West Berlin was once again at the center of significant architectural debates, and once again a center of institutionally recognized, as opposed to underground or protest-based culture. The IBA seemed to bring West Berlin out of the mire of its local politics, corruption, and infighting and into the international spotlight.

At the same time, the IBA, together with the jubilee celebration, helped to restore legitimacy to institutions of political and cultural power and thus provide a response to the critique of these institutions presented by the members of the alternative scene.[4] Throughout the 1960s and 1970s, West Berlin's well-publicized problems with government corruption and mass protests had left the impression that the West Berlin Senate was ineffectual, "foundering," and had lost control of the city (Nawrocki 1976). However in the wake of the 750-year celebration, the senate had done much to restore the faith of West Berliners, West Germans, and the world in its ability to govern the city successfully and without disenfranchising its citizens. West Berlin's political and architectural leaders had, it seemed, integrated the squatters' critique while at the same time regaining control of the urban space. Moreover, by acknowledging the squatters in such a grand and public fashion, the IBA had blunted the force of their critiques. For all these reasons, after the events of 1987, it could be once again argued that West Berlin represented mainstream Western values.

Obviously in terms of its main goal, the IBA was an attempt both to raise the city's public profile and to change housing policy. However, West Berlin's political importance in the context of the Cold War meant that the exhibition's function as an international public relations campaign ultimately overwhelmed local considerations. One telling detail in this regard is the fact that the IBA GmbH, the corporation formed to raise money for and execute the exhibition, was not authorized to make any changes to housing policy by, for example, reforming the process by which the government granted housing subsidies. According to architectural historian Wallis Miller, the city's housing administration "stood firmly between IBA GmbH and the developers, regulating the flow of concept into reality. . . . Responsibilities to produce an exhibition," she continues, "were not responsibilities to build subsidized housing" (Miller 1993: 207).

In part because of this administrative stricture, the IBA ultimately did not respond to many of the underlying issues that had spawned the housing crisis and the squatter movement, and thus many squatters viewed the exhibition as what one protest banner called "deception and capital-driven politics" (Bode 1987). Indeed, a number of West Berlin squats were throughout 1987 decked with similar anti-IBA banners, and protests of the IBA were held throughout the 1980s, in one instance disrupting a formal ceremony celebrating the exhibition (Hoffmann 1985; anon

1987: 11). Not only the IBA but the entire anniversary celebration was viewed with suspicion and derision by West Berlin's alternative scene, a fact that was clearly evident on 12 June 1987, when fifty thousand people filled the streets to protest Ronald Reagan's visit to the city and West Berlin's transformation into the "largest amusement park in the world" (Nawrocki 1987: 5).[5]

Such protests were, however, ultimately overwhelmed by the international significance of the celebration and of the city itself. For example, though tens of thousands of West Berliners protested his visit, Reagan's speech produced one of the most famous and lasting images of his presidency when, standing in front of the Berlin Wall at the Brandenburg Gate, he exhorted then-Soviet leader Mikhail Gorbachev to "tear down this wall." This widely publicized image, along with those of newly built and refurbished buildings, provided evidence of the IBA's and the anniversary's efficacy as international PR campaigns. However, one should note that to say that these events were primarily PR efforts is not simply to dismiss this as a shallow or unimportant goal. On the contrary, West Berlin's public image was an important part of its survival, since it was so dependent on West Germany's financial support as well as the military protection of the former Western Allies, and since securing such support meant fostering the perception that the exclave remained vital and important. Nonetheless it is also important to acknowledge West Berlin as a place that was not only internationally important, but that had its own unique local culture and politics, and in this way, to get beyond the notion of West Berlin as defined only by its governmentally and institutionally created urban image.

The IBA 87 was in many ways a microcosm of the city itself: both were supposed to be models or standards on a global scale, but in the end were special and unique, exceptions rather than rules. In fact, crucial to understanding any city is to understand this gap between the material reality of urban space and its ideological construction in the service of national identity or, as in the case of West Berlin, global political conflict. The example of the IBA reveals the tension within in a city that was a symbolic space and an ordinary town, one in which rubbish was collected. Both are key aspects of understanding West Berlin as it was and, indeed, united Berlin as it is today.

Notes

1. In addition to Nawrocki's and Krüger's, a host of other newspaper articles throughout the period predicted a dire future for West Berlin (anon. 1967; anon. 1978; Weis 1981). Similarly a

number of articles diagnosed West Berlin as suffering from an identity crisis (Weis 1976; Cleis 1981; Krupp 1986).
2. The term *deconstructivism* would not be coined until 1988 when an exhibition of the same name, which included IBA architects like Peter Eisenman, Zaha Hadid, and Daniel Libeskind, was held at the Museum of Modern Art in New York.
3. Designs for both Volkmann's and Valle's projects, as well as many of the IBA projects mentioned here, are included in Kleihues and Klotz 1986.
4. Paul Jaskot's discussion of the Jewish Museum in this volume provides a detailed account of one particularly interesting example wherein the IBA helped to shape the cultural institutions of West Berlin in the 1980s, and thus post-1990 Berlin.
5. An account in the *New York Times* puts the estimate of protesters far lower, in the twenty thousands (Schemann 1987).

Works Cited

anon. 1967. "West Berlin: Story of a City in Decline." *US News & World Report*, 4 December: 81–2.
anon. 1978. "Hauptstadt der Fixer." *Der Spiegel*, 2 January: 51–2.
anon. 1987. "Immobilien, Baukuhlen und Attrappen." *zitty*, October. Press Clipping, LArch Berlin B Rep 150/170.
Bode, Peter M. 1987. "Kreative Experimente kontra Spekulation." *Abendzeitung*, 29 January. Press Clipping, LArch Berlin B Rep 150/461.
Bodenschatz, Harald, Volker Heise, and Jochen Korfmacher. 1983. *Schluss mit Zerstörung? Stadterneuerung und städtische Opposition in West-Berlin, Amsterdam und London*. Giessen: Anabas.
Bruning, Fred. 1981. "Europe's Dead-End Kids." *Newsweek*, 27 April: 52–57.
Cleis, Andreas. 1981. "Westberlin auf der Suche nach neuer Identität." *Neue Zürcher Zeitung*, 6 October: 5.
Eisenman, Peter. 1987. "Das Symbol." In *Das Neue Berlin*: 86–90.
Engert, Jürgen 1981. "Ist Berlin noch eine deutsche Stadt? Jeder achte Berliner ist ein Ausländer." *Rheinischer Merkur*, 4 December: 3.
Görtemaker, Manfred. 2004. *Geschichte der Bundesrepublik Deutschland: Von der Gründung bis zur Gegenwart*. Frankfurt am Main: Fischer.
Gurtazch, Dankwart, ed. 1987. *Das Neue Berlin: Konzepte der Internationalen Bauausstellung 1987 für einen Städtebau mit Zukunft*. Berlin: Gebr. Mann.
Häußermann, Hartmut, and Elizabeth Strom. 1994. "Berlin: The Once and Future Capital." *International Journal of Urban and Regional Research* 18, no. 2: 335–46.
Hoffmann, Peter. "Report from West Berlin." 1985. *Architectural Record* 173 (Febr.): 67.
Kleihues, Josef Paul, and Heinrich Klotz, eds. 1986. *International Building Exhibition Berlin 1987: Examples of a New Architecture*. New York: Rizzoli.
Krüger, Karl-Heinz. 1983. "'Ich lerne langsam, dich zu hassen': Über den Niedergang von West-Berlin." *Der Spiegel*, 15 August: 36–53.
———. "Das Pathos endet an der Haustür." 1987. *Der Spiegel*, 1 June: 198–206.
Landesarchiv Berlin (LArch), B Rep 150: Organisationsbüro B 750.
Krupp, Hans-Jürgen 1986. "Berlin—Eine Stadt auf der Suche nach ihrer Wirtschaftlichen Identität." *Außenpolitik* 37: 327–41.
Mayer, Margit. 2000. "Social Movements in European Cities: Transitions from the 1970s to the 1990s." In *Cities in Contemporary Europe*, ed. Arnaldo Bangnasco and Patrick Le Gales, 131–52. Cambridge: Cambridge University Press.
Miller, Wallis. 1993. "IBA's 'Models for a City': Housing and the Image of Cold-War Berlin." *Journal of Architectural Education* 46, no. 4: 202–16.
Mulhak, Renate. 1983. "Der Instandbesetzungskonflikt in Berlin." In *Großstadt Und Neue Soziale Bewegungen*, ed. Peter Grottian and Wilfried Nelles, 205–52. Basel: Birkhäuser.

Nawrocki, Joachim. 1976. "Wird West-Berlin zum Hinterhof der Nation?" *Die Zeit*, 3 July: 3.
——. 1987. "Gewalt Zum Geburtstag." *Die Zeit*, 19 June: 5.
Page, Max. 2005. "Checkpoint Check Up." *Metropolis* (March).
Ribbe, Wolfgang. 2002. *Berlin 1945–2000: Grundzüge der Stadtgeschichte*, vol. 6, *Kleine Schriftenreihe der Historischen Kommission zu Berlin*, ed. Wolfgang Ribbe. Berlin: Berliner Wissenschafts-Verlag.
Rowe, Colin. 1984. "IBA: Rowe Reflects." *Architectural Review* 1076: 92–93.
Schemann, Serge. 1987. "24,000 Demonstrate in Berlin Against Reagan's Visit Today." *New York Times*, 12 June.
Schonlau, Manfred. 1987. "Die Berliner Wohnungsbauförderung." *Baumeister* 5 (May): 20–23.
Weis, Otto Jörg. 1976. "Identitätskrise einer Stadt." *Stuttgarter Zeitung*, 10 November: 1.
——. 1981. "Wohin man schaut: Nichts geht mehr." *Frankfurter Rundschau*, 3 September: 3.

PART FOUR

**Berlin After Unification:
Looking Back and Beyond**

Chapter 15

Stereographic City
Berlin Photography in the *Wende* Era

Miriam Paeslack

> In the process of considering place as an architectural artwork, we may be led to ask whether other artworks such as a painting, photograph, poem ... can also be a place—a virtual place. Isn't it true that we pause before them, rest in them, and are, in one sense of another, nurtured by them, as we rest and are nurtured by the towns and cities and landscapes we live in or visit? (Tuan 2004: 3)

In this essay I attempt to recreate the illusion of a stereographic three-dimensional space through a comparative reading of 1980s photography in West and East Berlin. The stereograph is photography's early invention of a 3-D viewer that simulates depth through two slightly misaligned identical images. Only by looking at these two images from a certain distance and with both our eyes open does our brain perceive three-dimensional space. The idea of the stereograph, which brings depth to two-dimensional imagery under conditions of correct viewing, thus translates into a more differentiated "three dimensional" understanding of pre-Wall Berlin. The goal of this essay is to bring such depth to a reading of Berlin by making visible the aesthetic and social-political differences of Berlin photography of the 1980s; but more importantly, by making visible the formal, aesthetic, and thematic suggestions of things that unite both views. Leaning on Clifford Geertz's anthropological concepts of "thin" and "thick" description, my analysis of the work of two Berlin photographers—one working in the East, the other in the West—during the 1980s aims at generating a "thick description" of life in divided Berlin through the idea of the stereograph (1973: 3–30). Understood as part of the same broader cultural network, these images, considered side by side, bring to life a city incredibly rich in cultural complexity. Yet they have commonly been discussed only from the perspective determined by the socially and politically opposite context of their creation. The notion of taking a stereographic view of Berlin incorporating views from both sides permits a renewed look at common perceptions of both the city and its imagery, and in so doing, underscores shared linguistic and cultural practices.

The stereographic image of East and West Berlin photography is not so much the result of similarities in subject matter—photographers captured people, traffic, and empty urban landscapes on both sides of the wall—but of the *mood* they convey. The locus of mood in the urban image is found here both in terms of form (the photograph, its formal qualities) and content (figures, scenarios, places); and in both cases can be variously indexed. The emotional and individual perceptions of the surroundings in East and West Berlin seem to both express notions of existential unsettledness and a stagnant sense of self, sharing a mood of upset and lacking a perspective for the future. Thus, as in the stereograph, they are emotionally "almost identical," but geopolitically "slightly misaligned." Retrospectively viewing photographs of East and West Berlin of the 1980s can result in a complex and three-dimensional image instead of a two-dimensional and dialectical one, which further reveals the social-political, cultural, and aesthetic gap between East and West.

Photographers educated in East Germany during the 1980s were trained with a strong focus on social documentary photography or reportage photography aiming at capturing the "decisive moment," a concept and practice popularized by French photographer Henri Cartier-Bresson.[1] The decisive moment for Cartier-Bresson was captured when "the eye cuts out a subject matter from [this] reality and the apparatus only needs to do its duty, to fix onto the surface of the film the eye's decision" (1999: 81). The job of the photographer in this process is to observe and capture reality with the camera, which Cartier-Bresson calls a "sketchbook," but not to manipulate it.

The photographer Helga Paris belongs to a group of photographers who remained true to this principle and to a body of work that since the mid-1960s depicted everyday life and ordinary people in the city. It is important to point out that during the 1970s, artists in East and West alike began exploring the documentation of performance and staged projects as photography expanded its scope beyond art photography, on the one hand, and photojournalism, on the other. Paris's work is representative of the large documentary fraction of photographers of her generation and is a notable example of an artist who, even though self-trained, fully absorbed the artistic and aesthetic discourses of her time, similar to her West German counterpart, Michael Schmidt.

The work of West German photographers who came to prominence during the 1970s and 1980s aesthetically embraced minimalism, conceptual approaches, and the documentation of performance. The Düsseldorf Art Academy photography professors Bernd and Hilla Becher's typological and conceptual documentations of industrial buildings had a tremendous impact on the next generation of photographers in the West. Even though their work also claims to be documentary, it lacks the journalistic, intuitive element in the vein of Cartier-Bresson. "In their abstracting representation of reality, due to the technical qualities of the photographic apparatus," the Becher school "created autonomous images almost completely detached from the subjective state of mind of its creator behind the camera." Unlike the immediacy of experience viewing a journalistic photograph, "it is only in the process of observing these images that they get reloaded with experiences and emotions and thus create new images and contextual connections" (Lange 2005: 85). The West German photographer Michael Schmidt, though not formally trained at an art school, reveals a similar "objective" approach to his subject matter and minimalist rigor in his formal composition. Schmidt began photographing in 1965, and is today considered one of the most important German photographers of the postwar generation.

Notwithstanding the significant conceptualizing differences in approaches to understanding photography, photographers in East and West did share experiences as well as aesthetic understanding of the urban image. In East Berlin, the urban chronicles of photographers from the 1970s to the early 1990s reflect the declining optimism and a retreat into psychological portrait studies and depictions of desolate urban landscapes. In the West, Michael Schmidt in his photo series and book *Berlin nach 45* (Berlin after '45) and some of his contemporaries turned their focus toward marginal sites at Berlin's city fringes or the Wall. In comparison to their East German colleagues with their humanistic eye, the Westerners do not focus on people but rather seem to avoid human traces in their photographs altogether. Despite, or maybe because of this existential challenge, one quality of photographs from East and West is particularly notable, namely, that they reflect a strong sense of place and address the city and the photographer's identification with it.

The different photographic manifestations of Berlin should not be understood literally or as a metaphor for the East-West polarity, but as a model to explain the complementarity of both sides. Rather than tracing aesthetic and political cross-fertilizations through what Greg Castillo in this volume has referred to as a diaphanous "nylon curtain," I am holding on to the two images of the stereograph for now at least, to eventually be able to sketch a full-fledged three-dimensional space of an urban condition in Berlin just before unification.

Paris's first politically critical photographic project is the reportage *Berliner Kneipen* (Berlin Pubs) in which she photographed the mixed crowd of regulars and occasional drop-ins in the traditional working-class pubs of Prenzlauer Berg.[2] The thematic focus of Paris's photographs is in part a response to pressure exerted on self-employed tradesmen and businessmen during the 1970s by the government to renounce their independence and be nationalized (Schube 2004: 14). Referring to the pub scenes, Inka Schube notes, "Paris sides with the owners of these institutions of informal get-togethers in a protective environment" (2004: 14). The safe climate is evoked in an image of a middle-aged woman in a local bar in East Berlin. Placed in the center of the picture frame, with fuzzy hair and a workingwoman's outfit, she shows us a bright smile, which is not put on for the camera but appears natural. The immediacy of the scene, the woman's casual comfort, and the smoke-filled backdrop of the pub, all communicate Paris's empathy for these people. This relationship between the photographer and the people photographed is one key prerequisite that marks Cartier-Bresson's work. He points out that "particularly in photographing people, there must be a relationship between the subject and the photographer, the *I* and the *you*, if the result is to be more than a superficial resemblance or likeness" (Newhall 1980: 283). Paris is one of them, and her camera frames an everyday life that is to disappear following the nationalization of pubs, resulting in its reorganization and subordination under a centralized party tutelage. Here we may begin to locate and define *mood* both in the formal characteristics of the image—grainy, determined by a strong black-and-white contrast, sometimes blurry in its spontaneous capture—and in the content where framing and the composition of figures puts the viewer into a place of intimacy with the subject. Mood is an expression of the photographer's experience of the urban condition and determined by a desire to conserve, and not merely the result of a personal interaction. These photographs generate a distinctive, emotionally charged, and at times weary image of the city as they focus on its inhabitants rather than on the urban structure.

It should be noted that photography in the GDR enjoyed a privileged position at least until the mid-1970s that allowed photographers more freedom of expression and was subject to less governmental scrutiny, particularly compared to the censorship visited upon fine artists, filmmakers, and writers.[3] The latter were more commonly exposed to state censorship and control (Flügge 2006: 11). However, Paris was by

Figure 15.1 Helga Paris, *Berliner Kneipen*. Courtesy of Helga Paris, Fotografien.

no means a revolutionary or an outspoken critic of the state. Nevertheless, one instance where Paris crossed the border and explicitly revealed her artistic independence from socialist realist doctrine was through her photo project in Halle/Saale, a medieval city in Saxony-Anhalt, which the GDR government systematically neglected and destroyed in order to make place for modern prefabricated housing. Paris's documentation of people and dilapidated buildings in the city attracted the party's disapproval and led to the closing down of an exhibition of that work a day before it was scheduled to open.[4] This event contributed to Paris's notoriety, a reputation she never intended to cultivate.

Berlin also held an aesthetic and phenomenological fascination for the West Berlin photographer Michael Schmidt. Schmidt founded the Werkstatt für Fotografie (Workshop for Photography) in Berlin's Kreuzberg district, which was to become an important place of transatlantic exchange, introducing for the first time young American photographers to Berlin. One phenomenon Schmidt introduced to his students was the New Topographics movement, a group of North American photographers such as Robert Adams, Lewis Baltz, Stephen Shore, and others who in the late 1960s and 1970s questioned the damage and degradation of landscapes. Schmidt's work clearly reflects the barren aesthetic of the New Topographics, which resonates very much with the approach of the West German Bechers who had been included in the New Topographics show. These images are all void of people, and instead of communicating a "decisive moment" they seem to allow an "insight about connections in reality without actually revealing them" (Lange 2005: 85), a feature photo historian Susanne Lange has detected in the Becher school's work.

One photograph, for example, in his publication *Berlin nach 45* (Berlin after '45) (Eskildsen 2005) was taken through a doorway in Kreuzberg, showing a direct view of the Berlin Wall. The strict symmetry and close composition—the doors practically framing the blocked view in the distance—makes this image appear hermetic, closed, and flat. The geometric abstractions of the square shapes of the doorway, the upper line of the Wall, and the concrete elements of the Wall convey a sense of containment.

Although Schmidt's attitude appears dispassionate, if not coldly analytical, photo historian Janos Frecot underscores Schmidt's reliance on his individual, subjective perception in his photographs when he quotes Schmidt saying, "One does not learn in the academy but from one's own

Figure 15.2 Michael Schmidt, *Wall*. Courtesy of Studio Michael Schmidt.

life experience" (Eskildsen 2005: 7). Even though Paris's and Schmidt's black-and-white photographs testify to a documentary language, neither is strictly speaking documentary. Documentary can be defined, according to Olivier Lugon, as showing the "desire to reveal 'things the way they are'" and providing "reliable, authentic information about them, avoiding any embellishment that might alter the integrity of reality" (Lugon 2005: 65). Instead both Schmidt's and Paris's photographs *interpret* "the city, its people, its stony forms and voids" (Eskildsen 2005: 8). Schmidt encapsulates in his photographs and their narrative sequences a "connection between historical memory and a search for evidence in the picture" (Eskildsen 2005: 9). His photographs do not speak of history directly, but *transform* history into pictorial form.

Two artistic approaches and subject matters, which at first sight seemed to derive from two diametrically opposed poles, turn out to share an element of identification, of attachment, and of similar emotional involvement with the city. Each, influenced by a cultural and aesthetic environment, shares a desire to maintain and document what is about to change. Both articulate their state of mind in a sober black-and white aesthetic language, but are rather emotional about, and attached to, their subject matter. Here the two slightly misaligned images of the stereograph align and build a fully-fledged three-dimensional space. This space is constituted by the mood of its creators. It presents the whole city of Berlin as a space shared by people equally concerned about the city's state during the 1980s, namely, its transformation, decay, and state of division.[5]

After reunification, Paris and Schmidt's interpretive documentary focus is replaced by image strategies that often engage more conceptually with Berlin. But instead of conceptual explorations of the nature of the city or socially engaged documentation, they assert new uses of photography to confront shifting identities, to preserve what is lost, and to challenge the assumption of the representability of the city as such. Photographers demonstrate different degrees of identification with Berlin and translate subjective experiences as well as more theoretical reflections about the city into images, for example by appropriating family snapshots in Berlin to make conceptual connections to the past or by photographing seemingly random sites in Berlin and arranging them into an ever-rearranged stream of images on an interactive CD-ROM. The radius of reflection now expands into the past and future as photographers incorporate historical material in their reflection on Berlin as well as project a sense of uncertainty about the shape of the reunited city in the future.

This new post-Wall consciousness is palpable in the work of two artists that have focused on Berlin in several projects. One is the East Berlin–born photographer Wiebke Loeper. *Lad*, Loeper's photo book, is composed of her own and her father's photographs. It is the result of the artist's visits to the site of her childhood in East Berlin. West German–born Elisabeth Neudörfl's interactive CD-ROM *Der Stadt* abstracts immediate urban experience into an unidentifiable flow of Berlin images and was photographed in both the former East and West Berlin.

Wiebke Loeper takes a retrospective, yet not sentimental perspective in her photo book *Lad* (1997), in which she appropriates mementos from her father's color slide collection of the 1970s, taken in the apartment in which she grew up. She then combines them with her own photographs and a biographical text. This project, completed in 1997, is a reflection on the artist's East Berlin home during a time just months before its demolition. What was a form of personal documentation about Berliners in Helga Paris's pubs is transformed here into a study of belonging and things past. While both artists are concerned with the past, Paris defines herself as profoundly shaped by the history of World War II and of the GDR, while Loeper addresses this identity-forming importance of history directly in her photographic work.

Another theme both East German–born artists share is the distinction between inner and outer life, interior and exterior. Paris suggests with her intimate studies of the life in Prenzlauer Berg's pubs that they are sacred places protected from governmental interference, but also threatened by their control. The necessity to segment inner and outer life is a central issue in Loeper's work.[6] The main focus of her project is the apartment and its immediate surroundings, her mother's presence there, and the memories triggered by the coloring of furniture, carpeting, and curtains. The interiors emerge as potent indices of the East Berliner's state of mind. They function as emotional microcosms in contrast to the mood of urban life outside, beyond the familial and circle of friends. One interior, a family snapshot in color that echoes the intimacy of Paris's pub photographs, is titled "My Mother at the Dining Table, Berlin 1971." It shows a set table in the foreground; modern, white furniture; corn-colored mashed potatoes on the table; and, from the depth of the room, a happily smiling young blonde—Loeper's mother. Everything in this photo suggests harmony and comfort.

The sense of security evoked in "My Mother at the Dining Table" is contrasted by another indoor shot taken by her father, of a young Wiebke on the occasion of her first day in elementary school. This photograph, although also an interior shot, captures a scene outside the familiar. It bears memories for Loeper, but unlike the one of the apartment, triggers ambivalence, if not discomfort. Young Pioneers, and second graders, are giving a presentation on the school's stage. The background is decorated

Figure 15.3 Wiebke Loeper, *Lad*. Courtesy of Studio Wiebke Loeper.

with the GDR's national emblem, the golden hammer and compass on red ground. In her text, Loeper comments on the intensity with which the state structured and controlled the lives of children. Here the interior embodies the tight grip of the socialist government. But she is careful to separate personal memories from historic accounts and statistics. Instead of creating a sentimental memento mori with *Lad,* she writes about the clear separation between "inner and outer world" during her life in the GDR, a phenomenon that has always fascinated her:

> The outer world of the school, the newspapers, posters, and of anything official in general, was only a part of my life. It was, however, determined by a threateningly large power. In this outer world, there were nevertheless people I liked a lot. They were the bridge between outer and inner world. The inner world, of parents and friends, was the real one for me. Nothing threatened this world in my view up until my elementary school enrollment. (Loeper 1997: 29)

The outer world, the city, and the "official life" thus is not perceived as real; it is highly mediated and its reading occupied by an official agenda.

In contrast to this focus on interiority and unlike this autobiographical project, Elisabeth Neudörfl's work, *Der Stadt* (Of the City, 1995–1998) addresses the contested, inhospitable urban space that resists identification. Comprised of 150 black-and-white photographs of Berlin (originally small format, then scanned and archived), displayed in a continuous band of images, *Der Stadt* is not a printed work, but accessible onscreen

Figure 15.4 Wiebke Loeper, *Lad.* Courtesy of Studio Wiebke Loeper.

through an interactive CD-ROM, which removes it further from the viewer's grasp than a book would. Identification with this Berlin is further obstructed by the fact that despite its frieze-like structure, this interactive work defies narrative reading. The sequence of images is programmed to run randomly, giving the work its particular navigation. Moving the cursor onto the frieze, the viewer can determine the speed, stop the stream of images, move upward and downward, or zoom into and enlarge sections of individual photographs. The observer can thus maneuver independently throughout the city images, though any attempt to return to an image already viewed results in a complete resequencing of the images. This structural inability to go back to previous images in this work evokes forms of inaccessibility also found in Schmidt's Berlin images. However, while Schmidt clearly indicated where he documented the city, enabling the viewer to follow his steps, Neudörfl's post-Wall narrative presents a new form of inaccessibility, one of disorientation, as it removes all local references, contexts, or signs of an identifiable historical period.

Der Stadt reveals Berlin to be a place of fragmentation, of transition, of disorientation. Its photographs depict Berlin in a variety of locations, times, and seasons: new dwellings, old inner-city streets, parks, construction sites, traffic, day and night, summer and winter. The city coalesces into a strange network, a system of pathways in space and time, in which the movements of the photographer are not retraceable. In contrast to Loeper, who gives the viewer access to the city through her own narrative, her interior spaces and interior life, Neudörfl provides no point of

Figure 15.5 Elisabeth Neudörfl, *Der Stadt*. Courtesy of Studio Elisabeth Neudörfl.

reference or identification whatsoever. Neudörfl's city dwellers are restless nomads, and as viewers, we embody their very experience as we are left without guidance through the continually reshuffled imagery: the script of our path throughout Berlin confines the viewer to random hits and undermines our desire as viewers to take a closer look at an image and revisit a particular site. Loeper's Berliners are at least provided with a historically anchoring narrative. But in order to understand Neudörfl's goal with this project, it needs to be asked if this is in fact about the identification with a particular city or not rather a reflection on contemporary urban experience as such. The latter seems to be the case as a younger generation of post-Wall photographers does not have the same feeling of being rooted in Berlin as did their predecessors, and it employs its medium in media-reflexive rather than documentary ways.

However, Loeper and Neudörfl both clearly relate to their predecessors' urban image-making impulses in the formerly divided city. Loeper's and her father's images recreate the historical and contemporary site of her childhood. This project as well as Paris's is born out of a classic impulse of the journalistic or snapshot photographer: to preserve and remember. Neudörfl's piece echoes the serial approach of Bernd and Hilla Becher; only that it turns their intention—to archive and to make comparable—ad absurdum. This tactic generates a profoundly different understanding of Berlin in comparison to Schmidt's work and identifies Neudörfl's allegiance to the New Topographics approach of neutral, critical, analytical detachment.

The concept of stereography outlined through a comparison of the photographic works discussed above proves to be useful for recognizing the shared themes and logics of Berlin photography's pre-Wall history. But unlike earlier methods of comparative art historical analysis and pedagogy such as Heinrich Wöllflin's slide comparison, the stereograph helps detect more than formal and stylistic differences as it presupposes the two images' belonging together. Wöllflin's slide comparison abstracted the image from its context in order to view mostly formal similarities, and was driven by an art-historical consciousness that believed in a continuum and in a linear advancement in art making. The idea of Berlin photography of the 1980s as a stereographic phenomenon allows an interdisciplinary viewing of images. It sheds light on the complexities of a city that cannot be defined by political polarities and different cultural and aesthetic approaches to image making and consumption alone. Berlin's urban condition and cultural production at the time resisted—and still resists—any such willful analysis.

Notes

1. Henri Cartier-Bresson (1908–2007) was the cofounder of the photo agency Magnum Photos together with Robert Capa, Davis Seymor, and George Rodger. His first monograph was called "The Decisive Moment" and was published in 1952.
2. Some of these photographs are published in the 2004 exhibition catalogue *Helga Paris: Fotografien*, edited by Inka Schube.
3. Art historian Matthias Flügge points out that "the guardians of a socialism distinguished by an almost religious veneration of words were slow to recognize photography as being art and long—one might say fortunately here—underestimated its power of shaping people's consciousness and awareness" (2006: 11).
4. Paris was rehabilitated and the show reopened only in 2006 and was accompanied by the catalogue *Diva in Grau: Häuser und Gesichter in Halle*.
5. Even though Schmidt's *Berlin nach 45* is void of people, he does not exclude people in his photographs on principle. For example *Waffenruhe* (Cease Fire) is a project and publication that focused on young people in Berlin Wedding during the 1980s.
6. This emphasis on the interior is a romantic visual, literary, and philosophical motif found in the German concept of *Innerlichkeit*, which refers to both *inwardness* and *interiority*, and is typically used in conjunction with early nineteenth-century literary turns toward themes of individual sensibility.

Works Cited

Bartsch, Wilhelm, Heinz Czechowski, Elke Erb, and Jörg Kowalski, eds. 2006. *Helga Paris, Diva in Grau: Häuser und Gesichter in Halle*. Halle/Saale: Mitteldeutscher Verlag.
Cartier-Bresson, Henri. 1999. "Der entscheidende Augenblick." In *Theorie der Fotografie III 1945–1980*, ed. Wolfgang Kemp, 78–82. Munich: Schirmer/Mosel.
Eskildsen, Ute, ed. 2005. *Michael Schmidt, Berlin nach 45*. With an essay by Janos Frecot. Munich: Steidl.
Flügge, Matthias, ed. 2006. *Sibylle Bergemann: Photographien*. Berlin: Akademie der Künste.
Geertz, Clifford. 1973. *The Interpretation of Cultures: Selected Essays*. New York: Basic Books.
Lange, Susanne. 2005. *Was wir tun, ist letztlich Geschichten erzählen . . . Bernd und Hilla Becher Einführung in Leben und Werk*. Munich: Schirmer/Mosel.
Loeper, Wiebke. 1997. *Lad*. Leipzig: Hochschule für Grafik und Buchkunst.
Lugon, Olivier. 2005. "'Documentary': Authority and Ambiguities." In *Documentary Now! Contemporary Strategies in Photography, Film and the Visual Arts*. Rotterdam: Nai Publishers. Reflect #04. 64–73.
Newhall, Beaumont. 1980. "Vision Plus the Camera: Henri Cartier-Bresson 1946." In *Photography: Essays & Images*, ed. Beaumont Newhall, 283–87. New York: The Museum of Modern Art.
Schmidt, Michael, and Einar Schlef. 1987. *Waffenruhe*. Berlin: Berlinische Galerie, Fotografische Sammlung, in association with Dirk Nishen Verlag.
Schube, Inka, ed. 2004. *Helga Paris: Fotografien*. Berlin: Holzwarth.
Tuan, Yi-Fu. 2004. *Place, Art, and Self*. Santa Fe: Center for American Places.
Warner Marien, Mary. 2002. *Photography: A Cultural History*. New York: Prentice Hall.

CHAPTER 16

Divided City, Divided Heaven?
Berlin Border Crossings in Post-*Wende* Fiction

Lyn Marven

Since the Berlin Wall came down, it has been recreated and remembered as much within fiction in retrospective depictions of divided Berlin as it has been preserved or memorialized within the city itself. This essay examines how texts written about pre-*Wende* Berlin since the fall of the Wall use the motif of crossing the border to depict the divided city. Border crossings represent and recall the symbolic Wall, Brian Ladd's term for the always intangible political border, in the absence of the material Wall.[1] Texts considered here evoke the significance of the political symbolic border rather than the sight of the concrete division, but often do so by emphasizing the physical experience of the crossing.

At once traumatic gap and link between the two halves of the city, the crossing both divides and unites; moreover, in these contemporary texts, it bridges past and present. I concentrate on three aspects: first, texts that represent Berlin as united even while still divided by focusing on the topography of the city, or by depicting the border as intrusive; Irina Liebmann, Monika Maron, and Emine Sevgi Özdamar illustrate the ambivalent function of the border and challenge the political division in retrospect. Secondly, representations of the border as an aporia, a traumatic gap in the memory of crossing and, latterly, in the city's rewritten history, which occur in texts by Liebmann and Julia Franck. Finally, images of the sky over Berlin, which illustrates that the inner city–interstate border is literally ungrounded and immaterial: both Liebmann and Özdamar refer to this literary-historical motif, as does Antje Rávic Strubel's hijack novel *Tupolew 134* in which the sky is the medium of crossing from one side to another.

These texts serve as a reminder that the border, never merely synonymous with the Wall, was porous as well as historically contingent. Subject to conditions and restrictions, West Berliners (like Sven Regener's Herr Lehmann), West Germans like the agent who attempts to help Strubel's hijackers escape, and foreigners such as Özdamar's autobiographical protagonists were still allowed into the GDR; a privileged few East Germans, like Liebmann and Maron, were also able to travel to the West. While these largely West-to-East visits were temporary—the protagonist of Kerstin Hensel's *Falscher Hase* (Meatloaf) is a rare exception who moves East to live, just before the Wall goes up—others crossed permanently from East to West legally as refugees (Franck's protagonists) or illegally (Strubel's hijackers).

Texts written since the fall of the Wall and reunification (the *Wende*) stress the unity of Berlin's topography both in the fabric of the city and through figures who cross from one side to the other, sometimes permanently, sometimes temporarily. In Irina Liebmann's autobiographical novel *In Berlin* (1994), the protagonist *the Liebmann* leaves East Berlin for West Berlin in 1988 to pursue a relationship, only to return repeatedly, and cross back again permanently after the Wall comes down. The text uses the Berlin transport system as an index of change since the *Wende*. Remembering an earlier journey to West Berlin on a day visa, the text retrospectively imposes what would be a normal post-*Wende* journey five stops along the S-Bahn line onto the divided city: "She was standing at the border crossing by seven in the morning, Friedrichstrasse station, the departure hall was empty, black slushy snow outside, at Savignyplatz station she got out, the station was the property of the GDR, dirty, normal in other words" (Liebmann 2002: 142–43). Even during the division, the transport system continued to connect both halves, albeit not as seamlessly. Liebmann emphasizes the presence of the GDR in West Berlin, extending via the S-Bahn that also links the two syntactically: she travels from Friedrichstrasse to Savignyplatz, East to West Berlin, within one sentence.[2] Liebmann's text ends by imagining a journey from Schönefeld, formerly the airport for East Berlin, across Berlin by S-Bahn shortly after reunification, reuniting the two halves through this movement: "If you want you can go from Schönefeld to Zoo [station], if you don't get out you will see the whole of Berlin" (Liebmann 2002: 174).

Like Liebmann—it may be significant that both are from the former GDR—Monika Maron's autobiographical essay "Geburtsort Berlin" (Place of Birth Berlin, 2003) emphasizes the unity of Berlin's topography. Maron does so in two ways: first, by portraying border crossings as impositions upon the city that force inhabitants into labyrinthine journeys: recalling a rare visit West, "It took me an hour and a half to go by tram to Friedrichstrasse, from there by S-Bahn to Wollankstrasse, to arrive where I set out, in Pankow: more precisely, ten meters beyond Pankow" (Maron 2003: 64). Such detours recur in texts challenging the validity of the border; the Wall becomes ridiculous as an obstacle within the city that nonetheless cannot prevent movement from East to West. In Thomas Brussig's *Helden wie wir* (Heroes Like Us, 1995) the opening of the Wall on 9 November 1989 is depicted as merely undoing the extreme "diversion via the Czech-West German border" (Brussig 2001: 314–15) to get from one part of Berlin to the other. Emine Sevgi Özdamar also presents the border as entailing unnecessary detours, in this case because of the divisive regulations about who was allowed to cross at which checkpoint; while she, as a foreigner, could cross into East Berlin at Checkpoint Charlie, her friend Peter has to go over at Heinrich-Heine-Strasse only to rejoin her on the other side.

Maron's text portrays as absurd, and thus also, in retrospect, unsustainable, the division that cuts through individual streets and separates Prenzlauer Berg from its identical "twin" Kreuzberg. She stresses the physical similarity of the different halves of the city: "I can remember vividly an earlier night during a car ride through Kreuzberg when I suddenly caught sight of a junction that was the identical twin of a junction in Prenzlauer Berg, and then I thought I recognized Warschauer Strasse and really understood for the first time in fact that the two halves of the city were part of a whole, that their parts belonged to the same body" (Maron 2003: 70–73).

Here Maron infers a concrete belonging-together that is emphasized by the description of the city as a (single) body. The passage continues: "At night, when darkness swallowed the colors and only the grey-black contours of the lines of the streets and the silhouettes of the houses stood out in the dark, the city revealed what had remained hidden from me during the day under the intact facades, the bright billboards, and behind the magnificent arrangements in shop windows" (Maron 2003: 73). Nighttime, another key trope in representations of the city, reveals that the East lies under the West; like Liebmann, Maron's unification of the city, effected through the text, posits an expansion of the East into the West, suggesting too that the former East Berlin survives under the expanded West.

Emine Sevgi Özdamar's Berlin texts present the crossings from a deliberately naive outsider's perspective; as a Turkish immigrant, she is granted an atypical view of the city from both sides. *Seltsame Sterne starren zur Erde* (Strange Stars Stare Toward Earth), subtitled "Wedding–Pankow 1976/77," is a fictionalized account of her time living in West Berlin and working at the Volksbühne; her daily commute from West to East on a twenty-four-hour pass recalls in reverse the pre-Wall days when many workers, known as *Grenzgänger* (border crossers), lived in the East while working in the West. The narrator links the two halves through her person: conversations are carried on across the border through her, and "West Berlin problems are solved in East Berlin" (Özdamar 2003: 181). In keeping with the narrator's deliberately naive political stance, her decisions to cross the border are idiosyncratic, personal, and often spur-of-the-moment. Her first trip into the East is an attempt to get away from dogs barking in the yard. The weight of detail in the long description of the journey that follows belies the apparent casualness of the decision, however, and as Margaret Littler has demonstrated, barking dogs are far from a random detail, but rather symbolic of the Nazi past that haunts the narrator in West Berlin (Littler 2007: 184).

The whole premise of Özdamar's text is the proximity of East and West, and the sheer frequency of her border crossings at Friedrichstrasse normalizes them; the length of descriptions decreases with familiarity to the point that she no sooner thinks about crossing than is there: "I thought it would be better to go to East Berlin. There I walked around on Unter den Linden for a while" (Özdamar 2003: 164). At the same time, however, she also portrays the division as insuperable: "I could never picture the two halves together and imagine that my seven friends in West Berlin only lived three stops away from here. It would have taken twenty minutes on foot" (Özdamar 2003: 18). For the narrator, whose perspective is limited to 1976–77, reunification is unthinkable. Laura Bradley suggests, "The narrator's position as an outsider allows her to observe life in East Berlin with a detachment that may not be so far removed from that of a post-*Wende* reader" (Bradley 2007: 288). With respect to the border then, her inability to imagine that changes might occur mirrors a post-*Wende* inability to imagine the now overcome division, in contrast to Liebmann and Maron.

While Özdamar and others such as Julia Franck in *Lagerfeuer* (Campfire, 2003) depict border crossings in extreme detail, many contemporary texts portray it rather as a traumatic gap. Descriptions of border crossings resemble trauma in several ways: trauma is inaccessible to memory and cannot be integrated into a narrative of the past; it exists as a blank, registered belatedly, or returning as surprisingly literal flashbacks. Liebmann repeatedly refers to the border as "the border hole" (*Grenzloch*); and literary effects can signal the narrative aporia as in Özdamar's subtitle "Wedding–Pankow 1976–77." The em-dash separates as well as binds; it screens the fact of crossing while also drawing attention to that elision.

In Liebmann's text, changes in tense depict this traumatic effect. When the character Liebmann first leaves for West Berlin, the narrative shifts from reporting her thoughts in the present tense into the future. The shift in tense represents the protagonist's anticipation and impatience, and the dissociative, dislocated experience. The future tense describes what will happen—imputing knowledge to the past—and the narrative then moves on as if what is described has already happened: "will see her daughter opening her mouth because the train doors are slowly shutting—we're off!" (Liebmann 2002: 77). The moment of crossing in the present is elided. It is the border that is inassimilable and unrepresentable, not just when leaving the GDR; journeys back into East Berlin from the West are similarly traumatic:

> All of a sudden she cried, shouted and stood up, the glass sign with Eisenacher Strasse on it was lit up already as she ran down the steps to the underground, the train came as always, then suddenly the border, the passport control booths, then everything pitch black, on foot past a hoarding, warm air, heard a tram screech and then saw it too, it stopped right in front of her, a man flung open the door from inside and yelled at her, and she realized then where she was: Invalidenstrasse (Liebmann 2002: 133).

In the shock of passing, the border is registered as a blackout both realistic and symbolic; the crossing registers belatedly with the reader, too, on the realization that the character has accomplished the complicated journey from Eisenacher Strasse in West Berlin to Invalidenstrasse in East Berlin within one sentence.

Two texts by Julia Franck also depict the border as a gap: in the short story, "Hausfreund" (Family Friend), told from a child's perspective, two sisters sleep while their mother and her lover drive out of East Berlin on 1 May. The difficulties of the political transit are elided in the child's viewpoint, who does not realize the significance of the unknown sights of West Berlin: "Tempelhof, Marienfelde. No idea where that is" (Franck 2002: 101). The impact of the text derives from reader's knowledge to fill in the gaps—which in this case also equate to the literal gaps on GDR maps of Berlin, where West Berlin was left blank. Franck's novel *Lagerfeuer* portrays a family escaping (as Franck's own family did) from East to West across Berlin. The refugee camp Marienfelde becomes an extension of the no-man's land, the inbetweenness of the border (Grätz 2006: 247, 251); in the course of the novel, the family never actually "arrives" in the West. Quite how much the border and what is beyond remains unknown is indicated in the chapter title for their border crossing, "Nelly Senff Crosses a Bridge" (Franck 2003: 7). The title refuses and ironizes the political significance of the border by designating it as merely a bridge, but for Nelly the indefinite article also designates an unknown: Nelly does not even know what is underneath the Bornholmer Bridge, which crosses train tracks, not water as she believes.

Since Christa Wolf's *Der geteilte Himmel* (Divided Heaven, 1963) at least, the sky has represented symbolically the arbitrary, unnatural, and porous nature of the border in Berlin. Wolf's text also contains two gaps that refuse the representation of the border: not only Rita's blackout (or suicide attempt) on hearing the news of the Wall going up, but also, crucially, her journey back from West Berlin, a point of intensity in the text, is a blur to Rita herself and obscured in the narrative: "She must have gone through the barrier and up the stairs then. She must have taken a train that took her to the right station. . . . She didn't sleep, but she wasn't fully conscious. The first thing she noticed after a long time was a bright, still pool in the dark countryside" (Wolf 1973: 188).

As Almut Hille notes, the Berlin sky was perceived ambivalently as both divided and shared (the two senses of the German *teilen*), but retained a utopian potential for border crossings. Historically the border was particularly porous by air, with balloons and sound carrying across (cf. Gröschner and Stange). More prosaically, the weather recurs as a motif in Özdamar's Berlin texts: "So by day I lived in East Berlin at the theater, and at night I returned to West Berlin to Kati and Theo. Every time when I came out of the underground I was amazed: 'Ah, so it snowed here in the West, too. Ah, so it rained here too'" (Özdamar 2001: 57). Pan Am flights above Pankow in Liebmann's *In Berlin* demonstrate that airspace cannot be divided as on the ground: flight patterns of necessity destabilize the border. As a result, the view from the air allows a glimpse of a whole city: "On the return flight to Tegel she sees the whole of Berlin for the first time. First the concrete wall, strip of land, floodlights, then a landscape of roofs, red. . . . PAN AM flying lower, dipping left and then right, now over East Berlin, West Berlin, border, she stares and stares at the image below, the diamond, the form underneath it all" (Liebmann 2002: 92–93).

Airspace constitutes the contested political border in Antje Rávic Strubel's novel about a real 1978 hijacking, *Tupolew 134* (2004). Here the East-West border above Berlin is crossed by a plane en route from Gdansk to Schönefeld and forcibly diverted to Tempelhof in West Berlin; the border crossing is a flight in both senses. The novel presents the prehistory of the escape, the events leading up to the hijacking on 30 August, and the trial of the two protagonists Lutz and Katja; the self-conscious narration is fragmented into multiple strands headed "down below" (*ganz unten*), "below," and "above." Strubel's hijackers are caught between the West's historical encouragement of dissidents to flee the communist East, thereby refusing to recognize the border, and its new antiterrorist measures in wake of the Mogadishu hijacking in 1977, which proscribed certain forms of border crossing. *Tupolew 134* also invokes the literary history of divided Berlin in allusions to *Der geteilte Himmel*.

This most audacious of border crossings combines the two aspects already discussed: the view from above allows the whole city to be seen, while the uncertain location of the border in the air makes the crossing an aporia. When hijacker Lutz sees the city from the cockpit, it is evoked as a body—the same motif used by Maron to emphasize its indivisibility:

> 'Like a scar. A huge great scar.'
>
> 'You won't see that on the ground.'
>
> He was standing behind the pilot's back, next to a row of instruments, levers and buttons. He was standing by the left-hand window, and when he stood back he saw himself reflected in the window pane, and if he came closer he could make out the border below, undeveloped, mined land, and a light stretch which was the wall. (Strubel 2006:159)

The border is a scar, a reminder of a wound that in fact knits the body of the city together. Moreover the superimposition of Lutz's own reflected figure on the image of the city through the window links the two. While Liebmann highlights the view of the whole city, it is the paradoxically invisible border that Strubel focuses on: from above it can be seen, whereas on the ground it is the Wall that must embody and make it visible.

Crossing the invisible border in the air leads to uncertainty: Lutz and the hostage stewardess can only guess when they have traveled into Western airspace—or the sky above the West: "We must be over the border already," says the stewardess to Schaper. "Then we're in the West," he replies (Strubel 2006:158). The double sense of the German *über* as "above" *and* "beyond" (*over* in both English senses) neatly encapsulates their position. Both Lutz and the stewardess register the border only after having crossed it: this belatedness suggests a traumatic gap, an impact only evident in retrospect, and emphasized further when they land. Like Franck's Nelly and her delayed arrival through Marienfelde refugee camp, those on board are still in limbo until they officially enter the West, signaled by extended use of the pluperfect: "When the airplane had landed and had come to a standstill on the outskirts and the military vehicles were already on their way, but hadn't reached the aircraft yet, it had been very quiet on board. No-one had said anything. No-one had stood up. The turbines were shut down" (Strubel 2006: 274). Most of the other passengers return to the GDR.

Strubel's novel invites comparison with Christa Wolf's *Der geteilte Himmel* in several ways: through its factory setting in the GDR, the love triangle implicated in the border crossing, and, of course, through the symbolism of the sky. In Wolf's novel, the (prior) division of the sky is invoked as the justification for the division on the ground, sealed by the construction of the Wall: "'At least they can't divide up the sky,' Manfred said mockingly. The sky? This whole arc of hope and desire, of love and sorrow? 'They can,' she said quietly. 'The sky splits first of all.'" (Wolf 1973: 187). By this same logic, Strubel's novel and her hijacker protagonists refute the validity of the political division by overcoming it in the air, though once on the ground the exigencies of political division are reasserted.

The two texts also share iconic motifs of space flight: in Wolf's text, Yuri Gagarin's flight into space in early 1961 is a symbol of hope, a utopian technological image that counters the politicization of the heavens and the reality on the ground, as well as functioning as a reminder of the space race and the East's role in the Cold War. Strubel's text refers to the cosmonaut Sigmund Jähn, whose space flight took place days before the hijacking. Jähn orbited the Earth from 26 August 1978 to 3 Sept 1978; the first citizen from either FRG or GDR in space, he symbolized GDR pride, but also transcended division, being seen by both sides simply as German.[3]

The contemporary narrative perspective of the text is posited as extraterrestrial—in the final fragment of the text it is labeled "überirdisch"—which does not connote superiority, rather a distance that undermines realism. The description of photos of Germany taken from space during Jähn's flight—"They were photographed so precisely that none of the photos resembled the originals" (Strubel 2006: 70)—is echoed by the narrative perspective: "Even from here, on high, you can't get a full view. There are details, some are better illuminated, the rest stays in the dark" (Strubel 2006: 87). Despite being based on real events, Strubel's text does not aim at realism, but rather undermines the reliability of memory through the trial narrative thread and emphasizes the liberties of fiction. In this refusal to fix a version of events, it is a challenge to the certainties of narratives about division.

All of these texts employ unfamiliar perspectives and stories to reshape the history of division, between East and West, German and non-German, above and below. Liebmann's visits to the West were far from the norm; Özdamar's Turkish perspective contrasts with German experiences; Strubel's protagonists are exceptional and criminal. They highlight the personal against the political background of the Cold War division, and expand the German-German, inner-Berlin border crossing to include the international dimension of this global frontier.

Katharina Grätz suggests that depictions of border crossings and the Wall have in fact increased since 1989 (2006: 244), while Dennis Tate suggests that continued depictions represent "in the broader psychological sense of the term, a border-crossing agenda which is still a long way from being resolved" (2004: 101). The aspects examined here—retroactive (re-)unification; the border as an absence in text and memory, and the division of sky and earth—suggest that the interpretation of the border, and with it, the division of the city, is still at stake. Border crossings retain their traumatic impact within the narrative of Berlin. Although these texts *do* depict crossings at times in detail, they also suggest that division remains a problematic memory, that the concrete history cannot be confronted directly; hyperdetailed accounts like Franck's are as much a symptom of trauma as narrative aporia. Images of border crossings thus represent the ambiguity of retrospective views of Berlin: these texts recall the difficulties of the pre-*Wende* division, in danger of being lost as the city knits itself back together, and as contentious GDR memory is marginalized, while also implicitly writing into the past—and thereby affirming—the future reunification of the city. Although the border is largely erased from the contemporary form of the city itself, then, it is nonetheless preserved in the intensity of affect in literature; as Maron writes: "In the meantime the severed connections between the two halves have long since been reconnected and the center of the city belongs to everyone once more. But still when I cross over one of the lines where the Wall once stood a strange feeling comes over me" (2003: 73).

Notes

1. "Most of the hundred miles of border fortifications remained largely intact for months. What had disappeared, rather, was the symbolic Wall—which meant that the concrete and the symbol were no longer the same thing" (Ladd 1997: 10).
2. Compare Özdamar's reference to West stations, the so-called ghost train stations, "left behind" in the East (Özdamar 2001: 57).
3. Jähn plays a similar uniting function in Wolfgang Becker's film *Goodbye Lenin!*

Works Cited

Bradley, Laura. 2007. "Recovering the Past and Capturing the Present: Özdamar's *Seltsame Sterne starren zur Erde.*" In *New German Literature: Life-Writing and Dialogues with the Arts,* ed. Julian Preece, Frank Finlay, and Ruth J. Owen, 283–95. Oxford: Peter Lang.
Brussig, Thomas. 2001. *Helden wie wir.* Frankfurt am Main: Fischer.
Franck, Julia. 2002. "Der Hausfreund." In *Bauchlandung.* Munich: dtv. 89–101.
———. 2005. *Lagerfeuer.* Munich: dtv.
Grätz, Katharina. 2006. "Das Andere hinter der Mauer: Retrospektive Grenzkonstruktion und Grenzüberschreitung in Julia Francks *Lagerfeuer* und Wolfgang Hilbigs *Das Provisorium.*" In *Wende des Erinnerns? Geschichtskonstruktionen in der deutschen Literatur nach 1989,* ed. Barbara Beßlich, Katharina Grätz, and Olaf Hildebrand, 243–57. Berlin: Erich Schmidt.
Gröschner, Annett. 1998. "'Wie geht's, Ihr Ostsäcke?' Westberlinerinnen, Westberliner und Luftballons zu Besuch an der Mauer." In *Grenzgänger. Wunderheiler. Pflastersteine,* ed. Annett Gröschner, Stefan Orendt, Bernd Roder, 223–53. Berlin: Basis Druck.

Hille, Almut. 2006. "Suche nach der Gegenwart: Ost-West-Berlin in literarischen Texten der Migration." In *Weltfabrik Berlin: Eine Metropole als Sujet der Literatur,* ed. Matthias Harder and Almut Hille, 239–56. Würzburg: Königshausen & Neumann.

Ladd, Brian. 1997. *The Ghosts of Berlin: Confronting German History in the Urban Landscape.* Chicago: University of Chicago Press.

Liebmann, Irina. 2002. *In Berlin.* Berlin: Berlin Taschenbuch.

Littler, Margaret. 2007. "Cultural Memory and Identity Formation in the Berlin Republic." In *Contemporary German Fiction: Writing in the Berlin Republic,* ed. Stuart Taberner, 177–95. Cambridge: Cambridge University Press.

Maron, Monika. 2003. "Geburtsort Berlin." In *Geburtsort Berlin,* 49–75. Frankfurt am Main: Fischer.

Özdamar, Emine Sevgi. 2001. "Mein Berlin." In *Der Hof im Spiegel,* 55–61. Cologne: Kiepenheuer & Witsch.

———. 2003. *Seltsame Sterne starren zur Erde: Wedding–Pankow 1976/77.* Cologne: Kiepenheuer & Witsch.

Stange, Heike. 1998. "Grenzgänge am Gleimtunnel." In *Grenzgänger. Wunderheiler. Pflastersteine,* ed. Annett Gröschner, Stefan Orendt, and Bernd Roder, 355–92. Berlin: Basis Druck.

Strubel, Antje Rávic. 2006. *Tupolew 134.* Munich: dtv.

Tate, Dennis. 2004. "Travelling on the S-Bahn: German Border Crossings before and after Unification." In *Border Crossings: Mapping Identities in Modern Europe,* ed. Peter Wagstaff, 81–104. Oxford: Peter Lang.

Wolf, Christa. 1973. *Der geteilte Himmel.* Munich: dtv.

CHAPTER 17

Interview with Barbara Hoidn

*Philip Broadbent and Sabine Hake
conducted the interview on 16 April 2008*

Broadbent/Hake: Would you describe your work in 2000 to 2001 as head of a team in the Housing Department of the Senate Department for Urban Development in Berlin, responsible for the handling of several large-scale urban renewal programs?

Hoidn: My unit was made possible through new funding possibilities that were not available before 2000. One has to recall that most of the European programs were not related to cities, but were launched for projects on the regional level or even to fund agricultural projects. In 1999, the European Union acknowledged for the first time the labor market and the problems of cities, and they started to support a program called "The Social City." Berlin was among the first cities to apply for those programs. My unit was, in fact, in charge of applying for these funds and then translating them into projects. In 2000, Berlin assigned fifteen areas to the Social City program, and allocated funds to the direct disposition of the people in the respective neighborhoods. Berlin was very generous and allocated EUR 500,000 per area. In this first year of the program, we were promoting a new strategy of urban design. We had to promote it to other departments, including the Department of Economy, the Department of Labor, and the Department for Family and Youth, in order to pool funds for the Social City program.

Broadbent/Hake: Just to clarify, your funding came from the European Union and not from the federal government?

Hoidn: It was matched with funds from the federal government because at the same time they launched the program on the federal level in 2000. It was then matched with local or community funds.

Broadbent/Hake: For a comparison, which other cities were involved in this first round? You mentioned Berlin.

Hoidn: In Germany basically all the cities with more than 500,000 inhabitants were involved, such as Hamburg, several cities in the Ruhr Region, Cologne, Essen, Duisburg.

Broadbent/Hake: But it was a Europe-wide program?

Hoidn: It was a Europe-wide program especially sought after by France and Germany because they were the ones to address issues of metropolitan areas. Then of course soon after, countries such as the UK, Denmark, and The Netherlands would follow, but they already had programs on the national level addressing these issues.

Broadbent/Hake: There is obviously one thing that distinguished your situation from all the other European cities, and that is that Berlin was now again a unified city. How did that affect your work? Could you say something about the locations of the various projects?

Hoidn: Right after reunification from 1994 till 2000, I was head of the Architecture Workshop in the office of the Senate Building Director [Hans Stimmann], which basically dealt with the construction of new buildings, and which was of course the focal point of master planning at the time in Berlin. The workshop was not so much about the impact or consequences of reunification. It was more about directing private investments into a shared concept of the Senate for steering development.

Broadbent/Hake: But what were some of the difficulties, because it seems that the earlier phase was more directly related to unification and differences between East and West Berlin?

Hoidn: Absolutely. I think one of the big controversies was establishing a dialogue with private investors coming from every part of the world. The controversy started around a shared image of which direction the city should go. The image of a European city was not easily communicated to developers who would see Berlin just as an opportunity, as an international real estate project, to be compared with other developments going on at the same time in, for example, Shanghai, Dubai, or the Docklands in London, which were created to become a real estate investment opportunity and to increase real estate value. That was not of course the first intention in Berlin. So, there was a debate over whether to have a city with projects that compete with each other, that stand out, or a consensus model with buildings that are made to create or to recreate a functional system of both public spaces and buildings, of residential space mixed with commercial space.

Broadbent/Hake: Berlin's situation was unique given that following reunification, the reconstruction of the city as a whole was very much anchored in a message for how Germany is going to be, so Berlin became almost a metaphor for the success of reunification. How was that suggested through these architectural and redevelopment plans for Berlin?

Hoidn: I think the metaphor was probably best addressed in the projects for the federal government. There were three competitions: the first one for the Reichstag,[1] the second one for the positioning of the Chancellery[2] and the offices of the German Bundestag,[3] and then there was a huge competition for the Spreeinsel,[4] in which concepts were sought for how to integrate other government agencies. I think Berlin had a strong voice in that whole debate because Berlin always voted for reusing existing facilities and reintegrating the government offices into the center, while at the beginning the Bonners were looking for more remote locations.

Broadbent/Hake: Could you perhaps give us a concrete example related to some of the projects you were involved with initially where we can see how different interests and different expectations were brought to various competitions?

Hoidn: First, there were two very significant projects. One was located three blocks away from the Gendarmenmarkt. The three adjacent buildings are the Galeries Lafayette,[5] the department store Quartier 206, and the Friedrichstadt-Passagen.[6] The project was already started under the East Berlin city government. The three investors initially insisted that they had to build a complex that would cover all three blocks and the streets between them.

Broadbent/Hake: Like a closed mall?

Hoidn: Like a closed mall. I think one of the most typical requests of the investors was to introduce the American shopping mall concept to the downtown area. There was a big fight to convince them that one single building should actually not be larger than one of the historic blocks, and that Berlin is interested in keeping the streets part of the public sphere. The compromise was to connect the three blocks underground. That's why you now have the Friedrichstadt-Passagen. Similar arguments revolved around Potsdamer Platz, which also had three large investors. The Daimler-Chrysler area was treated as one lot and Sony as one lot.

Broadbent/Hake: The Deutsche Bundesbahn?

Hoidn: No, the Bundesbahn[7] is only a tenant. I can't recall the name, but there were three large owners. Sony also insisted on covering basically the whole area, and we know they were successful; we now have this sort of tent-like structure. Daimler-Chrysler was very reluctant, but finally agreed to build various blocks and to implement public streets, which was not possible with the Sony Center.[8]

Broadbent/Hake: And if you look at the Friedrichstadt-Passagen now they're not exactly thriving commercially. And there was one battle they of course did win, which was the Potsdamer Platz Arkaden.[9] Initially the plans were not to have a glass roof, but the investors won out in that project.

Hoidn: And another typical example to highlight the strategy of the Senate Building Director was to ask for a separation of the program for a site into various building projects. For example, one would have one apartment building, one hotel, one office building and so on. A good example of that strategy is the so-called Heimsblock, the one with the restaurant Borchardt on the ground floor, which integrated two already-existing structures occupying the site. I think that is ideally how it should have been accomplished.

Broadbent/Hake: Part of the problem, of course, that makes Berlin so unique in this building phase is how to deal with the historical legacy, not only the legacy of National Socialism or divided Berlin, but also how to restore the legacy of the Weimar Republic and of course going back into the nineteenth century. They've made some interesting inroads architecturally to invoke that. Could you give some examples?

Hoidn: How the projects of the Weimar Republic were actually ... ?

Broadbent/Hake: No, for example I'm thinking of the Verdi Gewerkschaftshaus[10] on the Potsdamer Platz. The current form tries to evoke a building that once stood on the site.

Hoidn: I think Berlin has a kind of tradition of acknowledging the buildings that were on a particular site, and this strategy was implemented during the International Building Exhibition. That exhibition launched a lot of research and triggered a series of exhibitions on particular parts of the city and on the great history of Berlin, not only the political history but also the architectural, cultural, and other histories. I think that is part of the culture in Berlin that we all enjoy so much. There is this respect for existing buildings.

Broadbent/Hake: Not like in other cities such as London, for example, that don't do that.

Hoidn: It's amazing how much so-called ordinary people know about the history of their built environment.

Broadbent/Hake: So far we have talked a lot about investors, how to work with investors and how to persuade them to move away from American ideas about what shopping centers should look like toward a more distinctly European vision. Let's talk a little bit about some of the people involved directly in the rebuilding, but also the people working in the Senate offices. Was this primarily a West German team? Did you have East Berlin architects or administrators join the Berlin Senate? Were there any instances where you had really different ideas about either architecture—whether postmodern or historicist—or urban planning, where it was really a clash of two different models of training architects but also two very different urban visions?

Hoidn: In terms of reunification, one has to say the Senate was actually one of the best employers because they basically integrated all the employees from the East Berlin administration. Both in the Architecture Workshop as well as in the Social City program almost 50 percent of the employees were from former East Berlin. They were very cautious in terms of expressing their opinion about urban design, not so much in internal discussions but to the larger public. I also have to admit that there was not so much controversy about the larger strategy called critical reconstruction because it involved so many legal requirements, be it dealing with restitution or reconnecting existing infrastructure. The morphology of the concept of critical reconstruction was never in question. There were sometimes controversies over the density of the lots, especially if requested by future developments because investors and developers would of course always go for increased density. If the projects under development were to be on lots that were destroyed by the war or by the Wall, there was never really a problem to come up with a concept that was close to the previous buildings. There was of course a lot of controversy about demolishing symbolically charged former GDR buildings, and controversies erupted over buildings on Unter den Linden, the former Palace of the Republic, and the Tacheles building,[11] another very prominent project in Oranienburger Strasse. But at the time when I worked at the Senate, the projects had a relatively small radius. The controversy started only later with the Planwerk when the Senate developed the plan to define a wider downtown area, and when it then touched the residential neighborhoods of Karl-Marx-Allee and Leipziger Strasse.

Broadbent/Hake: In your planning did you actually have meetings with some citizen initiatives? You said earlier that there were projects in various parts of the city. Could you say a bit about the different requests, demands, or complaints expressed on these occasions?

Hoidn: That was part of our mission statement in the workshop. We had monthly talks about projects even when they were still hot, and when they were just about to the go into the approval process. There were monthly architecture talks. There were quarterly so-called *Stadtforen*, city forums, which were not so interesting for the public but of great interest to planners and professionals. Nonetheless the architecture talks were very well received and attended, and we had a lot of criticism from former architects from the Bauakademie in East Berlin because they thought that the projects were all too stiff, too modern, too monotonous, or not colorful enough. That was something that was addressed very often. Their argument was always that we had just come out of a prefabricated era, and now what you are offering us is not so different from the standardized typologies we know. They were also of course not so convinced of a strategy to reconstruct the footprint of the historical downtown because it seems they were already forecasting what was going to happen later or where development would stop. Would it stop before the Palace of the Republic? Would it go beyond that magic border because at that time the Museum Island was considered to be lost to the West Berliners, but the other area was still safe. They were very critical about the style of architecture.

Broadbent/Hake: It is interesting that Alexanderplatz has become this kind of crisis space in postunification urban planning. I am thinking of Hans Kollhoff and others, and it doesn't seem that anything is happening.

Hoidn: Alexanderplatz at that time was considered to be a conduit for a ll those investors who thought that Berlin was a little bit too cautious, that we could have more intense commercial development in the center, and who thought that Potsdamer Platz was still too small. So, Alexanderplatz served compensatory functions, and in that respect one can tell that the Senate was probably right to be so reluctant about high rises or towers.

Broadbent/Hake: Do you think Berlin was too cautious, or do you think the caution exercised in the reconstruction was justified?

Hoidn: I think the caution exercised was right because, on a very pragmatic level, Berlin wanted to spread the investment over a larger area and not just a few prestige projects. They were a little too cautious about the eaves height as a measure, which was very rigid. One could have negotiated in some parts, and I don't think it is a particularly strong urban effect to have Friedrichstrasse aligning all the way down for two kilometers. Recalling some of the encounters with investors, I do not think there was much of a choice, but in general I think it was good to be cautious.

Broadbent/Hake: Of course many architects, including Daniel Libeskind, have said that this was a wasted opportunity, that this would have been a moment for greatness and bold innovation. Instead what the international community of architects encountered was, from their perspective, this petty Berlin insistence on the maximum eaves height and all these local restrictions. What is your response to that?

Hoidn: Daniel Libeskind is talking like an architect who always creates extraordinary opportunities for himself, but this kind of extraordinariness is not what an urban planner should look for. In the bibliography of the history of urban design, the first principle is always that the urban planner should try to be neutral, to find guidelines that work for many if not all, and that the architect then has to find the moment for specificity, for something extraordinary. We have a lot of examples where that really worked very well. I think that Pariser Platz is a very good place to look for exactly this kind of extravagance as well as the ordinariness.

Broadbent/Hake: And perhaps there is an understandable reluctance for Berlin to have such a vast number of monumental projects. Of course it has historical echoes that may seem unwanted.

Hoidn: I think one of Berlin's great characteristics is that it does not have a grand monumental scale or buildings that look for greatness and monumentality.

Broadbent/Hake: To go back to your position both in the mid-1990s and also as head of the team of the Housing Department, from your perspective what were the most pressing issues in dealing with the reconstruction of East Berlin as opposed to West Berlin? Were there differences, points of contestation?

Hoidn: The entire interest of private investors was of course focused on the historical downtown. Two-thirds of it was former East Berlin, so that is where the entire master planning efforts went. The Senate made an effort to look for a mix of investments that would create jobs and would draw people to dwell and live there. I think the most pressing subject was to establish a top-down master plan with the concept of having the central train station there, placing the government offices there to create a synthesis of all these categories, and then to debate the plan and actually synchronize it with private investment. In terms of planning, that was an extraordinary exercise.

Broadbent/Hake: And also unprecedented really in twentieth-century history.

Hoidn: In an existing location, yes. Berlin also learned a lot from, let's say, Barcelona's urban renewal project where they undertook little infill projects, proposed concepts for public spaces to open up some areas such as the old Gothic Quarter, and then implemented some new developments. But that was done piecemeal. To have a downtown area where you have a major infrastructure project and at the same time these billion-Euro private investment projects such as Potsdamer Platz, was a logistic masterpiece, I have to say.

Broadbent/Hake: Looking back, especially at the early years when all these competitions were going on, we had the Info Box, and there were all these public tours on construction sites—what do you think was a mistake in retrospect? Where did the Senate make the wrong decision?

Hoidn: I think the Senate was a little bit too optimistic and too dependent on estimates of population growth. It was forecasted that Berlin would grow to 4 million by 2008 and then grow another million in five years, and that was, as we all know, not the case. Based on that demographic estimate, Berlin launched a housing program that also included housing projects on the periphery, and seen from today that was really counterproductive to central developments because the housing project brought a lot of other costs with it. For example, we created areas that lacked public transportation, and that drew a lot of middle-class income from the central areas to those remote areas. It eventually also led to a reversal in the hype around the city center because now it is promoted very strongly, and I think almost to the neglect of the other districts of Berlin. The political and public promotion of the center led eventually to the one central train station, the one central airport, the one central Museum Island and so forth, so the diversity of the other areas is not really in the focus of the Senate. I think that is another mistake. The first mistake with these housing developments was well intended because they tried to provide publicly funded housing to ease the market a little bit. Of course, for these new developments, it was not possible to implement them in the central areas because it is far too complicated, and there you only had small lots and so on. So they were all located on the periphery, and I think we could have used those funds much better in the central districts.

Broadbent/Hake: What was the thinking behind the creation of a central train station, because in a way that was new to Berlin? Berlin had had a number of stations that accommodated passengers, whether they were coming from the north, the south, the east, or the west. But to have a station that would then be representative of Berlin as a center is almost trying to create or suggest that there is and has always been a clearly definable center, which really is not the case. If we look, for example, at Berlin at the beginning of the twentieth century, there was the center at the Kurfürstendamm, then there was the Alexanderplatz, and it was a socially stratified city.

Hoidn: That central train station has been a dream since the 1920s. The opportunity was discussed in the 1930s, then again in the 1940s, and then it was not possible any longer because of the division of the city. So, it was a concept that was on the table almost immediately. In the late twentieth century there were also the technical possibilities to do that. It was always difficult to connect the north-south and the east-west transit lines, so it was almost unavoidable that this plan was again picked up.

We should also remember that this north-south axis was one of the pet projects of West Berliners because they wanted to use it as a kind of highway, tunneling under the Tiergarten and so on. There were plans and surveys and feasibility studies available for the ground, and the various departments of the Senate thought that this would be a major attraction for the federal government as well as for private investors.

Broadbent/Hake: Do you consider reconstruction now complete? Where are we right now in relation to these two moments that you were involved with?

Hoidn: No, I don't think reconstruction is complete. Maybe all the voids in central Berlin are filled, but now I think it is time to look at all the existing but still empty buildings in the vicinity of Friedrichstrasse. You just have to go five minutes to the west or to the east, and it is dark and quiet at night. So, I think one should make an attempt to bring in people, and to increase the residential possibilities because that would mean reconstruction of the downtown. I also think that the physical gap between Alexanderplatz and the districts behind it such as Friedrichshain and then Prenzlauer Berg could use some planning proposals.

Broadbent/Hake: Thank you very much for giving us this interview.

Notes

1. The Reichstagsgebäude (Reichstag Building), seat of the German parliament, was initially designed by Paul Wallot in 1894, but reconstructed by Norman Foster between 1995 and 1999.
2. Federal Chancellery. Architect Axel Schultes, completed 2001. Seat and residence of the German Chancellor.
3. Paul Löbe-Haus. Architects Axel Schultes and Charlotte Frank, completed 2001.
4. An island on the Spree River and the historic and political center of Berlin.
5. Department store on Friedrichstrasse. Architect Jean Nouvel, completed 1996.
6. Friedrichstadtpassagen Quartier 206 is a luxury department store. Architects Pei Cobb Freed & Partners.
7. Der Bahn Tower (German Railway Central Office). Architect Helmut Jahn, completed 2000.
8. Sony-sponsored building complex of offices, restaurants, and entertainment. Architect Helmut Jahn, completed 2000.
9. Shopping mall complex. Architect Renzo Piano, completed 1998.
10. Park Kolonnaden. Architect Giorgio Grassi, competed 2001. 2001–2004 headquarters of the Verdi Trade Union.
11. Originally designed as a department store by Franz Ahrens (1907–8), it was later the headquarters of the East German Freie Deutsche Gewerkschaftsbund (Free Federation of German Trade Unions). Although scheduled for demolition in 1990, the building is now under the direction of an artists' initiative. It houses an art center, a nightclub, and cinemas.

Notes on Contributors

Ulrich Bach is Assistant Professor of German in the Modern Languages Department at Texas State University. He received his PhD from UCLA with a dissertation on "Tropics of Vienna: Austrian Colonial Utopias." His research focuses on book history and postwar German cinema. Publications include an article on Leopold von Sacher-Masoch in *German Quarterly* 80, no. 2 (2007): 201–19 and a forthcoming publication on the erotica collector Eduard Fuchs.

David E. Barclay is Executive Director of the German Studies Association and is Margaret and Roger Scholten Professor of International Studies in the History Department at Kalamazoo College, Michigan. He is the author or editor of many publications on nineteenth-century Prussia and twentieth-century social democracy. He is currently working on a history of West Berlin from 1948 to 1994.

Deborah Ascher Barnstone is Associate Professor at Washington State University where she teaches architectural design, history, and theory. She holds a PhD in architectural history and theory from Delft University of Technology (2004) and is a principal with Ascher Barnstone Architects. Her primary research area is twentieth-century German architecture. Scholarly publications include: *The Transparent State: Architecture and Politics in Postwar Germany* (2005); "Text and Architecture at the Behnisch Bundeshaus," *Interfaces* (Winter 2005); and "From the Zero Hour: Transparency, Gender and Architecture," in *Art, Nation and Gender* (2004).

Philip Broadbent is Assistant Professor in the Department of Germanic Studies at the University of Texas at Austin. He received his PhD from University College London with a dissertation on postunification Berlin narratives. Recent publications address narrative representations of post-1990 Berlin, "Phenomenology of Absence: Benjamin, Nietzsche and History in Cees Nooteboom's *All Souls Day*," *Journal of Modern Literature* 32, no. 3 (2009) and "Generational Shifts: Representing Post-*Wende* Berlin,"

New German Critique 35, no. 2 (2008): 139–70. He is currently working on a book project on contemporary German and English fiction.

Greg Castillo is Associate Professor at the College of Environmental Design at the University of California, Berkeley and Research Associate at the United States Studies Centre at the University of Sydney. He received his PhD in Architectural History from the University of California at Berkeley in 2000. While at Berkeley, he worked as research assistant to the late Spiro Kostof, an association that led to Castillo's authorship of second-edition revisions to Kostof's *A History of Architecture* (1995), currently the bestselling college survey textbook in its discipline. Castillo's most recent book, *Cold War on the Home Front: Cultural Revolution in Mid-century Domestic Design* (2008) explores the attempt to divide Germany through the introduction of American- and Soviet-derived domestic design cultures.

April A. Eisman is Assistant Professor in Art and Design at Iowa State University. An art historian, she works on the relationship between art and politics in the twentieth and twenty-first centuries, with a particular emphasis on the German Democratic Republic. She received her PhD from the University of Pittsburgh in 2007 with the dissertation, "Bernhard Heisig and the Cultural Politics of East German Art." Recent publications include articles on Heisig, the contemporary Chinese artist Feng Mengbo, and the impact of 11 September on the American news media.

Jennifer V. Evans is Associate Professor of Modern European History at Carleton University in Ottawa, Canada. She is currently working on two book-length projects, one, under contract with Palgrave Macmillan on sexual space in postwar Berlin, and the other on the regulation of homosexuality in Nazi and Cold War Germany. She has written articles and book chapters on a range of topics in the history of sexuality, including "The Moral State: Men, Mining, and Masculinity in the Early GDR," *German History* 23, no. 3 (2005): 355–70 and "*Bahnhof* Boys: Policing Male Prostitution in Post-Nazi Berlin," *Journal of the History of Sexuality* 12, no. 4 (2003): 605–36.

Heather Gumbert is Assistant Professor of History at Virginia Tech. Her research focuses on the history of television and its emergence and impact on political culture in the former German Democratic Republic. She is the recipient of the Barnes F. Lathrop Prize of the University of Texas at Austin for her dissertation "East German Television and the Unmaking of the Socialist Project" and is currently revising it for publication.

Sabine Hake is the Texas Chair of German Literature and Culture in the Department of Germanic Studies at the University of Texas at Austin. She is the author of five books, including *German National Cinema* (2008, second revised edition) and *Topographies of Class: Modern Architecture and Mass Society in Weimar Berlin* (2008). She has published numerous articles and edited volumes on German film and Weimar culture. Her current book project deals with the fascist imaginary in postfascist cinema.

Barbara Hoidn shares the O'Neil Ford professorship with Wilfried Wang in the School of Architecture at the University of Texas at Austin; she is also a principal with HoidnWangPartner Berlin. She studied architecture and city planning at the University of Karlsruhe in Germany and has taught at the ETH Zürich, the Rhode Island School of Design, and the Graduate School of Design at Harvard University. In 1994 she joined the strategy department of the Senate Building Director of Berlin as Head of the Architecture Workshop. From 2000 to 2001 she was head of a team in the housing department of the Senate Department for Urban Development in Berlin responsible for the handling of several national and European urban-renewal programs for Berlin.

Mariana Ivanova is a PhD candidate at the Department of Germanic Studies at University of Texas at Austin. Her research focuses on the exchange between DEFA and East European film studios, transnational cinema, and postwar German history and culture. She has presented on topics such as DEFA's coproductions, censorship in East German cinema, film adaptation, and genre cinema.

Elizabeth Janik received her PhD in modern European history from Georgetown University in 2001. She has taught German and European history at George Mason University, James Madison University, and the International Summer University of the Free University in Berlin. She currently writes and conducts research for the Hampton Roads State of the Region report at Old Dominion University in Norfolk, Virginia.

Paul Jaskot is Professor of Art History at DePaul University. He is the author of *The Architecture of Oppression: The SS, Forced Labor and the Nazi Monumental Building Economy* (2000) as well as coeditor *of Beyond Berlin: Twelve German Cities Confront the Nazi Past* (2007). His research focuses on problems related to political economy and art as they intersect with the history of National Socialist Germany and its impact on postwar culture. Currently he is completing a project on the political reception of the Nazi past and postwar German art and architecture.

Lyn Marven holds a DPhil from Oxford and is a Lecturer at the University of Liverpool, United Kingdom. Her research focuses on contemporary literature, especially by authors of non-German origins and from the former GDR; she is currently working on images of Berlin in contemporary narrative. She is the author of *Body and Narrative in Contemporary Literatures in German: Herta Müller, Libuše Moníková and Kerstin Hensel* (2005), the coeditor (with Brigid Haines) of *Libuše Moníková: In Memoriam* (2005), and the translator of *Berlin Tales* (2009). She has also published a number of articles on contemporary literature, women's writing, representations of the body, collages, and photography.

Claudia Mesch is Associate Professor of Art History at Arizona State University. Her research focuses on postwar modernism and its ties to surrealism and to European intellectual history. She is coeditor of *Joseph Beuys: The Reader* (2007). Her book on *Modern Art at the Berlin Wall: Demarcating Culture in the Cold War Germanys* (2008) examines art produced in divided Germany, the most contested site of the Cold War. She is founding editor of the e-journal *Surrealism and the Americas,* and is at work on a study of European intellectuals' preoccupation with Native American culture.

Miriam Paeslack received her DPhil from the University of Freiburg and is currently Visiting Professor in Visual and Critical Studies at the California College of the Arts (CCA) in San Francisco/Oakland; she previously taught at the Hochschule für Grafik und Buchkunst in Leipzig. She has published on the subject of late nineteenth-century and contemporary urban photography and questions of identity and space in journals such as *The Journal of Architecture, Fotogeschichte,* and *Visual Resources* (editor, special issue on "Before and After the Wall: German Photography in Discourse and Practice," 12, no. 2 [2006]).

Emily Pugh received her PhD in Art History from the CUNY Graduate Center in New York in 2008 and is currently a postdoctoral research associate at the Center for the Advanced Study of the Visual Arts at the National Gallery in Washington, D.C. Her research interests include the role of architecture in visual culture and use of buildings as cultural symbols, as well as the relationship between architectural styles and national identities. A manuscript based on her dissertation is currently under contract with the University of Pittsburgh Press.

Heiner Stahl received his DPhil in Contemporary History and Political Science from the University of Potsdam and worked on a DFG-financed research project from 2004 to 2007. The title of his 2007 dissertation is "Youth Radio Programmes in Cold War Berlin. Berlin as a Soundscape of Pop (1962–1973)."

Maike Steinkamp received her DPhil from the University of Bonn with a dissertation on the reception of "degenerate" art in art criticism, exhibitions, and museums in the Soviet Sector and the later GDR, titled *Das unerwünschte Erbe* (2008). She is currently working at the Department of Art History, University of Hamburg. From 2001 until 2004 she worked as Assistant Curator at the Kunst- und Ausstellungshalle in Bonn and at the German Historical Museum in Berlin. Her research interests include German art and cultural history of the twentieth century, history of museums and collections, and photography.

Index of Proper Names: People, Places, and Institutions

Abesser, Doris, 81
Alexanderplatz, 19, 89, 90, 93, 95, 104, 108, 200, 202, 203
Aly, Götz, 126, 127, 133
Arndt, Adolf, 103, 105
Aust, Stefan, 126, 138

Baader, Andreas, 128, 137, 138
Balanbanoff, Angelica, 140
Barsky, Sergei, 36, 41
Barthel, Kurt, 47
Baumeister, Willi, 31
Baumgarten, Paul, 105, 107, 108
Behnisch, Günter, 108
Benjamin, Walter, 17, 103
Berdina, Sofia, 140
Berkman, Alexander, 141
Berlin Wall, 1, 2, 4, 5, 28, 46, 52, 69, 71–76, 78–86, 94, 96, 101, 105, 109, 135, 137, 139, 145–48, 152, 153, 157, 165, 171–73, 176, 177, 181–92, 199
Beyer, Frank, 88n2
Bitter, John, 37
Bloom, Claire, 121
Blume, Renate, 85
Bolz, Lothar, 102
Borchers, Cornell, 120
Box, Muriel, 122
Brancusi, Constantin, 24
Braque, Georges, 24
Brandenburg Gate, 71, 73, 75, 117, 165
Brecht, Bertolt, 34, 35, 41
Bresson Cartier, 172–74
Britten, Benjamin, 38, 40
Brussig, Thomas, 186
Bundeshaus Bonn, 5, 104, 106, 109
Butting, Max, 40, 42

Camaro, Alexander, 31
Carow, Heiner, 88n2
Cézanne, Paul, 24
Clay, Lucius, 79
Copley, John Singleton, 28
Cultural League for the Democratic Renewal of Germany, 24, 25, 27, 32n5, 40–42
Cummings, Burton, 28

DEFA, 5, 78–87, 88n2, 96, 118
Demandowsky, Ewald, 116, 120
Dessau, Paul, 41, 44
Dickinson, Desmond, 121
Dieter, Fritz, 98n3
Dietrich, Marlene, 115, 123
Dutschke, Rudi, 125–27, 129–33, 137, 139
Dymshits, Alexander, 36, 41
Dziuba, Helmut, 88n2

Edel, Uli, 138
Ehmsen, Heinrich, 32n7
Eisenman, Peter, 147, 161, 163
Eisler, Gerhart, 95
Eisler, Hanns, 35, 40, 43–44
Ensslin, Gudrun, 137
Enzensberger, Hans Magnus, 126, 131
Ephraim Palais, 149
Esche, Eberhard, 85
Extraparliamentary Opposition (APO), 126

Figner, Vera, 140
Franck, Julia, 184, 185, 187–88, 190, 192
Frank, Benno, 37
Franke, Günter, 98n3
Freud, Sigmund, 142–43
Frick, Henry Clay, 141
Friedrichshein, 94, 95, 99, 203

Friedrichstadt, 147, 148, 154n4
Friedrichstadt-Passagen, 196, 197, 203n6

Gass, Karl, 79, 80, 82, 84
Gauguin, Paul, 24
Gerlach, Philipp, 147, 151–53
Giedion, Sigfried, 103
Goldmann, Emma, 140, 141
Gorbachev, Mikhail, 165
Graffunder, Heinz, 5, 101, 102, 107–10
Grohmann, Will, 28
Grotewohl, Otto, 102

Hadid, Zaha, 147, 163, 166n2
Hansaviertel, 4, 46, 48–50, 116, 122, 158
Hassemer, Volker, 150, 154n6
Hathaway, Henry, 120
Henselmann, Hermann, 4, 89, 91, 98n1, 98n3
Hermann, Ernst, 42, 44n6
Hofer, Karl, 25, 32n7
Höffer, Paul, 39–40, 42
Honecker, Erich, 76, 102, 107, 108
Hoppe, Hans, 102
Hopper, Edward, 28

Internationale Bauausstellung, 5, 146–52, 156, 157, 159–65

Jaap, Max, 79
Jähn, Sigmund, 191, 192n3
Jaspers, Kristina, 122, 123
Jewish Museum, 5, 145–53, 154n2, 157, 166n4
Jobst, Gerhard, 50
Johnson, Van, 122
Jugert, Rudolf, 119, 123n4

Kaiser, Jakob, 31
Käutner, Helmut, 119
Khrushchev, Nikita, 46, 52, 106
Klein, Gerhard, 87n1
Kleihues, Josef Paul, 147, 148–49, 166n3
Knef, Hildegard, 5, 13, 14, 115–23
Kollhoff, Hans, 154n5, 200
Kommune I, 126, 129, 130, 133, 137
Korn, Arthur, 103
Kosel, Gerhard, 98n3
Krabbe, Hanna, 139

Kreuer, Willi, 50
Kupsch, Felix, 139
Kurfürstendamm, 122
Kurras, Karl-Heinz, 125–26
Kurella, Alfred, 73, 76, 77n1

Laux, Karl, 43
Libeskind, Daniel, 5, 150, 152, 153n1, 154n8, 166n2, 200
Liebmann, Irina, 6, 184–89, 190, 191
Liebermann, Max, 146
Liebknecht, Karl, 107
Liebknecht, Kurt, 50, 101, 104
Lindenstrasse, 147, 148, 152, 153
Loeper, Wiebke, 6, 179–82
Luxemburg, Rosa, 140

Maetzig, Kurt, 5, 80, 81–82
Mahler, Horst, 127, 130
Mahler, Karl, 48–49
Maron, Monika, 6, 184, 185, 186, 187, 190, 192
Meinhof, Ulrike, 5, 136–138, 139, 141–143
Meyer-Dennewitz, Gabriele, 73, 74, 76
Michel, Horst, 53
Michelson, Annette, 140, 141
Moholy-Nagy, László, 103
Momper, Walter, 128
Motherwell, Robert, 28
Müller-Rehm, Klaus, 51
Müller-Stahl, Armin, 83

Nay, Ernst Wilhelm, 31
Neal, Patricia, 121
Neudörfl, Elisabeth, 6, 178, 180–82
Neumann, Werner, 98n3
Niemeyer, Oscar, 4, 51
Nikolai Quarter, 149
Norden, Albert, 64n7, 95
Notowicz, Nathan, 42, 44n6

O'Keefe, Georgia, 28
Ohnesorg, Benno, 125, 126–30, 137
Ottinger, Ulrike, 138
Özdamar, Emine Sevgi, 6, 184–87, 189, 191, 192n2

Pagnol, Marcel, 118

Palace of the Republic, 5, 100–10, 199
Paris, Helga, 6, 172, 174–75, 177, 178, 182, 183n4
Pariser Square, 200
Paulus, Ernst, 139, 141
Pechstein, Max, 26, 32n4
Perlberg, William, 120
Picasso, Pablo, 24
Pollock, Jackson, 28
Potsdamer Platz, 1, 11, 121, 197, 198, 200, 201
Powers, Tyrone, 121
Praunheim, Rosa von, 160
Prokofiev, Sergei, 36, 40

Rainer, Yvonne, 5, 127, 136–44
Reagan, Ronald, 165
Rebay, Hilla, 27
Red Army Faction, 126, 127, 130, 136–139, 141, 143
Reed, Carol, 121
Reichstag, 5, 105, 107, 196
Reuter, Ernst, 79, 128
Richter, Gerhard, 136
Richter, Roland Suso, 88n2
Rodin, Auguste, 24
Rossellini, Roberto, 17

Sander, Helke, 138
Sannwald, Daniella, 122, 123
Scheerbart, Paul, 103
Schlöndorff, Volker, 138
Schmidt, Michael, 6, 173, 175–77, 181–83
Schneider, Helmut, 79
Schneider, Peter, 126, 128, 129, 131
Schoszberger, Hans, 51
Schütz, Klaus, 128, 130, 131
Schwippert, Hans, 101, 104–06, 108–10
Seaton, George, 120
Shahn, Ben, 28
Sheeler, Charles, 28
Shostakovich, Dmitri, 36, 38–39, 41
Siegmann, Gerhard, 52
SMAD, 24, 27, 29, 36, 41
Söhnker, Hans, 119
Socialist Unity Party of Germany (SED), 5, 27, 29, 41–44, 50, 52, 59, 62, 64n6, 70–76, 77n1, 89–92, 133

Speer, Albert, 50
Stalinallee, 4, 46–48, 50, 51, 53, 89, 91, 93
Staudte, Wolfgang, 118
Stravinsky, Igor, 34, 38, 40
Strempel, Horst, 29
Ströbele, Christian, 127
Strubel, Antje Rávic, 184–85, 189–191
Stuart, Gilbert, 28
Stuckenschmidt, Hanz Heinz, 39, 40, 43, 45n8
Székely, Kathy, 83

Taut, Bruno, 103, 108
Teacher's House, 104
Television Tower (East Germany), 5, 89–98, 98n1–4, 108
Teufel, Fritz, 130
Thiel, Heinz, 87n1
Thein, Ulrich, 81
Tiergarten, 11, 12, 49, 122, 147, 203
Tiessen, Heinz, 40, 42, 44n7
Tigerman, Stanley, 161
Tjulpanov, Sergei, 36
Tobey, Mark, 28
Topography of Terror, 148
Trökes, Heinz, 31
Trotta, Margarethe von, 88n2, 138
Tshombe, Moïse, 129

Uhlmann, Hans, 31
Ulbricht, Walter, 50, 52, 69, 73, 90, 91, 93, 95, 98, 101

Valle, Gino, 161, 166n3
Vogel, Frank, 5, 80, 82, 83, 86, 88
Volkmann, Abel, 161, 166n3

Weber, Klaus, 4, 69, 70–74, 77n1, 76, 77n2
Wiens, Paul, 83
Winnicott, D.W., 144
Wohl, Albert, 146
Wolf, Christa, 85, 189, 190
Wolf, Konrad, 5, 80, 82, 83, 85
Wölfflin, Heinrich, 182

Zadkine, Ossip, 24
Zasulich, Vera, 140
Zimmermann, Mac, 31

www.ingramcontent.com/pod-product-compliance
Lightning Source LLC
Chambersburg PA
CBHW072000290426
44109CB00018B/2081